The Stoic Theory of Beauty

The Stoic Theory of Beauty

Aistė Čelkytė

EDINBURGH
University Press

Edinburgh University Press is one of the leading university presses in the UK. We publish academic books and journals in our selected subject areas across the humanities and social sciences, combining cutting-edge scholarship with high editorial and production values to produce academic works of lasting importance. For more information visit our website: edinburghuniversitypress.com

© Aistė Čelkytė, 2020, 2022

Edinburgh University Press Ltd
The Tun – Holyrood Road
12(2f) Jackson's Entry
Edinburgh EH8 8PJ

First published in hardback by Edinburgh University Press 2020

Typeset in 11/13 Adobe Sabon by
Servis Filmsetting Ltd, Stockport

A CIP record for this book is available from the British Library

ISBN 978 1 4744 6161 0 (hardback)
ISBN 978 1 4744 6162 7 (paperback)
ISBN 978 1 4744 6163 4 (webready PDF)
ISBN 978 1 4744 6164 1 (epub)

The right of Aistė Čelkytė to be identified as the author of this work has been asserted in accordance with the Copyright, Designs and Patents Act 1988, and the Copyright and Related Rights Regulations 2003 (SI No. 2498).

Contents

	Acknowledgements	vi
	Note to the Reader	vii
1	Beauty and Its Problems: Introduction	1
2	The Problem of Indifferents	26
3	The Beautiful and the Good	47
4	'The wise man is no true Scotsman': The Stoics on Human Beauty	78
5	Beauty in Stoic Theological Arguments	101
6	The Stoic Definition of Beauty as *Summetria*	144
7	Aesthetics in Stoicism and Stoicism in Aesthetics	171
	Bibliography	192
	Index Locorum	208
	General Index	214

Acknowledgements

As this book is a heavily revised version of my doctoral thesis, *Chrysippus on the Beautiful: Studies in a Stoic Conception of Aesthetic Properties*, I would like to thank my supervisor, Professor Stephen Halliwell, whose advice to develop a rigorous work ethic above all else has seen me through the long process of completing this project. I am grateful to a number of people who discussed this work with me and offered their comments, especially Alex Long, Chris Gill, Sarah Broadie, Tomohiko Kondo and Kei Chiba. I would also like to thank the members of the ancient philosophy group in Utrecht, especially Teun Tieleman, for their support and enouragement.

A version of Chapter 6 of this work has previously been published as a journal article in the *Classical Quarterly*.

Note to the Reader

All Greek and Latin text comes from standard modern editions (unless otherwise indicated): Oxford Classical Texts for Plato, Aristotle, Diogenes Laertius, Plotinus, Seneca; Teubner editions for Sextus Empiricus, Epictetus, Olympiodorus, Cicero; Loeb edition for Plutarch; *Commentaria in Aristotelem Graeca* edition for Alexander of Aphrodisias. All translations are indicated in notes. Secondary literature is quoted in the notes by author's name and date. Names of ancient authors are given in full, while abbreviations of their titles mostly follow the conventions of the *Oxford Classical Dictionary*, fourth edition, edited by S. Hornblower, A. Spawforth and E. Eidinow (Oxford: Oxford University Press, 2012).

Fragments collections and other notable abbreviations are as follows:

DK   H. Diels and W. Kranz (eds) (1951–2), *Die Fragmente der Vorsokratiker*, 3 vols, Berlin.
K   C. Kühn (ed.) (1821–33), *Claudii Galeni Opera Omnia*, 20 vols, Leipzig.
LS   A. Long and D. Sedley (eds) (1987), *The Hellenistic Philosophers*, 2 vols, Cambridge.
MM   Galenus, *Methodus Medendi*.
SVF   H. F. A. von Arnim (1903–24), *Stoicorum Veterum Fragmenta*, 3 vols, Leipzig.
U   H. Usener (ed.) (1887), *Epicurea*, Leipzig.

UP Galenus, *De Usu Partium*.
W   C. Wachsmuth (ed.) (1884), *Ioannis Stobaei Anthologii libri duo priores qui inscribi solent Eclogae physicae et ethicae*, 2 vols, Berlin.

I

Beauty and Its Problems: Introduction

'A theory of beauty would be a good thing to have . . .'
                    Denis Donoghue, *Speaking of Beauty*[1]

Stoics and their place in ancient aesthetics

Beauty is often taken to be a part of the standard philosophical curriculum, yet there are not many comprehensive histories of Western thought on the subject. One of the more recent of such studies is Wladyslaw Tatarkiewicz's *The History of Aesthetics*. In this work, Tatarkiewicz presents a taxonomy of the theories and conceptualisations of beauty. The 'original Greek concept of beauty' is the first type of theory. Tatarkiewicz explains this type of theory by contrasting it with the prevalent understanding of beauty in Europe from the eighteenth century, which constitutes the second type of theory in his classification. He claims that the former is broader than the latter, as it is applicable not only to shapes, sounds and sights, but also to thoughts and customs.[2] The second type of concept of beauty, meanwhile, includes aesthetic experiences only.[3] So far, Tatarkiewicz's account is, by and large, fairly standard. The third category in his taxonomy, however, is a surprising one. While the first category summarises Greek literature and philosophy in an overarching manner, as if all Greek texts shared a single concept of beauty, the third category singles out one line of thought within the Greek tradition. It is the Stoic theory of beauty. According to

Tatarkiewicz, the Stoics presented an aesthetic concept of beauty, but their theory recognised only visual beauty,[4] and, for this reason, the Stoic theory constitutes a distinct category in his taxonomy.

Tatarkiewicz's taxonomy of the theories of beauty can be questioned and criticised in multiple ways,[5] but the peculiar addition of Stoicism to what would otherwise be a relatively standard classification of the theories of beauty is thought-provoking. One might wonder whether the Stoic[6] account was indeed sufficiently different from the other concepts employed by Greek philosophers and writers to deserve its own category. Before investigating whether the Stoics deserve a category of their own, however, it is important to examine Tatarkiewicz's motivation for singling out Stoicism.

Tatarkiewicz is not very explicit about his motivation, but it is likely that he describes the Stoic conceptualisation of beauty as restricted to the visual realm due to the tension between the standard interpretation of Stoic philosophy and the presence of the aesthetic vocabulary in Stoic arguments. Tatarkiewicz points out in his *History of Aesthetics* that the Stoics' 'philosophical principles were not suited to make aestheticians of them'.[7] This statement was very likely inspired by the Stoics' reputation as strict moralists who argue that it is crucial to remain unaffected by life's joys and sorrows alike. If Stoicism is viewed in this way, it would be natural to assume that the Stoics adopted an equally indifferent attitude towards beauty and, thus, their principles led them away from aesthetics.

The understanding of Stoicism as a philosophy which requires its followers to be ascetics who shun ordinary human experiences, however, does not take into account all of the available evidence. One might be led into thinking this way by noting that the Stoics classified beauty as a preferred indifferent,[8] which seems to suggest that a Stoic ought not to be concerned about beauty. At the same time, there is a surviving Stoic definition of beauty as *summetria* of parts with one another and with the whole accompanied, at least in some cases, by the examples of visual beauty. These two pieces of evidence might be the reason why Tatarkiewicz writes that the only concept of beauty subscribed to by the Stoics was an aesthetic concept of visual beauty. Such a stance on beauty would be unique, so it is unsurprising that Tatarkiewicz presents the Stoic idea as not being comparable to any other theory and deserving of its own category.

There are, however, some additional Stoic arguments that are not mentioned by Tatarkiewicz. In these arguments, beauty terms are employed to describe phenomena that are not visual and, in some cases, are related to morality, thus indicating that the Stoic concept of beauty might have been more complex than Tatarkiewicz acknowledges it to be. There are at least two groups of problematic evidence.[9] First, the texts that record the definition of beauty as *summetria* also state that just as the *summetria* of limbs accounts for the beauty of the body, so an analogous phenomenon accounts for the beauty of the soul. Second, the infamous Stoic paradox stating that only the wise man is beautiful suggests that the Stoics presented some reflections on the question of what human beauty amounts to which took into account much more than visual appearance. The claim that only the wise man is beautiful is not compatible with the concept of beauty as an aesthetic property restricted to visual appearance alone. Therefore, the Stoics either conceptualised beauty in a more complex way than Tatarkiewicz suggests, or they had more than one concept and some of those concepts accounted for more than visual beauty.

Interestingly, this evidence also shows that beauty is not contrasted with morality in Stoic arguments, as one might expect given the Stoic view that conventional goods are of indifferent value. In fact, there is little evidence that prominent early Stoics such as Chrysippus wrote about beauty as possessing or lacking intrinsic value.[10] One of the extant arguments states that only the beautiful (τὸ καλόν) is the good, but, as will be argued in Chapter 3, the context of this argument shows that it concerns an inference about the properties of the good rather than the equation of beauty with morality. Beauty, in this case, plays an instrumental role in making such inferences. There is also a group of surviving theological arguments which state that the beauty of the world, especially astronomical phenomena, is an indication of the manner in which the world was generated. All these ideas suggest that the Stoics employed beauty terms to denote attributions of value and to construct logical inferences. The Stoic concept of beauty, therefore, must have been much broader than Tatarkiewicz allowed. It was also more problematic, but in philosophically interesting ways. First, there is a tension between some fundamental Stoic ethical doctrines and the prominent role that beauty terms play in certain Stoic arguments, which raises the question of the relationship between morality and aesthetic value. Second, the employment of aesthetic terms in wide-ranging contexts raises the question of the unity of the underlying theory. In order to determine the scope of the Stoic theory, it is necessary to consider the broad context in which they occur. This concerns not only the historical context (which will be discussed in later chapters) but also the philosophical one, in the sense of the problems that the aesthetic phenomenon poses and the manner in which these problems are typically approached.

Ancient aesthetics

Before delving into the philosophical problems concerning beauty, it is necessary to address the potential issue that concerns the area of this study, that is, ancient aesthetics. Any work on ancient aesthetics inevitably faces the question of whether the term itself is not anachronistic and inappropriate. Before discussing the tradition of the theories of beauty and how Stoic thought might fit into it, it is necessary to address the concern of whether ancient thought can be a part of aesthetics in general. The most famous and often-cited proponent of the view that philosophers and thinkers did not make proper aesthetic enquiries until the eighteenth century was Paul Oskar Kristeller, who argued as follows:

> We have to admit the conclusion, distasteful to many historians of aesthetics but grudgingly admitted by most of them, that ancient writers and thinkers, though confronted with excellent works of art and quite susceptible to their charm, were neither able nor eager to detach the aesthetic quality of these works of art from their intellectual, moral, religious and practical function or content, or to use such an aesthetic quality as a standard for grouping the fine arts together

or for making them the subject of a comprehensive philosophical interpretation.[11]

While some scholars treat this view as a serious challenge to ancient thought,[12] it has also been convincingly criticised in a large variety of ways. James Porter, for instance, has astutely criticised both Kristeller's premises and conclusions.[13] Stephen Halliwell has not only criticised Kristeller's argument itself,[14] but has also argued that the ideas of Plato and Aristotle are both relevant to the preoccupations of modern philosophers and address the foundational questions of aesthetics and philosophy of art.[15] As Anastasia-Erasmia Peponi has argued, despite the fact that in the eighteenth century aesthetics was conceived of as a discipline that investigates the fine arts, it does not follow that 'aesthetic' cannot be applied to historic material. Although the Greeks did not have an exact equivalent of the modern notion of 'fine arts', there is evidence that at least some thinkers grouped activities we call 'fine arts' and were interested in the effects produced by the beautiful properties of, for instance, poetry.[16]

There is, of course, always a risk of anachronism in attributing concepts to the ancients that originated much later. At the same time, there is a risk of denying that ancient philosophers were able to conceptualise certain positions just because their ideas originated in different contexts.[17] The sensitivity to context is necessary in any historical study, but this is due to the fact that the context often illuminates the richness of the thought. By itself, it cannot exclude certain debates from being part of a wider tradition. Kristeller's view that ancient thought ought to be separated from later developments in aesthetics because the ancients mixed aesthetic questions with moral, intellectual, practical and other questions, hence making their enquiries not purely 'aesthetic', can be challenged in this way too. In the introduction to *A Companion to Ancient Aesthetics*, the editors Pierre Destrée and Penelope Murray present a careful and context-sensitive study of the nature of ancient debates on aesthetics, including a discussion of the difference between the ancient and the modern traditions. And while ancient aesthetics is shown as a distinct tradition in its own right, it is also quite clear that it can be studied as a tradition of aesthetics. Its differences do not limit the ability of the ancient thinkers to offer interesting and valuable insights on the nature of aesthetic properties and art. In fact, in recent years, several substantial studies on both literary criticism and philosophical aesthetics have been published, and they are an additional proof that ancient aesthetics is a productive field of research.[18] Given the amount of work that has been done on this topic, it seems that Kristeller's challenge is not a great obstacle for including ancient thought in the general history of aesthetics.

More importantly, the way in which ancient thought is approached in the more recent and novel studies in aesthetics shows this challenge to be somewhat dated. Contemporary philosophers rarely subscribe to the restricted meaning of 'aesthetics'. The very idea that aesthetics is a clearly demarcated area of philosophy has been shown to be problematic.[19] Some of the more recent novel projects in aesthetics ignore these boundaries altogether and, as a result, show Kristeller's historical concept of aesthetics to be an untenable position.

Denis Dutton's monograph *Art Instinct*, for instance, is a rather innovative approach to the analysis of art production and experience. In this work, Dutton attempts to find solutions to standard questions raised by philosophers of art by employing insights provided by Charles Darwin's theory of natural selection. Since Dutton approaches aesthetic questions with a methodology which suggests that the practical and biological functions of objects are very significant for understanding artistic and aesthetic value, ancient ideas and theories that often treat aesthetics as connected to the considerations of the nature of human beings are as relevant as the ideas of their successors. Dutton not only briefly discusses Plato's critique of the arts in the *Republic* and Aristotle's theory of *mimesis* in the *Poetics* as works that exemplify some important problems and insights regarding human experience of the arts,[20] but even states that 'Plato and Aristotle invented aesthetics as analysis of the arts.'[21] This is not as rash an assertion as it might appear at first sight. In Dutton's theoretical framework, the fact that these philosophers do not approach aesthetic questions in the same manner as eighteenth-century thinkers is not a reason to exclude their thought from aesthetics, because his own project would not count as 'aesthetics' either according to Kristeller's definition. If Plato and Aristotle raised issues and proposed ideas that are significant for thinking about aesthetic properties and art, then it does make sense to speak of Platonic and Aristotelian aesthetics. Of course, not all classicists and experts on ancient philosophy will readily agree with Dutton's naming of Plato and Aristotle as the *inventors* of aesthetics,[22] but the way in which Dutton weaves ancient thought into his project shows that the scope of ancient discussions is by no means a reason to exclude them from the field of aesthetics.

Beauty and ethical puzzles

Questions about the nature of beauty have many ramifications in the philosophical analysis of value. The attribution of beauty to an object or a phenomenon implicitly assigns a certain value to that object.[23] This raises the question of the grounds on which beauty is a value and, in certain cases, this question is of great importance. For instance, if beauty prompts scientists to choose one theory over another, then the way in which beauty renders one theory more valuable than another is not trivial. Of course, in order to determine in what sense beauty renders an object valuable and choice-worthy, it is necessary to understand what kind of a property beauty is and how it comes into being.

In some cases, ethical discourses employ beauty terms to describe morality and thus problematise the relationship between beauty and morality.[24] One of the most powerful examples of the potential ambiguity between the references to beauty and morality is the ancient Greek term τὸ καλόν. This term is not easily translatable, and it is difficult – and, perhaps, not necessary – to interpret it in a single way.[25] In some cases, τὸ καλόν can be understood as denoting moral excellence, but there are instances in which it implies cultural and aesthetic values. In the term καλοσκἀγαθος, for instance, καλός often loses aesthetic connotations entirely, as this term can be used to denote, for instance, a high class.[26] When it stands alone, the adjective καλός can refer to good looks, but, at the same time, Kenneth Dover notes that '*kalos* and *aiskhros* are applied very freely indeed by the orators to any action, behaviour or achievement which evokes any kind of favourable reaction and praise or incurs any kind of contempt, hostility or reproach'.[27] In addition to this, in some contexts, this word can also refer to suitability and convenience.[28]

In the case of philosophical texts, the relationship between the good and the beautiful is complex not only linguistically, but also conceptually. These terms underpin conceptualisations of properties and the relationship between them. The treatments of the good (τὸ ἀγαθόν) and the beautiful (τὸ καλόν) in the works of Plato[29] and Aristotle[30] have received quite a lot of attention in recent scholarship. The views of Plotinus, especially his account of the perception of beauty, are also studied quite often.[31] These studies show that the philosophical use of beauty terms is a rich area of research, but the problem of translating τὸ καλόν and interpreting what concept it underpins is not limited to one period or specific philosophers.[32] There are also problems that concern beauty qua property in general, that is to say, beauty is no less problematic from the point of view of metaphysics.

Metaphysics of beauty

Arguably, the most recognisable issue concerning beauty in the modern Western tradition is the question of the subjectivity or objectivity of aesthetic judgements. Unlike ancient philosophers, who tend to discuss aesthetic judgements as if they were unproblematically objective, some early modern philosophers famously argue that aesthetic judgements are more subjective than objective. David Hume, for instance, argues for the subjectivity of aesthetic judgements as follows: 'Beauty is no quality in things themselves: It exists merely in the mind which contemplates them; and each mind perceives a different beauty. One person may even perceive deformity, where another is sensible of beauty; and every individual ought to acquiesce in his own sentiment, without pretending to regulate those of others.'[33] Immanuel Kant, one of the more important figures in the history of aesthetics, also argues that the judgements of beauty are of a subjective kind.[34] Nowadays, it is generally recognised that the strong versions of either subjectivism or objectivism are untenable and a different approach, perhaps combining some elements of both positions, is needed. Despite the fact that these debates have somewhat lost their urgency, certain parts of them are still informing contemporary positions on the metaphysics of beauty, which is increasingly becoming a more popular area of research.[35]

Kant's distinction between judgements of free and dependent beauty, for instance, is a notable example of an idea from the early modern period that is employed in current debates on the metaphysics of beauty. Kant argues that judgements of beauty in flowers, birds, decorative design and music not set to words are some examples of free judgements of taste, because 'no concept is here presupposed of any end for which the manifold should serve the given object, and which the latter, therefore, should represent. . . . But the beauty of man . . . presupposes a concept of the end that defines what the thing has to be, and consequently a concept of its perfection; and is therefore merely adherent beauty.'[36] This notion of dependent beauty is used by some contemporary thinkers to deny the unity of all manifestations of beauty, which, arguably, is the central problem for the metaphysics of beauty. This problem arises from the following phenomenon.

A landscape, a person, a painting, a piece of music and a mathematical theorem can be beautiful. The nature of all these objects, however, is so different that it is not at all clear that one is referring to the same property when one is making these aesthetic judgements. This lack of clarity regarding the reference of the term 'beauty' is commonly recognised as one of the principal problems in aesthetics by philosophers, theorists of beauty and those who engage with the topic marginally.[37] The problem can be phrased in different ways, but fundamentally it consists of the question of whether all the diverse manifestations of beauty share a common subvening property that grounds and unifies them. A subsequent, and no less significant, question is whether there are principles of beauty; that is, whether there are sufficient and necessary conditions which fully explain and even predict the manifestations of aesthetic properties.

There are, thus, two ways of conceptualising beauty: a pluralist and a reductive theory of beauty. The accounts of beauty which I call pluralist state that the beauty of an object ought to be understood in terms of the non-aesthetic properties of that *kind* of object only, so that beauty in two objects of different kinds ought to be understood as two different kinds of properties. Broadly speaking, such accounts state that the instances of beauty found in objects of different kinds are different kinds of beauty that can only be understood in terms of the nature of those objects that happen to be beautiful. Consequently, it is impossible to have a single account which would explain all the instances of beauty. Jerrold Levinson presents a very clear version of such an argument. According to him, in the case of the comparison between human weight, animal weight and inanimate weight, it is obvious that the issue at stake is the same property – weight – because attributing weight to different objects does not change the meaning of the term 'weight'. Then Levinson argues that 'when it comes to the beauty exhibited by a person's face, a tidepool, a Cézanne still life, and a suspension bridge by Santiago Calatrava, it is almost impossible to avoid remarking that each is, indeed, beautiful in its own way'.[38]

A pluralist stance is especially often adopted when discussing human beauty. Nick Zangwill, for instance, suggests that human beauty is 'clearly dependent beauty. A person is beautiful not as an abstract sculpture, but as a human being.'[39] Here, he uses the Kantian notion of dependent beauty as a property that is always dependent on the *kind* of object in which it manifests itself and, therefore, not reducible to a single kind of property. These accounts, which I call pluralist, suggest that the instances of beauty originating from objects of different kinds are, in fact, different kinds of properties that are irreducible to a single principle. Similarly, those accounts which explain human beauty in terms of the Darwinian understanding of sexuality also imply a pluralist understanding of beauty.[40] The beauty of an object amounts to the excellence of its functioning as an object of its kind; for instance, human beauty amounts to physical features that signify health and a capacity to reproduce.[41]

Reductive theories of beauty, meanwhile, maintain that all

instances of beauty do share something in common. More importantly, such theories typically offer an account of beauty which would account for all (or most) instances of beauty. The metaphysical accounts of this type propose that all instances of beauty share a property, a cognitive process or a circumstance that allows beauty to supervene or construct the necessary and sufficient conditions for beauty in some other way. In general, reductive accounts have been mostly under attack for the last century. Yet a suggestion that the meaning attributed to the predicate of the sentence 'a person is beautiful' is different from the meaning attributed to the predicate of the sentence 'this theorem is beautiful' is by no means immediately obvious and requires further explanation. This is the driving motivation for the reductive theories. And while historically, reductive theories often relied on complex theoretical devices to unify the diverse manifestations of beauty (Platonic Form is arguably the best known example of such a theoretical device), which can be critised as unnecessarily burdensome, more recently, Jennifer McMahon has shown how a reductive theory of beauty – which draws inspiration from the ancient philosophical accounts – might be conceptualised within a physicalist worldview.[42] This project also suggests that the references to ancient debates can be used very productively today. Yet a thorough and precise understanding of ancient thought on the questions pertinent to aesthetics is necessary for such undertakings. This is true not only of well-known figures such as Plato (as well as the subsequent Platonist tradition) and Aristotle, but also of such schools as the Stoa. The Stoic use of beauty terms, after all, problematises the concept of beauty in a way which is similar to the issues raised by contemporary philosophers, because it raises the question of the unity of the manifestations of beauty. An enquiry into the ideas of such Hellenistic schools as the Stoa, therefore, is of interest not only from a historical but also from a philosophical perspective.

The scope of the study

The development of the Stoa is traditionally divided into three stages: the early period, the middle period and the Roman period.

Philosophers from each of these periods had different interests and characteristics. In addition to these distinctions, some individual philosophers are known to diverge from orthodox Stoicism.[43] For these reasons, it would be too speculative to assume that it is possible to speak of Stoic ideas as if they constitute a homogeneous system of thought. The historical scope of the study of Stoic aesthetics, therefore, is inevitably limited.

In order to analyse the Stoic concept of beauty in a coherent and historically plausible manner, I narrow down the scope of my analysis to the views that can be attributed to Chrysippus. The restriction to one philosopher ought to ensure that any coherence amongst the views that might emerge is not accidental. The choice of this particular Stoic is motivated by several reasons. First, since arguments from different areas of philosophy are investigated in this book, it is necessary to choose a philosopher who contributed to all these areas. Chrysippus fulfils such a requirement better than any other Stoic. He wrote not only profusely,[44] but also on a great variety of topics ranging from logic to political theory. All of the most important arguments that discuss beauty or use beauty vocabulary – from the definition of beauty as *summetria* to the argument that only the wise man is beautiful – can be attributed to Chrysippus. This does not mean that he is the author of these arguments, but the evidence shows that Chrysippus engaged with and subscribed to the ideas inherent in these arguments. These arguments can, therefore, be investigated as representing his views. Second, Chrysippus was the author of and a contributor to some of the most important Stoic metaphysical ideas. Some of the interpretations of Stoic arguments in this book require to be tested against Stoic metaphysics, and since the most relevant metaphysical doctrines can be attributed to Chrysippus, it is both convenient and more plausible to concentrate on investigating those Stoic concepts of beauty that can be attributed to him.[45]

Approaching the Stoic concept of beauty by means of Chrysippus' ideas has one more advantage. Chrysippus is a very significant figure in the development of early Stoicism; his views represent one of the most important stages in the history of this philosophical school. It could also be argued that Chrysippus' views exemplify the original Stoicism,[46] while middle and Roman Stoicism can be treated as distinct developments of Stoic thought.[47] This is not to say that the early Stoics were not influenced by their predecessors.[48] These connections are important and at least some of them will be investigated in the relevant chapters. It is worth noting from the outset, however, that one of the main theses of this work is that Stoic views were distinct. As is shown in Chapter 7 in particular, the comparison between the Stoic definition of beauty as *summetria* and the Platonic as well as the Aristotelian discussions of beauty show that the Stoic definition has a distinct form. The same is true of, for instance, the use of *summetria* in some Pythagorean texts. In order to appreciate the Stoic theory, it is necessary to note the ways in which the theorisations of beauty attributed to Chrysippus were novel and critical of his predecessors' views.

This approach does not suggest that the ideas discussed are Chrysippean alone. It has been shown that there is a strong connection between the views of Posidonius and Chrysippus, for example.[49] The focus on Chrysippus serves as a methodological tool to ground the discussion historically and to lend coherence to the reading of the sources. The figure of Chrysippus, thus, anchors this discussion and, at the same time, serves as the starting point of the enquiry. Once the main evidence is covered, it will become clear that Chrysippean aesthetics is Stoic aesthetics, because the arguments pertinent to aesthetics are the ones that originate from the central Stoic commitments and are shared by many Stoics. The differences will be noted but, broadly speaking, they are mostly exceptions that prove the rule.

Although there are many advantages to concentrating on Chrysippus, such an approach imposes some restrictions on the scope of this investigation. Some of them are methodological. Most notably, just like the works of many of the early and middle Stoics, the works of Chrysippus are not extant. The evidence for his views is preserved in the doxographical sources and the works of authors critical of the Stoics. The project of this book is a reconstruction of these views, which involves some critical discussion of the sources.

There is also some restriction of the scope of this project in terms of the topics discussed. While some Stoics engaged in the production and criticism of artworks, Chrysippus neither composed poetry nor wrote on literary criticism or philosophy of art. Chrysippus' predecessor Cleanthes is known for composing the *Hymn to Zeus*,[50] a philosophical poem on Stoic theology, while the Roman Stoic Seneca wrote tragedies.[51] Aratus' *Phaenomena*, although not a philosophical poem *per se*, exhibits strong Stoic influences.[52] Arguably, Stoic ideas even influenced the visual arts, as the statues in the library at Pergamum suggest.[53] It has also been argued that Stoic thought contained substantial reflections on questions of craftsmanship and the role of the artist,[54] influencing Renaissance aesthetic thought.[55] Perhaps the most substantial of all Stoic engagements with the arts is their contribution to the development of Hellenistic literary criticism and musical theory.

The discoveries of papyri at Herculaneum that contain literary and musical theories have ignited much interest in Hellenistic literary and art criticism in recent years. The most prominent example is Philodemus' treatises, which have opened the possibility of investigating not only the Epicurean, but also the Stoic philosophy of art.[56] This is due to the fact that, for example, in his *On Poems*, Philodemus criticises the Stoic poetic theory.[57] Diogenes Laertius preserves some corroborating evidence, as he records that Posidonius wrote on poetic theory.[58] Diogenes of Babylon also advocates substantial and original theories on sound, music and poetry that are very interesting in their own right. Diogenes examines the nature of the arts in a way which Chrysippus had not done, as far as the extant evidence indicates. Chrysippus' ideas were only one of several influences for the theories produced by Diogenes of Babylon[59] which constitute a significant development of the scope of Stoic enquiry.[60]

The Stoic philosophy of art is outside the scope of the current work, however. This study is primarily concerned with the ideas which Chrysippus developed in the context of the traditional Stoic areas of philosophy: metaphysics, epistemology and ethics.[61] That is not to say that Chrysippus never made any references to or produced insights into art or literature, but only that his treatment of these areas was rather superficial and accidental. It is known that he was, for instance, keen on quoting literature. A particularly vivid anecdote recorded by Diogenes Laertius suggests that, in one of his treatises, Chrysippus quoted Euripides' *Medea* so extensively that a reader referred to it as 'Chrysippus' *Medea*'.[62] There is hardly any indication, however, that Chrysippus was interested in the *Medea* for its literary value. It is more likely that he cited it for instrumental purposes to support his own philosophical agenda.[63] The Stoics in general, including the Roman Stoics, showed interest in Medea and her story. This tragedy is cited and discussed by Epictetus,[64] while Seneca wrote his own version of it.[65] Perhaps it was Chrysippus who started this trend amongst the Stoics, although the practice of citing poetry or tragedy in order to support philosophical points was by no means peculiar to the Stoics.

Although the list of titles of his treatises recorded by Diogenes Laertius reveals that Chrysippus wrote treatises titled *On Poems* (Περὶ ποιημάτων) and *On How to Listen to Poetry* (Περὶ τοῦ πῶς δεῖ τῶν ποιημάτων ἀκούειν), these titles are listed under the subheading of 'Ethics dealing with the classification of ethical concepts'[66] by Diogenes, which suggests that the agenda of these treatises was primarily to discuss Stoic ethics rather than to comment on literary works for their own sake. Similarly, the treatise *On Rhetoric* (Περὶ τῆς ῥητορικῆς)[67] is listed under 'Ethics dealing with the common view and the sciences and virtues thence arising'.[68] Diogenes' classification suggests that the Stoic interest in literary works was strongly influenced by ethical discussions, although with no surviving evidence, it is impossible to judge with certainty the exact content of these treatises.[69] Chrysippus also composed a treatise titled *On Beauty* (Περὶ καλοῦ), but it was probably dedicated primarily to ethical issues. The best-known extant part of this treatise is the argument that only the beautiful is the good, and our sources indicate that this argument was intended to support the Stoics' tenet that only virtue is the good.[70] The treatise *On Beauty* may have dealt with the aesthetic properties of virtue, yet it seems unlikely that Chrysippus also wrote on the philosophy of art in this treatise.

The way in which Dionysius of Halicarnassus criticises Chrysippus also suggests that he was not an authority on rhetoric. Dionysius explains Chrysippus' failure as a writer by noting that he wrote on syntax, 'the grouping of propositions, true or false, possible and impossible, admissible and variable, ambiguous and so forth',[71] rather than on *synthesis*, 'the art of composing an aesthetically satisfactory (ἡδεῖα καὶ καλή) text'.[72] So even in antiquity Chrysippus was known as a philosopher concerned with logic rather than rhetoric or literary criticism. For this reason, the scope of this study is limited to the nature of aesthetic properties in metaphysical, epistemological and ethical arguments. It does not extend to the philosophy of art, although the conclusions of this study will be relevant for the Stoic philosophy of art as well.

Chapter plan

The first section of this work is dedicated to the discussion of the Stoic theory of value, especially in regard to the category of 'indifferents' which includes beauty. Chapter 2 is focused on the question that naturally arises in this case, namely, the challenge that the very categorisation of beauty amongst the objects of indifferent value poses for aesthetics. The Stoics notoriously claim that only virtue is good, while only vice is bad and everything else, including health, wealth, beauty and life itself, are mere indifferents. The inclusion of beauty in this list seems to indicate that the Stoics were not interested in theorising beauty. This does not necessarily follow. A thorough reading of the material shows that beauty is not treated as irrelevant in general; our evidence only shows that it is a value inferior to virtue. This interpretation is supported by a fairly large amount of evidence, including the later Roman Stoic texts, such as the works of Epictetus. Most importantly, this interpretation shows that the Stoic theory of value and aesthetics are not mutually exclusive areas of study.

Chapter 3, 'The Beautiful and the Good', starts with the question of the relationship between τὸ καλόν (typically signifying moral beauty, sometimes translated as an ethical term) and τὸ κάλλος (physical beauty). The focus of this chapter is the vague relationship between aesthetic and moral values. The Stoic stance on this problematic issue is best exemplified by the argument 'that only the beautiful is the good' (μόνον τὸ καλὸν ἀγαθὸν εἶναι).

The reconstruction suggests that, despite the fact that different interpretations of this argument are given in the doxographical material, the syllogism which accompanied the argument in the original Chrysippean version points to a very specific idea. In this argument, beauty plays the role of a distinguishing sign peculiar to the true good. Beauty signifies the true good and makes it distinct from merely apparent goods. It supports the Stoic tenet that virtue is the only genuine good by claiming that beauty distinguishes true good from other, merely apparent, goods.

Chapter 4 is dedicated to analysing the so-called Stoic paradox that only the wise man is beautiful, which implies that young, conventionally attractive youths are not. Plutarch's testimonial and critique of these views claims that they commit what in contemporary terms is sometimes called the 'No True Scotsman' fallacy, that is, an arbitrary redefinition of terms, in this case, aesthetic terms. This chapter offers an alternative and more charitable interpretation of these claims. This reading involves the notion of aesthetic functionality, that is, the idea that an object's aesthetic value is determined in reference to the kind of object it is. This interpretation of the Stoic wise man paradox is consistent with the central Stoic tenets about virtue and happiness.

Chapter 5 is dedicated to analysing theological arguments in which aesthetic vocabulary plays a prominent role. In these arguments, the beauty of the world is used to make an inference about its rational generation. To be precise, the arguments state that the presence of beauty in the world indicates that the world must have been generated by means of a rational principle and not by the random motion of atoms (as argued by the Epicureans). This reading is followed by the examination of the issues of how beauty is used to form this inference and what theoretical implications the use of aesthetic terms in this context underpins. The findings here are consistent with the findings in the previous chapters, especially in regard to the notion of good order or, to be more precise, well-functioning order. Thus, a systematic Stoic theory of aesthetics begins to emerge. The most substantial evidence for this theory is discussed in the following chapter.

The Stoic definition of beauty as *summetria* of parts with each other and with the whole is undoubtedly a central concept in Stoic aesthetic discourse. In Chapter 6, the evidence for this definition is presented and discussed. Although the evidence is somewhat fragmentary, it is relatively abundant as there are four explicit citations of the definition and numerous shorter references equating *summetria* with beauty. This definition is important because it reveals how the Stoics theorised beauty metaphysically. Beauty is a property that supervenes on the composition of non-aesthetic properties. Since supervenience is generally considered to be a contemporary concept, the Stoic theory of categories helps to determine whether Stoic physics could support the conceptualisation of such a phenomenon. Finally, the criticism that Plotinus levelled at the Stoic definition of beauty, namely, that their theory cannot account for why a well-organised virtue, but not a well-organised vice, possesses beauty, is introduced and discussed. Arguably, there is one insight that has emerged in the previous chapters, namely, the notion of *functional* composition, which would allow the Stoics to respond to this Plotinian critique.

Consequently, the Stoic definition of beauty is best understood as the claim that aesthetic properties supervene on two aspects of an object: (i) the formal properties of the object (*summetria* of parts with each other) and (ii) the functional properties of the object (*summetria* of parts with the whole). The definition states that in order for an object to be beautiful, it must possess a harmonious composition for the kind of object that it is. This reading is corroborated by noting that the concept of functional beauty was a viable theoretical option for thinking about beauty for ancient philosophers, and showing that a number of references in the Stoic fragments suggest that they employed the notion of functional composition in their arguments. The final section of the book situates this theory in its context.

Chapter 7 presents the argument that the Stoic definition of beauty and the way in which beauty vocabulary is used in various arguments are remarkably consistent. This coherence suggests that while there is no extant Stoic treatise on aesthetics, their engagement with this area of philosophy must have been thorough and substantial. Their ideas both differed from and corresponded with other aesthetic theories in antiquity. First, the evidence of Polycleitus' theory about the origin of beauty is examined, including a discussion of how this theory is received and understood in Vitruvius' *On Architecture* and related sources. The evidence shows that Polycleitean *summetriae* were not so much an attempt to theorise beauty as such, but rather a technical instruction – consisting of a series of ratios – for creating a beautiful statue or painting. These ratios were numerous and depended on the object depicted. These *summetriae* relied heavily on mathematics and this approach to aesthetic properties found its way into philosophy. The Pythagoreans are especially noted for the importance they assigned to number. The fragments of early fifth-century figures such as Philolaus of Croton show, however, that Pythagorean views differed in some important respects from the ways in which artists such as Polycleitus accounted for aesthetic properties.

The same is true of the ways in which the notion of *summetria* is employed in the works of Plato and Aristotle, both of whom used the term in connection with theorising beauty, but in distinct ways. There is a large amount of recent scholarship on Plato's views on art, but the primary focus in this case is his views on the origin and significance of aesthetic properties in such dialogues as the *Philebus* and the *Symposium*. The definitions of beauty in Aristotle's works and the conditions for beauty that his extant works posit are also discussed. The comparison between Plato, Aristotle and the Stoics shows that although the term *summetria* can be found in the works of all of them, it is used differently and for different theoretical purposes. The upshot of this is that the Stoic definition of beauty as *summetria* was a distinct theory that accounted for aesthetic properties in reductive terms, that is, as a functional structure. It rivalled the Platonic accounts in which Forms played the central role. Plotinus' attack on Stoicism shows that this rivalry lasted for a long time, and that while Platonism dominated the philosophical scene in late antiquity, Stoic views survived in other contexts. This is evident in Galen's discussion of the recognisably Stoic view within alleged Hippocratic context. Having discussed the ancient tradition of aesthetics and the role of Stoic ideas within it, the chapter concludes with a brief discussion of the place of aesthetics within Stoicism and the place of Stoicism within aesthetics.

Notes

1. Donoghue (2003: 25).
2. Tatarkiewicz (1972: 165).
3. Tatarkiewicz (1972: 166).
4. Tatarkiewicz (1972: 166).
5. Possibly the most problematic aspect of Tatarkiewicz's classification and similar taxonomies is the way in which they treat ideas about beauty as stable and unified at any given historical period. For a more contemporary approach which advocates a pluralist understanding of aesthetic discourse see, for instance, Halliwell (2012: 16–17).
6. In this section, I use the generic term 'Stoic' while presenting the overall direction of my enquiry, but I will limit my historical scope to Chrysippus' ideas and give my motivation for this choice below.
7. Tatarkiewicz (1970: 193).
8. Diogenes Laertius 7.102=LS 58A.
9. These claims and their implications are discussed in depth in Chapters 4 and 6.
10. It is important to note that although beauty is classed as one of the preferred indifferents by the Stoics (Diogenes Laertius 7.102=LS 58A), this does not mean that the Stoics denied the value of beauty or prohibited its pursuit entirely. For an insightful study of the Stoic notion of preferred indifferents, cf. Brennan (2005, especially 130–1).
11. Kristeller (1951: 506). This view, put in general terms, predates Kristeller and can even be found in, for instance, Tolstoy's famous essay *What is Art?* ([original Russian edn 1897] 1995: section 2).
12. See Roman (2014: 12).
13. See Porter (2009).
14. Halliwell (2002: 7–11).
15. Halliwell (1991).
16. Peponi (2012: 2–6). See also Halliwell (2002: 7, n. 18) for evidence that the grouping of the arts into a single family can be found already in Aristotle's *Poetics* and attempts at such classification continued into late antiquity.

17. See, for the example, the case of aesthetic indifference and the Epicurean position on the proper approach to the arts in Čelkytė (2017).
18. See Porter's *The Origins of Aesthetic Thought in Ancient Greece: Matter, Sensation, and Experience* (2010); Konstan's *Beauty: The Fortunes of An Ancient Greek Idea* (2014); Anastasia-Erasmia Peponi, *Frontiers of Pleasure: Models of Aesthetic Response in Archaic and Classical Greek Thought* (2012); cf. edited volumes, including *Aesthetic Value in Classical Antiquity* (2012), edited by Ineke Sluiter and Ralph Rosen, and *A Companion to Ancient Aesthetics* (2015), edited by Pierre Destrée and Penelope Murray as well as *Greek Philosophy and the Fine Arts*, Volume 2 (2000), edited by Konstantine Boudouris.
19. Walton (2007).
20. Dutton (2009: 31–6). It is noteworthy that some early twentieth-century philosophers were also not averse to the idea that ancient philosophers might have had the same conceptualisations of aesthetic objects (such as art and beauty), cf. Collingwood (1925: 162).
21. Dutton (2009: 166).
22. It is noteworthy, however, that Halliwell (2009: 472) also suggests that Plato can be thought of as the founder of philosophical aesthetics.
23. Arguably, the most in-depth analysis of aesthetic value is still C. I. Lewis' *An Analysis of Knowledge and Valuation* (1946).
24. Contemporary discussions generally concentrate on the problem of ethics and aesthetics in art. See Bermúdez and Gardner (2003).
25. Martha Nussbaum, when discussing the supposed dichotomy between philosophical and literary endeavours, noted the following: 'For the Greeks of the fifth and early fourth centuries BC, there were not two separate sets of questions in the area of human choice and action, aesthetics questions and moral-philosophical questions, to be studied and written about by mutually detached colleagues in different departments. Instead, dramatic poetry and what we now call philosophical enquiry in ethics were both typically framed by, seen as ways of pursuing, a single and general question: namely, how human beings should live' (1990: 15). See also Sartwell (2004: 88–92).
26. Dover (1994: 41–5).
27. Dover (1994: 70).
28. Dover (1994: 71).

29. Rachel Barney, for instance, addresses the question of whether the way in which Plato associated these terms indicates that the Form of the Good and the Form of the Beautiful are identical (2010: 366). She concludes that the good and the beautiful are ultimately different properties, despite the fact that very often they coincide for the following reason: 'To be fine is to be the appropriate object and characteristic cause of admiration; to be good is to be the appropriate object and characteristic cause of desire' (Barney (2010: 377)). It is interesting to note that Aryeh Kosman's article 'Beauty and the Good: Situating the *Kalon*' in the same special edition of *Classical Philology*, although much broader in scope, also concludes that ancient philosophers did not equate the good with the beautiful, while maintaining that there is a close and important connection between the two properties (Kosman 2010: 356–7).

30. The usage – and especially the translation – of the term τὸ καλόν is a problematic and contentious issue in Aristotle's works as well. Terence Irwin argues that there is no single concept of beauty which underlies all the instances of beauty terms in Aristotle's corpus, and 'if . . . we are to do justice to Aristotle's use of *kalon* and to his arguments about different kinds of *kalon* things, we should probably prefer a uniform translation that does not suggest one type of *kalon* rather than another. Unsuitable uniform translations include "beautiful", "right", "noble", and all cognates of "honor". Suitable translations include "fine" and "admirable", and perhaps "fitting" (to mark the close connection between *kalon* and *prepon*)' (Irwin (2010: 396)). More recently, this drastic conclusion has been challenged by Richard Kraut (2013). He convincingly argues that such a uniform translation of τὸ καλόν is not coherent with Aristotle's points about the formal properties of τὸ καλόν and, more importantly, does not convey all the nuances of Aristotle's arguments. It is better, therefore, to choose an aesthetic translation of τὸ καλόν in some cases.

31. I have already mentioned a number of articles that deal with the question of aesthetics in Plato and Aristotle. See the analyses of Plotinian aesthetics by Kuisma (2003); Perl (2007); Gál (2011).

32. As Oleg Bychkov has argued, this is a very relevant issue in Stoic texts as well, and it is important not to translate τὸ καλόν uniformly as an ethical term (2010: 176).

33. Hume (1985: 230), original edn 1757.
34. 'If judgements of taste (like cognitive judgements) were in possession of a definite objective principle, then one who in his judgement followed such a principle would claim unconditioned necessity for it. Again, if they were devoid of any principle, as are those of the mere taste of the senses, then no thought of any necessity on their part would enter one's head. Therefore they must have a subjective principle, and one which determines what pleases or displeases, by means of feeling only and not through concepts, but yet with universal validity' (2007: §20, 237–8), tr. Meredith. The nature of this subjectivity is explained in greater detail later, at §§56–8, 338–51).
35. Such works as Arthur Danto's *The Abuse of Beauty* (2003), Crispin Sartwell's *Six Names of Beauty* (2004) and Nick Zangwill's *The Metaphysics of Beauty* (2001) are just a few examples of resurgent interest in beauty amongst philosophers.
36. Kant (2007: §16, 229–30), tr. Meredith.
37. Mothersill (2009: 171); Scruton (2009: 1); Clercq (2013: 302); Sheppard (1987: 56–7); Tatarkiewicz (1972: 166); Sartwell (2004: 10); Kintsch (2012: 636); Mynott (2009: 112).
38. Levinson (2011: 192–3). For a similar (although briefer) treatment of this question, see Clercq (2013). It is not uncommon for early twentieth-century philosophers to claim that, for instance, the beauty of art and the beauty of a butterfly do not excite the same kind of response; cf. Bell (1987: 12–13) for an example of such an argument.
39. Zangwill (2003: 336).
40. See McMahon (2005: 13), who attributes the origin of this idea to Freud.
41. Pinker (1997: 483).
42. McMahon (1999: 7–27).
43. Possibly the most famous rebel amongst the early Stoics was Aristo of Chios. See Sextus Empiricus *M*=11.64–7=*SVF* 1.361=LS 58F.
44. Diogenes Laertius (7.180) attributes more than 705 treatises to Chrysippus.
45. I assume that there is a conceptual coherence in Chrysippus' thought. For the problem of the unity of Stoicism, see Inwood (2012).
46. For a survey of the evidence for Chrysippus' reputation, see Gould (1970: 7–17).

47. Antiochus of Ascalon, for instance, converted from Academic scepticism to Stoic dogmatism. His beliefs appear to have had some original features originating from his diverse philosophical commitments; see Barnes (1989: 70–6; 78–89).
48. For a more general discussion, see Harte, McCabe, Sharples and Sheppard (2010). This influence is discussed in the field of aesthetics too. Zagdoun (2000: 80) noted that the Stoics borrowed elements from other philosophers, but '*la définition stoïcienne du beau dans son ensemble est originale et serait incompréhensible sans une référence constante aux fondements du stoïcisme*'.
49. See, for example, Tieleman (2003: ch. 5, esp. 198–200).
50. See Asmis (2007).
51. See Staley (2009: 11–23) for a study of Seneca's theorisation of tragedy.
52. Fowler (1989: 115, 163–6).
53. Onians (1979: 88–94).
54. Zagdoun (2000) is the most exhaustive study on this topic. See especially Zagdoun (2000: 48–69; 239–50).
55. Close (1971: 176–9).
56. Richard Janko's editions of Philodemus' *On Poems 1* (2000) and *On Poems 3–4* (2011) are arguably the most important foundational works in this area. Elizabeth Asmis has also written profusely on Philodemus' views, cf. for instance Asmis (1995), (1998) and (2004).
57. Asmis (1990) argues that the author of this theory might have been Aristo.
58. Diogenes Laertius 7.60.
59. Janko (2000: 181).
60. De Lacy (1948) presents a summary and a discussion of literary and musical theories developed by the later Stoics.
61. This terminology is, of course, contemporary. The evidence suggests that the early Stoics called these areas 'physics', 'logic' and 'ethics' (Diogenes Laertius 7.39). Although the Stoic classification did not overlap exactly with the boundaries of the contemporary subdisciplines of philosophy (cf. Ierodiakonou (1993)), in this work I use the modern equivalent 'metaphysics' when I write on the topics which are typically considered metaphysical today, but which the Stoics would have labelled as 'physics'.

62. Diogenes Laertius 7.180.
63. Blank (2011: 262): 'In both Chrysippus and Plutarch, one is not meant merely to *read* poetry; rather, one should *use* poetry as a stock of materials for improving the mind and for making plausible the force and structure of ethical notions.' The Stoics, moreover, were criticised for such a view of poetry by some Hellenistic scholars, according to Gutzwiller (2007: 35–6). See Nussbaum (1993: 148–9) for the argument that the early Stoics subscribed to a cognitive view of poetry and 'while apparently treating the poets as wise men and sources of insight, Stoic thinkers never really admit the possibility that poetry might actually have something to teach *them* – not just about diseases, but about full health, not just about aberration but about the complete human life.' For a thorough study of how exactly Chrysippus used certain passages from *Medea* for the explication of his doctrines, see Gill (1983), (1996: 226–36) and (2006: 259–65). See Tieleman (1996: 219–48) for a study of Chrysippus' exegesis and adoption of Homeric and Hesiodic verses for his philosophical purposes.
64. *Disc.* 1.28.6–10.
65. For a philosophical reading of Seneca's *Medea*, see Gill (2006: 422–36).
66. Diogenes Laertius 7.199, tr. Hicks: Ἠθικοῦ λόγου τοῦ περὶ τὴν διάρθρωσιν τῶν ἠθικῶν ἐννοιῶν.
67. Diogenes Laertius 7.202.
68. Diogenes Laertius 7.201, tr. Hicks: Ἠθικοῦ τόπου περὶ τὸν κοινὸν λόγον καὶ τὰς ἐκ τούτου συνισταμένας τέχνας καὶ ἀρετάς.
69. See Hunter and Russell (2011: 12).
70. See Chapter 3 for the discussion of this evidence.
71. Dionysius of Halicarnassus *Comp.* 4.20–1, tr. Usher.
72. Wiater (2011: 241).

2

The Problem of Indifferents

'Mankind, including every description, wish to be loved and respected by something; and the common herd will always take the nearest road to the completion of their wishes. The respect paid to wealth and beauty is the most certain, and unequivocal; and, of course, will always attract the vulgar eye of common minds.'
   Mary Wollstonecraft, *A Vindication of the Rights of Woman*[1]

The Stoics offered substantial contributions to many areas of philosophy, yet they are undoubtedly best known for their ethics. So much so that the term 'stoic' entered the common vocabulary as an adjective for describing indifference and resilience to tough circumstances. This term undoubtedly refers to the notorious Stoic argument that only virtue is the good because one of the more controversial consequences of this argument is that the things conventionally considered to be the good are indifferents. The Stoic indifferents include health, wealth, beauty and life itself. This claim has wide-reaching consequences, including some implications for aesthetic judgements. Seemingly the most pressing consequence of the claim is that it leaves no room for aesthetics. After all, if aesthetic value is not a genuine type of value, then what is there to say about it? A closer inspection of the Stoic argument concerning values, however, shows that this is not as significant a problem as it might at first appear.

The good, the bad and the indifferent

The most extensive descriptions in the extant evidence come from Diogenes Laertius and Arius Didymus' *Epitome of Stoic Ethics*, preserved by Stobaeus. Diogenes Laertius introduces the Stoic doctrine by noting that, according to the Stoics, existing things can be divided, in accordance with their value, into good, bad and neither. While virtues such as prudence (φρόνησις) or justice (δικαιοσύνη) belong to the first category and vices to the second, the things listed in the third category are as follows: 'life, health, pleasure, beauty, strength, wealth, reputation, noble birth, and their opposites'.[2] Then Diogenes references the Stoics who wrote on these views: Hecato in his seventh book of the treatise *On the End* (Περὶ τέλους), Apollodorus in his book *Ethics* (Ἐν τῇ ἠθικῇ) and Chrysippus (no specific treatise of his is mentioned).[3] This list is most likely not exhaustive, and it shows that this doctrine was widely adopted by the Stoics.[4]

Although all the value categories have some pertinence to Stoic thought on aesthetics,[5] the category of the indifferents ought to be addressed first because it raises the question that is fundamental for studying Stoic aesthetics: namely, the question of the Stoic attitude towards aesthetic values. One very significant point to note from the outset is the vocabulary. The term for beauty, τὸ κάλλος, used in these texts denotes bodily beauty. The differences between various kinds of beauty and the reasons they are important will be addressed in due course, once the necessary evidence has been discussed. For now, it is enough to note that bodily beauty is an appropriate place to start because it is the simplest, or at least the most familiar, kind of beauty. Determining its status as a value will pave the way for enquiring into more complex types of beauty, such as abstract and moral beauty.

The starting point of this study, therefore, is the question of the meaning of the category 'indifferent' and how the Stoic conceptualisation of beauty was affected by beauty's belonging to this category. The mere fact that the Stoics introduced such a category is notable. It distinguished them from their contemporaries and earned them their reputation as controversial philosophers. In order to appreciate the Stoic stance, it is important to note that their taxonomy of values has various subcategories and, arguably, the most notable subcategory is that of the indifferents which are 'preferred'. Diogenes Laertius' list of the three categories of the Stoic value system is immediately followed by the remark that these examples of indifferents are of the species 'preferred'. Then he offers a further elaboration of the category 'indifferent' as follows:

διχῶς δὲ λέγεσθαι ἀδιάφορα· ἅπαξ μὲν τὰ μήτε πρὸς εὐδαιμονίαν μήτε πρὸς κακοδαιμονίαν συνεργοῦντα, ὡς ἔχει πλοῦτος, δόξα, ὑγίεια, ἰσχὺς καὶ τὰ ὅμοια· ἐνδέχεται γὰρ καὶ χωρὶς τούτων εὐδαιμονεῖν, τῆς ποιᾶς αὐτῶν χρήσεως εὐδαιμονικῆς οὔσης ἢ κακοδαιμονικῆς. ἄλλως δὲ λέγεται ἀδιάφορα τὰ μήθ' ὁρμῆς μήτ' ἀφορμῆς κινητικά, ὡς ἔχει τὸ ἀρτίας ἔχειν ἐπὶ τῆς κεφαλῆς τρίχας ἢ περιττάς, ἢ ἐκτεῖναι τὸν δάκτυλον ἢ συστεῖλαι, τῶν προτέρων ἀδιαφόρων οὐκέθ' οὕτω λεγομένων· ὁρμῆς γάρ ἐστιν ἐκεῖνα καὶ ἀφορμῆς κινητικά. διὸ τὰ μὲν αὐτῶν ἐκλέγεται, <τὰ δὲ ἀπεκλέγεται>, τῶν [δ'] ἑτέρων ἐπίσης ἐχόντων πρὸς αἵρεσιν καὶ φυγήν.

'Indifferent' is used in two senses: unconditionally, of things which contribute neither to happiness nor unhappiness as is the case with wealth, reputation, health, strength and the like. For it is possible to be happy even without these, though the manner of using them is constitutive of happiness and unhappiness. In another sense those things are called indifferent which activate neither impulse nor repulsion, as in the case of having an odd or even number of hairs on one's head, or stretching or contracting a finger. But the previous indifferents are not spoken of in this sense. For they are capable of activating impulse and repulsion. Hence some of them are selected and others deselected, but the second type is entirely equal with respect to choice and avoidance.[6]

The same doctrine is recorded and described in a similar way in Arius Didymus' *Epitome of Stoic Ethics*. The content is almost exactly the same, with the exception of the examples of the genuinely indifferent things. In the text preserved by Stobaeus, those are pointing a finger in one rather than another direction, or picking something, such as a leaf or a twig, up in some way.[7] According to both of these accounts, there are two kinds of indifferent things: those that are subject to impulse or repulsion and those that are not. The latter are indifferent in the common sense, as the example of having an even or odd number of hairs shows. People generally place no value on such things and, therefore, they do not care whether they have an odd or an even number of hairs. The former, meanwhile, belong to the peculiar Stoic sense of indifferent, and it is quite important to distinguish between the two types of indifferents in order to appreciate the Stoic position.

The Stoic indifferent is the kind of object or phenomenon which provokes a reaction in a person. This reaction consists of two stages. The first stage is either pursuit or avoidance and the second stage is either choice or rejection. The latter follows the former and constitutes an attitude a person adopts towards a certain object in respect to that object's value. To be more precise, when a person encounters some object, the first reaction is either to pursue it or to avoid it. Yet one is not obliged to act in accordance with this first impression. In this way, one can 'select' or 'deselect' whether to adopt a certain attitude towards the object or, in other words, one forms a choice.[8] As the very first sentence of Diogenes' passage indicates, the goal of the act of choosing is happiness. The things that are indifferent in the Stoic sense of the term are of indifferent value in respect to happiness.

The two attitudes one can have towards an object, the pursuit and the choice, form the foundation of the Stoic doctrine of value. Notably, the two attitudes have different objects. Whereas anything can be pursued, only virtue is an object of choice.[9] Consequently, the enquiry into the role that aesthetic properties play in the Stoic ethical system has to be twofold. On the one hand, there is the question of the connection between virtues and aesthetic properties; on the other hand, there is also the question of the consequences of the claim that beauty is a preferred indifferent. Virtue, a genuine good, and its relation to aesthetic properties[10] will be discussed in the following chapter. The remainder of this chapter will be focused on the objects that one 'deselects', that is, the ones that are indifferent in the Stoic sense of the word. These are the objects of pursuit and avoidance, yet they are not choice-worthy, which raises the questions of how their value ought to be understood and what is the significance of the fact that beauty is found amongst the objects of pursuit.

Polemics

The list of the objects that are indifferent only is rather long and contains various things that are conventionally considered to be good or bad. Certainly the best way to appreciate such an idiosyncratic position is by contextualising the argument and thus noting what position the Stoics were reacting to with their claims.

Arguably, the primary target is the Peripatetic school and its founder, Aristotle. Although Aristotle agrees with those who maintain that happiness consists of virtue,[11] he adds that some external goods are also necessary for happiness. Friends, wealth or political power are necessary assets without which it is impossible or at least very hard to attain happiness. Such properties as low birth, unattractiveness or childlessness, meanwhile, necessarily detract from happiness.[12] This is due to the fact that the lack of certain external goods constitutes an impediment to happiness while happiness consists in complete and unobstructed activities.[13] Aristotle's position is motivated by reasoning that the lack of certain goods impedes the disadvantaged person's ability to exercise the actions that would, in ideal circumstances, constitute happiness. Those who deny this, for one reason or another, are talking nonsense, according to the arguments in the *Nicomachean Ethics*.

The Stoics were, of course, such nonsense-speakers.[14] Cicero's *On Ends* contains evidence that the disagreement between the Peripatetics and the Stoics was a noted debate. In this treatise, the Stoic spokesperson Cato presents an account that contrasts the Peripatetic and the Stoic accounts of the good, especially in respect to such issues as bodily well-being and the property of being rich. The contrast between the quite common-sensical Peripatetic and the fairly radical Stoic accounts raises the question of why the latter disagreed with the former or, to put it otherwise, what exactly is the error, according to the Stoics, that the Peripatetics make in their account of the good. It is interesting to note that the Stoics did not necessarily present their position as radical. On the contrary, there is extant evidence of Chrysippus claiming that the Stoic position is the one in accordance with common conceptions,[15] that is, the true impression imprinted on all human minds.[16]

One might be tempted to dismiss such a claim, but it is worth considering in what ways the Stoic system could appeal to common conceptions. Arguably, by bearing in mind that the Stoic position is motivated by an appeal to common conceptions, one can obtain a more nuanced insight into the Stoic critique of Peripatetic ethics, which goes as follows in the *On Ends*. First, Cato reports that, according to the Peripatetics, life cannot be complete without the conventional goods (*illi enim corporis commodis compleri vitam beatam putant*), which is in line with what is to be found in the *Nicomachean Ethics*. Then he states that, according to the Stoics, external goods are not relevant at all to having a happy life.[17] Subsequently, Cato adds the following arguments:

> *etenim, si et sapere expetendum sit et valere, coniunctum utrumque magis expetendum sit quam sapere solum, neque tamen, si utrumque sit aestimatione dignum, pluris sit coniunctum quam sapere ipsum separatim. nam qui valitudinem aestimatione aliqua dignam iudicamus neque eam tamen in bonis ponimus, idem censemus nullam esse tantam aestimationem, ut ea virtuti anteponatur. quod idem Peripatetici non tenent, quibus dicendum est, quae et honesta actio sit et sine dolore, eam magis esse expetendam, quam si esset eadem actio cum dolore. nobis aliter videtur, recte secusne, postea; sed potestne rerum maior esse dissensio?*

If wisdom and health are both worth seeking, then the two together are more worth seeking than wisdom alone. But if each commands some value, it does not follow that the two together are worth more than wisdom on its own. In judging that health commands a certain value, but not deeming it a good, we thereby consider that there is no value great enough to take precedence over virtue. This is not the Peripatetic position. They have to say that an act that is both virtuous and painless is more worth seeking than a virtuous act accompanied by pain. We think differently. Whether rightly or wrongly is a question to be considered later. But there could hardly be a greater difference between the two views.[18]

As Cato points out, the crucial difference between the Peripatetic and the Stoic positions is fairly straightforward. At first sight, the argument that positing two, rather than one, components for happiness somehow diminishes the value of one of those components might seem weak, but this is not the entire point of the argument. Cato's point concerns the relationship that these components share with happiness, and he is pinpointing a peculiar consequence of the Peripatetic position. Whereas the Stoic claim that virtue is the only good posits virtue as both the necessary and the sufficient condition for happiness, the Aristotelian model of happiness implies that there are two components that together form necessary and sufficient conditions for happiness. This means that virtue is not sufficient for a happy life. Thus Aristotle, according to the Stoic view, downgrades virtue from having a very strong relation to happiness to a somewhat open-ended one. Cato's point is, therefore, a pertinent one. This position is, moreover, consistent with the Stoic rejection of external goods as necessary for happiness. In addition to this, this position has another notable consequence, namely the notorious claim that even women and slaves have access to rationality.[19] In this respect, the Stoics differed significantly from their predecessors and contemporaries. Hardly any extant evidence explains the motivation for adopting such a genuinely egalitarian stance. It is, however, in line with the way in which the Stoics theorise rationality and criticise, for instance, the Peripatetics. If virtue can only lead to happiness when it is accompanied by other attributes, then the role it plays in regard to happiness is necessarily only partial. Stoic egalitarianism, by contrast, makes rationality a much more powerful phenomenon. It is clear that despite not rejecting conventional cultural practices in general,[20] the Stoics were firmly committed to the view that no external circumstance or hindrance stands in the way of one's happiness.

Although the Stoic stance was notorious, they cannot be credited with being the first school to question the value of the conventional goods. On this point, the Stoics were greatly influenced by

Socrates, and their indebtedness to Socratic thought has been noted before in the scholarship.[21] In Plato's dialogues, Socrates consistently pronounces that the conventional goods (health, wealth, beauty and so on) are, in fact, neither good nor bad by themselves, but they can participate in the good or the bad or neither.[22] In the *Euthydemus*, it appears that these things become good or bad depending on whether ignorance or wisdom guides them.[23] A very similar argument is presented by Seneca, and it is worth looking at this text more closely as it contains not only a notable similarity but also some remarkable differences.

In the letter explaining the difference between the Stoic concept of the good and the other, more conventional, concepts,[24] Seneca provides a brief but pointed distinction between the genuine goods and the indifferents. Having explained that defining the good as that which rouses the soul's impulse towards itself is insufficient because harmful activities can also arouse the soul's impulse, Seneca states that the following Stoic definition is better: 'the good is that which stimulates a mental impulse towards itself in accordance with nature and is worth pursuing only when it begins to be worth choosing'.[25] Seneca illustrates this distinction with the examples of military, diplomatic and judiciary services which by themselves are of indifferent value, but when these activities 'are conducted honourably, they start to be good and make the transition from being uncertain to being good'.[26]

Seneca's argument appears to be Socratic because it contains the statement that an act changes from the class of the indifferents to the class of the good when it is conducted in a certain way.[27] Yet there are also similarities to the description of the Stoic value system preserved by Diogenes Laertius: most notably, Seneca also implies that there is a difference between the relationship that a person has with the conventional goods and the genuine good. This is especially evident in the definition of the good which Seneca describes as the one acceptable to the Stoics, and which is cited in the paragraph above. The things that are pursued (*patendum*) belong to the category of the conventional goods, but only the proper good belongs to the category of the things that are chosen (*expetendum*).[28] The language which described virtue as the only and proper good as choice-worthy is very important, because it suggests that the conventional goods are still not choice-worthy, even when they are found in what Seneca described as the category of the good which is underpinned by rational acts and approach.

Seneca's use of the term 'good' is a little confusing, but this is due to the context. He is teaching the Stoic doctrine by contrasting it with the conventional notions of the good and, for this reason, he uses the term 'good' in both the conventional and the Stoic sense of the term.[29] The choice-worthiness of the conventional goods, however, can only arise from their association with virtue; nothing inherent in these acts can make them the good. Seneca calls acts such as virtuously performed military service 'the good' in order to explain to Lucilius the virtue that does all the work in creating the value of the act. The conventional goods do not become the good in the Stoic sense, because the agent never stands in the same relationship to them (which are objects of pursuit) as to the genuine good (which is the only choice-worthy object). Here the difference between the Socratic and the Stoic claims is starting to emerge.

As Tad Brennan points out, the Socratic stance is significantly different from the Stoic view in two respects. First, the Stoics would never say that wealth is sometimes good, 'for, among other things, if this portion of wealth on this occasion really were a good, that is, really benefited its possessor, then an agent would have reason to feel that the loss of that wealth on that occasion, or the failure to attain that wealth on that occasion, really was a loss of something genuinely good; and this is not a conclusion the Stoics would support'.[30] Second, there is a difference between the Socratic claim that wealth is a good thing and the Stoic claim that the correct use of wealth is a good thing. The value lies in the action and action alone, according to the Stoics, and it can never transfer to an object of that action.[31] The relationship that a person forms with a certain object is of crucial importance for understanding the Stoic category of indifferents, as the extant evidence shows.

Indifferent preferences

The polemics with other schools illustrates how sweeping is the Stoic treatment of value. No room is left for ascribing genuine value, that is, the status of the good, to the conventional goods. At the same time, it is worth bearing in mind that the description of Stoic value emphasises that one makes a choice with happiness in view. The Stoic notion of indifferents denotes the relationship between the objects in the category of the indifferents and happiness, not the relationship that a person has with those objects *per se*. This means that a person is making an error by thinking that, for example, being rich will constitute her happiness. She is not making an error by thinking that being rich is preferable to being poor in general. This point is elaborated by the Stoic spokesperson Cato in Cicero's *On Ends*. He explains that there is no reason to avoid performing certain actions just because they are not good (or, equally, avoid things even if they are not genuinely evil). Certain actions, he argues, have the property of 'reasonableness', which means that one can give a rational motivation for that action. Then he adds the following: 'since there may yet be something useful about what is neither a virtue nor a vice, it should not be rejected. Included in this category is also a certain kind of action, such that reason demands that one bring about or create one of the intermediates.'[32]

Arguably, nothing clarifies the Stoic stance on the indifferents better than the notorious disagreement within the school. Aristo of Chios diverged from the orthodox Stoics by denying that any of the indifferents can have the status of being preferred, even in a secondary way. The refusal to recognise any hierarchy within the sphere of indifferents marks Aristo as an outlier within the Stoic tradition, so much so that, in Cicero's *On Ends*, Cato says that Aristo's refusal to recognise the hierarchy of indifferents throws the whole of life into chaos.[33] Aristo's position appears to have been supported by the argument that the value of things such as health depends on the circumstances of the person. Consequently, health has no inherent value that might originate from its nature. For this reason, one ought not to assign a permanent value and thus establish a hierarchy of values within the category of the indifferents, according to Sextus Empiricus' report of Aristo's views.[34] In Diogenes Laertius' record of Aristo's views, there is an illuminating illustration. The wise man, according to Aristo, is like a good actor who plays a part in the proper way regardless of whether he puts on the mask of Agamemnon, the commander of the Achaeans in the Trojan War, or Thersites, a minor character in the *Iliad*, remarkable for lacking in both his looks and his character.[35] The idea behind Aristo's position is that the orthodox Stoic position concedes too much to the Peripatetic claim about the necessity of the conventional goods for happiness. It also illustrates Aristo's argument found in Sextus Empiricus very well. An orthodox Stoic in the shoes of Thersites would value good looks and wit,[36] but he would not do so in the shoes of Agamemnon. This shows that the value of the indifferents is entirely circumstantial and ought not to be ascribed to their inherent nature.[37]

There is some evidence to suggest that these Homeric characters were standard examples in the internal Stoic debates on value. Epictetus, for instance, also uses the examples of Thersites and another Homeric hero, Achilles, in the context of discussing the value of the indifferents. It is not clear whether Epictetus is targeting Aristo in particular by advocating the view that certain indifferents are, in fact, 'preferred', but this text is nonetheless an apt illustration of the difference between the positions of Aristo and the orthodox Stoics. More importantly for the purposes of the current work, this passage is a rare case of a Stoic philosopher discussing the notion of a preferred indifferent with an explicit reference to beauty.

Epictetus on beauty

This passage is found in Epictetus' treatment of the faculty of expression (that is, eloquence), or to be more precise, Epictetus' admonition of those who shun such skills and call them not worth acquiring. In order to illustrate their error, Epictetus employs an analogy with beauty as follows:

τὸ δ᾽ αἴρειν τὴν δύναμιν τῆς φραστικῆς καὶ λέγειν μὴ εἶναι μηδεμίαν ταῖς ἀληθείαις οὐ μόνον ἀχαρίστου ἐστὶ πρὸς τοὺς δεδωκότας, ἀλλὰ καὶ δειλοῦ. ὁ γὰρ τοιοῦτος φοβεῖσθαί μοι δοκεῖ, μή, εἴπερ ἐστί τις δύναμις κατὰ τὸν τόπον, οὐ δυνηθῶμεν αὐτῆς καταφρονῆσαι.

The Problem of Indifferents 37

τοιοῦτοί εἰσι καὶ οἱ λέγοντες μηδεμίαν εἶναι παραλλαγὴν κάλλους πρὸς αἶσχος. εἶτα ὁμοίως ἦν κινηθῆναι τὸν Θερσίτην ἰδόντα καὶ τὸν Ἀχιλλέα; ὁμοίως τὴν Ἑλένην καὶ ἣν ἔτυχε γυναῖκα; καὶ ταῦτα μωρὰ καὶ ἄγροικα καὶ οὐκ εἰδότων τὴν ἑκάστου φύσιν, ἀλλὰ φοβουμένων μὴ ἄν τις αἴσθηται τῆς διαφορᾶς, εὐθὺς συναρπασθεὶς καὶ ἡττηθεὶς ἀπέλθῃ. ἀλλὰ τὸ μέγα τοῦτο, ἀπολιπεῖν ἑκάστῳ τὴν αὑτοῦ δύναμιν ἣν ἔχει καὶ ἀπολιπόντα ἰδεῖν τὴν ἀξίαν τῆς δυνάμεως καὶ τὸ κράτιστον τῶν ὄντων καταμαθεῖν καὶ τοῦτο ἐν παντὶ μεταδιώκειν, περὶ τοῦτο ἐσπουδακέναι, πάρεργα τἆλλα πρὸς τοῦτο πεποιημένον, οὐ μέντοι ἀμελοῦντα οὐδ᾽ ἐκείνων κατὰ δύναμιν. καὶ γὰρ ὀφθαλμῶν ἐπιμελητέον, ἀλλ᾽ οὐχ ὡς τοῦ κρατίστου, ἀλλὰ καὶ τούτων διὰ τὸ κράτιστον· ὅτι ἐκεῖνο οὐκ ἄλλως ἕξει κατὰ φύσιν εἰ μὴ ἐν τούτοις εὐλογιστοῦν καὶ τὰ ἕτερα παρὰ τὰ ἕτερα αἱρούμενον.

But to do away with the faculty of expression and say that in reality it is nothing, is not only ungrateful to those who have given it to us, but cowardly too. For someone who would want to do that seems to me to be afraid that, if there is any such faculty, we may not be able to despise it. Such is the case, too, with those who claim that there is no difference between beauty and ugliness. What, could one be affected in the same way by the sight of Thersites and that of Achilles? Or by the sight of Helen and that of some ordinary woman? No, that is mere foolishness, indicating a lack of cultivation in people who are ignorant of the specific nature of each reality, and who fear that if one comes to appreciate its excellence, one will at once be carried away and placed within its power. No, the important thing is this, to leave each thing in the possession of its own specific faculty and then to consider the value of that faculty, and to learn what is the most excellent of all things, and to pursue that in everything, and make it the chief object of one's concern, regarding everything else as of secondary value by comparison, yet without neglecting even those other things, so far as possible. For we must take care of our eyes too, though not as being the most excellent thing, but for the sake of what is most excellent, because it cannot attain its natural perfection unless it uses our eyes with prudence and chooses some things instead of others.[38]

Epictetus argues that only an ignorant and boorish person would be sufficiently terrified of preferred indifferents not to recognise that

Achilles was more beautiful than Thersites. As mentioned above, this is very likely an attack on Aristo or those who held similar positions, as the motivation for preferring one indifferent over another is not only clearly explained but also vehemently advocated. More pertinent for current purposes is the fact that this passage spells out in greater detail the orthodox Stoic attitude towards bodily beauty as a preferred indifferent. In the cases of both eloquence and bodily beauty, the correct manner of action is to recognise the actual value of every object and to treat them appropriately, rather than to deny that the preferred indifferents are valuable in any sense whatsoever.[39] It is clear that Epictetus does not consider beauty to be of such a high value as to be the good. Beauty has no power at all to constitute one's happiness and therefore it is not choice-worthy in this text as well as in, for example, Diogenes Laertius' account of the Stoic theory of value. Beauty is, however, an object of pursuit. And this text is especially helpful in spelling out what this means. The fact that beauty inspires impulsion (and its opposite inspires repulsion) means it is a certain kind of value, and thus it is preferable to its opposite. The status of being a 'preferred' indifferent renders such properties as beauty genuinely preferable. It turns out, then, that it is not at all the case that the Stoics are indifferent to beauty.

Pleasure

Before concluding the analysis of the Stoic doctrine of indifferents, it is necessary to discuss briefly another item on the list that plays a fairly important role in aesthetic discourse: namely, pleasure. The Stoic treatment of pleasure is quite prominent in their ethics, primarily due to the polemics with their contemporary Epicureans. Their radical stance on the status of pleasure as a value has a bearing on the views that the Stoics, their adversaries and critics, put forth regarding the issue of aesthetic pleasure.[40] The Stoics have a distinct account of the nature of the inclination towards one rather than the other object which, arguably, directly addresses some of the central points of the Epicurean position.

Typically, pleasure plays a significant role in determining values, because of the argument that pleasure indicates what is preferable or not preferable by nature. Pleasure plays such a role in the accounts of the famous hedonist philosophers such as the Cyrenaics and the Epicureans. Very little evidence on the Cyrenaics is extant, but it is a notorious school, not least because it is the only philosophical school in the ancient Greek tradition that posited pleasure, rather than happiness, as the τέλος of human life.[41] Notably, these are primarily the bodily pleasures.[42] The existing sources suggest that the Cyrenaics only recognise the so-called kinetic pleasures and claim that bodily pains are greater than mental ones.[43] The distinction between katastematic and kinetic pleasures features prominently in the Epicurean philosophy and can be explained as follows: the katastematic pleasures are derived from the absence of pain, and the kinetic ones are derived from active sensations.[44] The Cyrenaics are notable for the prioritisation of the latter, but the Epicureans take a rather different approach.

The Epicurean account states that, if studied carefully, the pattern of desires shows that they ultimately refer to the health of the body and the calmness of the mind, and these conditions constitute happiness. Pleasure, therefore, is the good.[45] Pleasure is not, however, the good in an unqualified way. Epicurus establishes an elaborate hierarchy of pleasures and a hard distinction between natural pleasures that constitute happiness and the others that are only marginally relevant or, in some cases, completely irrelevant to happiness.[46] This hierarchy results in the claim that, according to Epicurus, the greatest pleasures are in fact derived from mere sustenance of the body and the calm of a philosophising mind.[47] The katastematic pleasures, therefore, play a crucial role in the Epicurean account of happiness.[48] In this respect, the Epicureans differ significantly from the Cyrenaics.[49]

Although accounts of the hedonists differ, they share one common assumption, namely, that pleasure is the sole indicator of what is choice-worthy by nature or, in other words, the good. And it is precisely this very fundamental notion, that pleasure is indicative of and constitutes the good, which is the target of the Stoic treatment of pleasure. The Stoics deny that it is pleasure that motivates living beings even in their most basic pursuits. Instead, all living beings strive for self-preservation or, to put it differently, what is in accordance with their nature. Pleasure is a mere by-product of attaining the things that are in accordance with nature.[50] Those who posit pleasure as the determiner of value, then, are making a mistake in missing the actual fundamental motivation of human and animal actions. Pleasure might follow the attainment of the good, but it is not the good itself. Consequently, it makes no sense to pursue pleasure *per se*.

It is important to note that the argument about the origin of value has immense consequences for the way in which conventional external goods are valued. Pleasure is genuinely irrelevant to the making of judgements of value, because it is a property that may or may not supervene on what is the actual good. The people who pursue wealth, for example, because of the pleasure that it might bring them, are making a gross misjudgement of what would actually benefit them, as pleasure by itself has no power to constitute the good. Seneca's texts are often useful for providing examples of the central tenets of Stoicism, and he supports this argument with the vivid illustration of a baby animal that strives to stand even against pain.[51] The inclination for morality and right action develops from these natural inclinations.[52] This leads to the question of how the Stoics account for this natural attraction to those things that are in accordance with one's nature. This question, however, requires a substantial discussion, and therefore it will be addressed in the following chapter.

Concluding remarks

Several noteworthy points emerge from the reading of the Stoic sources presented in this chapter. One of them is that the doctrine of indifferents or, more specifically, the claim that beauty is one of the indifferents, did not constitute an obstacle for the Stoics in holding views on aesthetic issues and, consequently, it is far from being crucial to understanding the Stoic stance regarding aesthetic value. It is certainly not irrelevant, yet it tells us fairly little about the Stoic understanding of aesthetic value. This is a positive conclusion for the study of questions pertinent to aesthetics. This reading shows that the fact that the Stoics categorised beauty as a preferred indifferent does not constitute an impediment to their interest in beauty. Such a categorisation tells us neither how a good Stoic ought to judge aesthetic properties (in the sense of determining whether an aesthetic property is present or not) nor what constitutes the value of aesthetic properties. Stoic views on aesthetic properties simply cannot be explained in terms of their ethics, and therefore need to be studied separately.

In addition to this quite significant starting point, the doctrine of indifferents contributes two pertinent points to the enquiry into Stoic thought on aesthetic judgements. First, one of its consequences is that the pursuit of beauty does not lead to happiness. This might lead one to assume that the Stoics were not interested in the issues pertaining to beauty at all, but such a reading presents Stoicism in its most radical form (represented by Aristo of Chios). The more orthodox version of Stoicism does not rule out discussing preferables, and even valuing them.[53] The belief that the pursuit of beauty does not lead to happiness, thus, is also far from a fatal blow to the interest in aesthetics more generally. In general, the accounts connecting beauty and morality are exceptional, although it is not impossible to find some examples.[54] It is more typical to come across theories that treat enquiries into ethical issues, such as what life one ought to lead, and enquiries into aesthetical issues, such as how aesthetic judgements are made, as separate. This is not to say that there can be no overlap, but rather that one cannot get answers to aesthetic questions by looking at ethical doctrines.

Second, beauty is far from an indifferent in the common sense of the word 'indifferent'; it is something we are propelled to by impulse, thus indicating that it is something attractive by nature. In some cases, it is quite clear what is naturally attractive about, for example, health or life. In the case of beauty, however, the answer is less clear. What is the cognitive content of the impulse towards beauty? What is it that we 'see' that renders the seen object beautiful? The notion of pursuit and the impulse to pursue lead to the question of the nature of aesthetic values qua values. In order to find answers to these questions, it is necessary to look past the doctrine of the indifferents and into other extant Stoic texts that use aesthetic vocabulary. The following chapter is dedicated to the discussion of the question that started emerging at the end of the previous section, namely: what is it that constitutes the inherent attractiveness of certain objects? The most important case of objects that display this peculiar kind of inherent attractiveness are virtues. For this reason, the following chapter focuses on those objects that are not only pursued but also chosen.

Notes

1. Wollstonecraft (2014: ch. 4), original edn 1792.
2. Diogenes Laertius 7.102, tr. Hicks: ζωή, ὑγίεια, ἡδονή, κάλλος, ἰσχύς, πλοῦτος, εὐδυξία, εὐγένεια· καὶ τὰ τούτοις ἐναντία.
3. Diogenes Laertius 7.102=LS 58A, tr. Long and Sedley. In the previous paragraph, Diogenes cites from Chrysippus' *On Beauty* (Περὶ τοῦ καλοῦ) the argument μόνον τὸ καλὸν ἀγαθὸν εἶναι, which is an ethical argument relating to the Stoic concept of the good. The topic of indifferents is quite closely related to this argument and therefore it is likely that Diogenes Laertius is citing from the same work of Chrysippus here, although this cannot be proven definitely.
4. One notable exception is Aristo of Chios, see below.
5. They will be discussed later in this work; see Chapter 3 for the discussion of the aesthetics of the good, and Chapter 6 for the discussion of the problem that vices posit to Stoic aesthetics.
6. Diogenes Laertius 7.104–5=*SVF* 3.119=LS 58B, tr. Long and Sedley.
7. Arius Didymus 2.7.7–7a (Pomeroy)=Stobaeus 2.79–80W=*SVF* 3.118; 3.140, tr. Pomeroy: ἀδιάφορα δ' εἶναι λέγουσι τὰ μεταξὺ τῶν ἀγαθῶν καὶ τῶν κακῶν, διχῶς τὸ ἀδιάφορον νοεῖσθαι φάμενοι, καθ' ἕνα μὲν τρόπον τὸ μήτε ἀγαθὸν μήτε κακὸν καὶ τὸ μήτε αἱρετὸν μήτε φευκτόν· καθ' ἕτερον δὲ τὸ μήτε ὁρμῆς μήτε ἀφορμῆς κινητικόν, καθ' ὃ καὶ λέγεσθαί τινα καθάπαξ ἀδιάφορα εἶναι, οἷον τὸ <ἀρτίας ἔχειν ἐπὶ τῆς κεφαλῆς τρίχας ἢ περιττάς, ἢ τὸ> προτεῖναι τὸν δάκτυλον ὡδὶ ἢ ὡδί, ἢ τὸ ἀνελέσθαι τι τῶν ἐμποδῶν, κάρφος ἢ φύλλον. κατὰ τὸ πρότερον δὴ λεκτέον τὰ μεταξὺ ἀρετῆς καὶ κακίας ἀδιάφορα λέγεσθαι κατὰ τοὺς ἀπὸ τῆς αἱρέσεως ταύτης, οὐ μὴν πρὸς ἐκλογὴν καὶ ἀπεκλογήν· δι' ὃ καὶ τὰ μὲν ἀξίαν ἐκλεκτικὴν ἔχειν, τὰ δ' ἀπαξίαν ἀπεκλεκτικήν,

συμβλητικὴν δ' οὐδαμῶς πρὸς τὸν εὐδαίμονα βίον... διότι κἄν, φασί, λέγωμεν ἀδιάφορα τὰ σωματικὰ καὶ τὰ ἐκτός, πρὸς τὸ εὐσχημόνως ζῆν (ἐν ᾧπέρ ἐστι τὸ εὐδαιμόνως) ἀδιάφορά φαμεν αὐτὰ εἶναι, οὐ μὰ Δία πρὸς τὸ κατὰ φύσιν ἔχειν οὐδὲ πρὸς ὁρμὴν καὶ ἀφορμήν.

8. See White (2012: 114–17) for the argument that, from the ontological perspective, selection concerns objects and choice concerns actions.
9. Inwood (1985: esp. 211–14).
10. The vocabulary for the aesthetic properties of virtue is different as well and it has to be discussed separately. This chapter, as noted above, is primarily concerned with the kind of beauty that is denoted by τὸ κάλλος.
11. *Nic. Eth.* 1098b30–1.
12. *Nic. Eth.* 1099a31–b6.
13. *Nic. Eth.* 1153b17–19.
14. On the Stoic interaction with the Peripatetics, see Tieleman (2016: 110ff.).
15. Plutarch *Mor.* 1041E=*SVF* 3.69=LS 60B; cf. Diogenes Laertius 7.53=LS 60C (not attributed to Chrysippus).
16. Common conceptions come about from the repeated exposure to simple impressions, and they only depict what is the case. A well-known Stoic argument from common conception concerns the existence of gods. All the people have a concept of a god, even if they disagree on the details, therefore, gods must exist (Cicero *Nat. D.* 2.12=LS 54C). This is based on the view that humans are born with *tabula rasa* and at first they acquire knowledge of the world empirically (Aetius 4.11.1–4=*SVF* 2.83=LS 39E). The regular reception of a certain impression, thus, results in a more epistemically solid common conception, which is revelatory of the true state of affairs or, in other words, can act as the criterion of truth (see Frede (1987: 166) for the explanation of how this might work).
17. Cicero *Fin.* 3.43.
18. Cicero *Fin.* 3.44, tr. Woolf.
19. Lactantius *Div. inst.* 3.25. See Schofield (1999: 43). Later sources arguing that girls and boys have equal capacities for learning show that this was an important and explicit commitment. See Musonius Rufus 4.1. See also Grahn-Wilder (2018: ch. 8).

20. This issue will be discussed in detail in Chapter 4 of this work on the Stoic wise man.
21. See Tieleman (2016: esp. 113–17) for the argument that the Socratic heritage was mediated by the Stoics' engagement with Aristotelian thought.
22. Plato *Grg.* 467C–468E; cf. *Men.* 87E–88A.
23. *Euthyd.* 281D–E.
24. The specific target here is the Peripatetics, see Inwood (2007: 307).
25. Sen. *Ep.* 118.9, tr. Inwood: *Bonum est, quod ad se impetum animi secundum naturam movet et ita demum petendum est, cum coepit esse expetendum.*
26. Seneca *Ep.* 118.11, tr. Inwood: *Haec cum honeste administrata sunt, bona esse incipiunt et ex dubio in bonum transeunt. Bonum societate honesti fit, honestum per se bonum est.*
27. Inwood (2007: 313) also points out that this is similar to the argument in Plato's *Men.* 88D–E, where *phronesis* is the virtue that renders other 'goods' genuinely good.
28. *Expetendum* is the Latin equivalent of *haireton*, see Inwood (2007: 311). See also Inwood (1985: ch. 6).
29. This is not conventional (see Inwood (2007: 313)), but Plutarch records a citation from Chrysippus' *On Good Things*, in which Chrysippus says it is permissible to apply the term 'good' to the preferred indifferents if one does this in order to distinguish them from the dispreferred indifferents with the common use of the terms (Plutarch *Mor.* 1048A=*SVF* 3.137=LS 58H).
30. Brennan (2005: 120).
31. Brennan (2005: 121).
32. Cicero *Fin.* 3.58, tr. Woolf: '*quoniamque in iis rebus, quae neque in virtutibus sunt neque in vitiis, est tamen quiddam, quod usui possit esse, tollendum id non est. est autem eius generis actio quoque quaedam, et quidem talis, ut ratio postulet agere aliquid et facere eorum.*'
33. Cicero *Fin.* 3.50.
34. Sextus Empiricus *M* 11.64–7=*SVF* 1.361=LS 58F.
35. Diogenes Laertius 7.160=*SVF* 1.351=LS 58G.
36. Presumably, the reference here is to *Il.* 2.212–23, where not only Thersites' appearance and poor character is described, but also his

jealousy of Achilles and Odysseus, as well as his verbal abuse of Agamemnon.

37. As the focus of this work is on the orthodox Stoics, the discussion of Aristo's views is fairly short. For discussions focused on Aristo's views, see Porter (1996); Ioppolo (2012) and the essay collection by Fortenbaugh (2006).
38. Epictetus *Disc.* 2.23.30–5, tr. Hard.
39. The same argument can also be found in Cicero *Fin.* 3.51, tr. Woolf: 'For some, though not all, of the items which are valuable, there is good reason to prefer them to other things, as is the case with health, well-functioning senses, freedom from pain, honour, wealth and so on. Likewise, with the items which are not deserving of value, some offer good reason to reject them – for example pain, illness, loss of a sense, poverty, ignominy and so forth – while others do not. This is the source of Zeno's term *proêgmenon*, and its contrary *apoproêgmenon*' (*quae autem aestimanda essent, eorum in aliis satis esse causae, quam ob rem quibusdam anteponerentur, ut in valitudine, ut in integritate sensuum, ut in doloris vacuitate, ut gloriae, divitiarum, similium rerum, alia autem non esse eius modi, itemque eorum, quae nulla aestimatione digna essent, partim satis habere causae, quam ob rem reicerentur, ut dolorem, morbum, sensuum amissionem, paupertatem, ignominiam, similia horum, partim non item. hinc est illud exortum, quod Zeno προηγμένον, contraque quod ἀποπροηγμένον nominavit*).
40. The Stoics had a taxonomy of pleasures (see Alexander of Aphrodisias *In Top.* 181.2–6) which appears to have been inherited from such figures of Prodicus; see Destrée (2015: 473).
41. Zilioli (2014: 149), on the basis of Diogenes Laertius 2.87–8.
42. Primarily, although not exclusively; see Zilioli (2014: 155) for the argument that the Cyrenaics recognise mental pleasures but, within their philosophical framework, mental pleasures can be reduced to physical ones.
43. Diogenes Laertius 10.136–7=LS 21R, see Wolfsdorf (2013: ch. 7).
44. Cicero *Fin.* 2.9–10=LS 21Q.
45. *Ep. Men.* 127–8=LS 21B; cf. Athenaeus 546F=U 409, 70=LS 21M (tr. Long and Sedley) where the following saying is attributed to Epicurus: 'the pleasure of the stomach is the beginning and root of all good, and it is to this that wisdom and over-refinement actually refer'

(ἀρχὴ καὶ ῥίζα παντὸς ἀγαθοῦ ἡ τῆς γαστρὸς ἡδονή· καὶ τὰ σοφὰ <καὶ> τὰ περιττὰ ἐπὶ ταύτην ἔχει τὴν ἀναφοράν).

46. See Epicurus *Ep. Men.* 127. This doctrine has some consequences for the Epicurean stance on aesthetics; see Čelkytė (2017).
47. Epicurus *Sent. Vat.* 33, 59=LS 21G; Epicurus *Men.* 129–131; Plutarch *Mor.* 1089D=U 68=LS 21N.
48. See, for example, Plutarch *Mor.* 1089D and Aulus Gelius *NA* 9.5.2 for the Epicurean claim that the greatest pleasure is the stable condition of the body (τὸ εὐσταθὲς σαρκὸς κατάστημα), see Konstan (2012) for the discussion of how specific pleasures are valued in view of this.
49. A detailed discussion of this question is outside the scope of this work, but see Zilioli (2014: 157–61).
50. Diogenes Laertius 7.85–6=*SVF* 3.178=LS 57A, reportedly from Chrysippus' *On Ends*.
51. Seneca *Ep.* 121.6–15=LS 57B.
52. Cicero *Fin.* 3.22–3. The Stoic notion of *oikeiosis* is the general way of theorising natural inclinations. See Inwood (1985: 184ff.).
53. According to the Stoics, the best way to make money is to be a king; see Stobaeus 2.109, 10–110, 4 W=*SVF* 3.686=LS 67W.
54. See, for example, Nehamas (2001) and (2007).

3

The Beautiful and the Good

'We aim at Order and hope for Beauty.'
Denman Ross, *A Theory of Pure Design*[1]

The term τὸ κάλλος, found in the Stoic category of the preferred indifferents discussed in the previous chapter, primarily refers to visual/bodily beauty, but it is not the only aesthetic term used by the Stoics. Another one, τὸ καλόν, arguably plays a more significant role due to its association with the good. By virtue of denoting the good, τὸ καλόν falls into the category of being choice-worthy. There is a small group of arguments designed to prove that only the beautiful[2] is the good (μόνον τὸ καλὸν ἀγαθὸν εἶναι). The first important point is the nuanced meaning of the term τὸ καλόν, and the argument for the aesthetic interpretation of this term in the context of this Stoic argument is given in the section below. The second point is the meaning and significance of the argument, which is far from clear. It is worth noting that ancient sources describe it as marginal. In Cicero's *On Ends*, for instance, one of the main sources for this argument, the Stoic spokesman Cato calls it one of the auxiliary proofs of the standard Stoic thesis that the only good is virtue.[3] Apart from Cicero, different versions of the argument are found in the works of Diogenes Laertius, Seneca and Plutarch. Despite certain differences, all the versions preserve the fundamental structure of the argument. This argument is always presented as a proof that only the beautiful is the good, and it always has the same conclusion: that the good is the beautiful, although the middle stages, being 'chosen', 'praiseworthy' and so on, vary from one testimonial to another. This formulation raises a number of questions. Our sources do not specify how the propositions of this syllogism are linked[4] or what precisely the conclusion of the argument implies. In addition to this, it is necessary to ask what relationship between the good and the beautiful this syllogism posits more generally, and what motivated the Stoics to employ an aesthetic term in the context of ethical discourse. Although the meaning of the argument is a little obscure, it is not only a promising source for determining the Stoic position on the relationship between the good and the beautiful – one of the fundamental questions in the field of aesthetics – but also for examining how ideas about beauty were embedded in Stoic philosophy.

Translation and interpretation

Before discussing the argument as a whole, it is necessary to discuss in greater detail both the term τὸ καλόν (which has been translated as 'the beautiful' so far) and the notion of 'the good'.

The good

The argument μόνον τὸ καλὸν ἀγαθὸν εἶναι has a connection with the idea that virtue is a special kind, the highest, of the goods. The notion of the highest good was not invented by the Stoics; it is a very important concept in ancient schools of thought,[5] and there are many different philosophical treatments of this concept. The Stoics were known for restricting the scope of the highest good to virtue alone. According to them, virtue is not only moral but also epistemic, because virtue consists of rationality.[6] In the previous section, it was shown that orthodox Stoics were not so radical as not to recognise some value in the conventional goods. Their highly nuanced understanding of the goods, one that allows more than virtue to be of some value, still demarcates virtue as a fundamental type of good. Virtues are fundamental goods because, unlike conventional goods, they ground happiness by virtue of constituting the τέλος of human life.[7] For this reason, they are choice-worthy[8] and not just objects of simple pursuit, like the conventional goods. Whether an object is choice-worthy or not might seem to be a matter of pure rational deliberation, but this is not entirely the case. There is some evidence suggesting that the Stoics also maintained that the good has an inherent attractiveness recognisable even to those not capable of rational deliberation. Sextus Empiricus refers to the Stoic view that even irrational animals find beauty (τὸ καλόν) choice-worthy. It is important to note that this argument is presented as a support to the Stoic claim that only the beautiful is the good. In the context of criticising the Epicurean and the Stoic arguments on the good, Sextus records and refutes the Stoic belief that only the beautiful is the good as follows:

ἀλλὰ καὶ οἱ μόνον τὸ καλὸν ἀγαθὸν δοξάζοντες δείκνυσθαι νομίζουσιν, ὅτι φύσει τοῦτο αἱρετόν ἐστι καὶ ἀπὸ τῶν ἀλόγων ζῴων. ὁρῶμεν γάρ, φασίν, ὥς τινα γενναῖα ζῷα, καθάπερ ταῦροι καὶ ἀλεκτρυόνες, καίπερ μηδεμιᾶς αὐτοῖς ὑποκειμένης τέρψεως καὶ ἡδονῆς διαγωνίζεται μέχρι θανάτου. καὶ τῶν ἀνθρώπων δὲ οἱ ὑπὲρ πατρίδος ἢ γονέων ἢ τέκνων εἰς ἀναίρεσιν ἑαυτοὺς ἐπιδιδόντες οὐκ ἄν ποτε τοῦτ' ἐποίουν, μηδεμιᾶς αὐτοῖς ἐλπιζομένης μετὰ θάνατον ἡδονῆς, εἰ μὴ φυσικῶς τὸ καλὸν καὶ ἀγαθὸν τούτους τε καὶ πᾶν τὸ γενναῖον ἀεὶ ζῷον ἐπεσπᾶτο πρὸς τὴν αὐτοῦ αἵρεσιν.

But even those who hold that only the beautiful is good think that it is proved by the irrational animals that this is desirable by nature. For we see, they say, how certain noble animals, such as bulls and cocks, contend unto the death even when they have no feeling of delight and pleasure. And those men who have given themselves over to destruction for the sake of country or parents or children would never have done so, when they had no hope of pleasure after death, unless the beautiful and good has naturally drawn them, and every noble animal, to desire it.[9]

The statement suggesting that even irrational animals perceive beauty as choice-worthy appears to refer to the well-known Stoic argument against the Epicurean tenet that pleasure is the good.

The Stoics responded to Epicurean hedonism by claiming that animals are drawn to what is in accordance with their nature, and they derive pleasure from that which is in accordance with the natural. Pleasure, therefore, is not a primary, but only a derivative impulse.[10] For the purposes of this chapter, the more interesting notion is the inherent attractiveness of τὸ καλόν. Once it is ruled out that the attractiveness of the good is motivated by pleasure, it becomes necessary to provide another explanation. According to the passage from Sextus above, the Stoics posit τὸ καλόν to do this job.

τὸ καλόν

The question of how to interpret τὸ καλόν overlaps significantly with the question of how to translate it. There is a tendency to translate the Greek word τὸ καλόν (and its Latin equivalent *honestum*) found in the Stoic texts as ethical terms, such as moral excellence or honour.[11] This is often a natural translation and it might seem that it is the best choice in the case of the argument μόνον τὸ καλὸν ἀγαθὸν εἶναι as well, bearing in mind how virtue-centred Stoic beliefs in ethics are.

I would argue, however, that the term has an aesthetic aspect in the context of this argument and, for this reason, it is more appropriate to translate τὸ καλόν (and, to a lesser extent, *honestum*) as 'the beautiful' in this case.[12] The choice of translation that emphasises the aesthetic aspect of the term is primarily motivated by the fact that this chapter is dedicated to the analysis of this aspect. Putting an emphasis on the aesthetic dimension of the term serves as a useful tool for illuminating and clarifying the conceptual commitments of the argument as a whole. One might worry that this is a circular methodology, especially if the upshot of the argument is just to show that τὸ καλόν is used as an aesthetic term here. This is not quite the case, however. The focus of this chapter is the investigation of the conceptualisation of the aesthetic properties that are inherent in virtue. That the term τὸ καλόν has an aesthetic aspect can be concluded for the following reasons.[13]

The most appropriate starting point for investigating whether a

The Beautiful and the Good 51

term has an aesthetic dimension or not would be to define what it is that we are looking for, that is, what 'aesthetic' refers to. There is, however, a risk of anachronism in adopting such an approach. The contemporary analyses of the 'aesthetic' are influenced by the aesthetic tradition springing from the eighteenth century and thus they might be not very helpful for examining ancient Greek ideas. For this reason, the starting point of the discussion of what the 'aesthetic' is in Stoic thought and, more pertinently, whether τὸ καλόν has this property, in the ancient texts containing the Stoic explanations of the special aspects of τὸ καλόν.

In Book 7, section 100 of the *Lives of Eminent Philosophers*, Diogenes Laertius cites a cluster of various Stoic claims that are in some way related to τὸ καλόν. The first, and the most relevant for current purposes, states the following:

καλὸν δὲ λέγουσι τὸ τέλειον ἀγαθὸν παρὰ τὸ πάντας ἀπέχειν τοὺς ἐπιζητουμένους ἀριθμοὺς ὑπὸ τῆς φύσεως ἢ τὸ τελέως σύμμετρον.

The reason why they characterise the perfect good as beautiful is that it has in full all the measures required by nature or has perfect proportion.[14]

This testimony appears to give either two reasons, or two alternative formulations of the same reason, for why the good is called 'beautiful' by the Stoics. The similarity of content in both parts of the disjunction seems to indicate that these are alternative formulations of the same concept. The second might be Diogenes Laertius' simpler re-formulation of the idea, although it is also possible that he was citing two different sources. In any case, both formulations are useful. The second one is more straightforward, since it contains a reference to *summetria*. This, notably, is a concept that features prominently in the Stoic definition of beauty. The concept, together with the whole definition, will be discussed in Chapter 6. For now, it is enough to note that this is a distinct concept and it has, without a doubt, strong links to aesthetic phenomena, as it is used to explain both visual beauty and the beauty of the soul.[15]

For the purposes of the current chapter, however, the first

formulation in Diogenes Laertius' text is more useful. The perfect good is said to be καλόν by virtue of possessing τοὺς ἀριθμούς. The good is defined by using the same vocabulary in another source, Stobaeus, who cites the Stoics as claiming that 'a right action is a proper function which possesses all the measures (τοὺς ἀριθμούς)'.[16] The term οἱ ἀριθμοί here must refer to something like proportionality, and, in that case, the passage states that the Stoics describe the good as καλόν, because it is proportional to what is in accordance with nature.[17] And although the aesthetic dimension of the Stoic notion of the good is rarely discussed, it is worth noting that this reading is in line with the standard prevalent understanding of the Stoic notion of the good.

In his seminal paper *On the Stoic Conception of the Good*, Michael Frede outlines the difference between the appropriate action and what the Stoics call the proper function as follows: 'roughly speaking, an appropriate action is one in doing which one does what is the right thing to do – namely, in general, one in which one goes for what is conducive to one's survival and avoids what is detrimental to it. But a right or virtuous action requires in addition that one does this with the right motivation, for the right reason; it requires that it be an action borne of virtue and wisdom . . .'.[18] In his subsequent discussion of this Stoic view, Frede notes that the evidence suggests that these actions possess internal order and consistency.[19] The Stoic right action, then, has certain formal[20] properties.

The term οἱ ἀριθμοί in Stobaeus' passage, thus, must explicitly refer to some kind of formal property, such as being proportioned in such a way as to be highly consistent and harmonious. In short, it must refer to being well-proportioned. The ground for ascribing the property of καλόν to the good is the fact that the latter shares something in common with the former, that is, οἱ ἀριθμοί, which is some kind of structural pattern. This is the ground for the aesthetic understanding of τὸ καλόν. And although it has been noted by Frede that τὸ καλόν (in the Stoic argument that only τὸ καλόν is the good) refers to a 'certain attractiveness which makes it an appropriate object for admiration, praise, and the like',[21] my inclusion of these texts into the discussion of Stoic aesthetics requires a further explanation.

The first worry here might be that τὸ καλόν can be an ethical concept even if it is formal. Formal properties play a prominent role primarily in the areas of logic and aesthetics, but it is not impossible to find ethical notions that have formal properties as well. Justice can be theorised as having formal properties. If, for example, in order for a city to be just, it would have to be ordered in a specific way, then justice – an ethical notion – acquires certain formal features.[22] My goal is not to rule out the ethical reading entirely, however. Rather, the aim is to point out that if a concept has formal features, it can have aesthetic properties too, by virtue of having those formal features. If proportionality is the underlying cause of aesthetic properties, then a proportionally ordered ethical concept can be beautiful just like a proportionally ordered chair could. The important point here is that the aesthetic reading does not rule out the ethical one, but it shows something that ethical reading by itself does not quite capture, that is, that the issue at stake is not just an order but a beautiful order. Perhaps a useful analogy here would be beautiful mathematical theorems. By calling a theorem beautiful, a mathematician signals that this theorem has some special property that comparable theorems lack, thus making them inferior to the beautiful theorem.[23] If we read τὸ καλόν as a notion that does the same job as 'beauty' in the case of an especially good mathematical theorem, then this helps to explain why calling the good τὸ καλόν accounts for its inherent attractiveness. The perfect good is said to be καλόν because it has formal properties ordered in accordance with what is required by nature, and it is this formal ordering that renders it attractive and thus recognisable even by irrational animals.

The formality of the notion τὸ καλόν, then, is crucial for this reading.[24] If there was no mention of οἱ ἀριθμοί, one could argue that τὸ καλόν here is used in the sense denoting what is 'fitting' or 'appropriate'. However, as a whole, the passage describes fitting 'numbers', that is, formal features. The issue at stake, therefore, is compositionality, which is an aesthetic concept. In addition to this, the reference to the *summetria* in Diogenes Laertius' report on the reason(s) why the good is καλόν already mentioned above cements the connection between the good and aesthetic properties.

In addition to this, if the term 'beautiful' was used merely as a metaphor for moral excellence, the intermediate stages of the argument, such as praiseworthiness, would be redundant or even misleading, because they evoke the notion of admiration. It could be argued that admiration can be directed at moral excellence, but this would not reflect the content of this argument well.[25] The argument already starts with the term 'the good', which means that the issue at stake is positive value with a moral aspect, and moves on to prove that the phenomenon denoted by this term has an additional property. This suggests that the argument proves that the good – the genuine Stoic good – has this special property. The argument is more nuanced than a simple statement that the good is moral excellence and, therefore, the term 'beauty' expresses more adequately the message of this argument. For these reasons, the aesthetic translation of τὸ καλόν is adopted in this chapter. My hypothesis is that aesthetic vocabulary adds a dimension to this argument that could not be expressed in more straightforwardly ethical language, and by using an aesthetic translation of the relevant terms I aim to explicitly engage with the question of what role the aesthetic overtones of the good are supposed to play.

Before concluding this part of the discussion, it is necessary to address the concern that a more neutral translation of the term τὸ καλόν, such as 'fine', is a better solution. While it is a fair option, it is worth noting that it does not actually solve any problems. If we chose this translation, we would still end up with the argument in which true goodness is marked by special language. It is hard to see why saying 'the true good is fine' is any more illuminating than 'the true good is beautiful'. Both versions ascribe a special feature to the good, but it is not obvious that the former does it more clearly than the latter. By thinking about τὸ καλόν as a more neutral concept, such as 'fineness', one might avoid some problems that arise when the ethical and the aesthetic are associated. Those problems will inevitably emerge again, however, when one comes to the part of Diogenes Laertius' passage which suggests that the Stoics claimed the good to be καλόν by virtue of being *summetros*.

Before moving on to the discussion of how this argument conceptualises the relationship between aesthetic properties and morality, another note about translation is necessary. An important source of the Stoic ideas on this topic are Seneca's works in which τὸ καλόν is rendered as *honestum*.[26] The aesthetic translation of this term is, in general, hardly appropriate. Yet given the fact that Seneca is discussing the very same concept that, in Greek, has an aesthetic aspect, his texts employing *honestum* will be used in this chapter as well. In the context of discussing this particular Stoic doctrine (and in this context alone), *honestum* is effectively read as having an aesthetic aspect, just like τὸ καλόν. Seneca writes in Latin and so he uses Latin vocabulary, but there is no apparent change in the content of the Stoic argument that he expounds. Although τὸ καλόν turns into *honestum*, it is still playing the same role in the Latin argument (demarcating the true good from other, only apparently good) as in the Greek. I will even argue later in this chapter that Seneca, writing in Latin, presented the argument in a way which resembles the original Chrysippean meaning more accurately than Diogenes Laertius, writing in Greek. This is not the argument for adopting such a translation in all cases of *honestum*, as such an argument would, of course, not be correct. It would, equally, not be correct to give a different meaning to the argument because it is translated into Latin. For the sake of philological sensitivity, I leave the term *honestum* untranslated, but I do not consider this term to be problematic for my project of investigating what conceptual understanding was signified by the aesthetic vocabulary of the original, Chrysippean version of the argument μόνον τὸ καλὸν ἀγαθὸν εἶναι.

The argument

Various versions of this argument are often found in the context of discussing happiness, especially in connection with the Stoic claim that only the wise man is happy.[27] It is important to note, however, that the argument itself is not specifically about the happiness or beauty of the wise man; rather, the argument μόνον τὸ καλὸν ἀγαθὸν εἶναι (abbreviated as KA) establishes a more general truth, and then its conclusion is applied to the wise man as well as other cases.[28] The scope of this chapter is limited to analysing the argument in its abstract form by focusing on conceptual connections. The question of how the relationship between the good and the beautiful manifests itself in specific instances according to the Stoics is addressed in the following chapters.

Two issues ought to be noted: the authorship, and the unity of the argument. The author of this argument is unknown. The sources, nonetheless, provide some information about who employed it. The most common attribution is to Chrysippus, as he is mentioned by both Diogenes Laertius and Plutarch. Both of them even record the name of the specific treatise, that is, *On Beauty* (Περὶ τοῦ καλοῦ). There is not enough evidence to suggest that Chrysippus was the author of this argument, but it is not unlikely, especially bearing in mind that other Stoics who, according to our sources, advocated this argument in their works lived after Chrysippus.[29] The fact that this argument is recorded by Cicero and Seneca indicates that it was known in Roman Stoic circles as well.

This raises the question of whether this argument always maintained the same meaning, even when employed by different Stoic philosophers coming from different intellectual backgrounds. On the one hand, all the versions of this argument appear to have a similar form and exactly the same conclusion. Diogenes Laertius and Plutarch record the syllogism as titled 'that only the beautiful is the good'. Cicero does not name the argument in the same way, but he uses the phrase in close proximity for describing the results of the argument in both *On Ends* and *Tusculan Disputations*.[30] Although Seneca does not provide the syllogistic part of the argument, he extensively comments on the meaning of the claim that only the beautiful is the good in his *Letters*. Another example, a passage of Philo, contains only the title of this argument, 'that only the beautiful is the good'.[31] This indicates that the argument was treated by many philosophers as representing a view commonly held by many Stoics. It is possible that different Stoics ascribed different conceptual interpretations to the KA argument. In fact, I show that ancient sources interpret this belief in two different ways in the following section. The syllogistic part of this argument, however, has clear implications, and I argue that it shows one of these interpretations to be more accurate than the other.

The Beautiful and the Good 57

Diogenes Laertius and Seneca

In his work *The Lives of Eminent Philosophers*, Diogenes Laertius provides a wide spectrum of Stoic views on beauty. First, he states that according to the Stoics, the good is the beautiful, because it is proportionate to the use made of it.[32] In the following paragraph, he explains that the Stoics said that the good is the beautiful because it has all the 'measures' required by nature (τοὺς ἐπιζητουμένους ἀριθμοὺς ὑπὸ τῆς φύσεως) or has a perfect *summetria*,[33] cited in full above. Then he presents four subspecies of the beautiful (τὸ καλόν) under which good deeds are accomplished. The next definition states that the beautiful is that which renders its possessor praiseworthy,[34] and then, in another sense, it denotes good aptitude for one's proper function.[35] The last definition in this passage states that the beautiful is that which lends additional grace to something, as in the case of the wise man.[36] These definitions are interesting and important in their own right,[37] but the most relevant passage for the topic of the current chapter is the paragraph which follows this cluster of different definitions. It states the following:

Λέγουσι δὲ μόνον τὸ καλὸν ἀγαθὸν εἶναι, καθά φησιν Ἑκάτων ἐν τῷ τρίτῳ Περὶ ἀγαθῶν καὶ Χρύσιππος ἐν τοῖς Περὶ τοῦ καλοῦ· εἶναι δὲ τοῦτο ἀρετὴν καὶ τὸ μετέχον ἀρετῆς, ᾧ ἐστιν ἴσον τὸ πᾶν ἀγαθὸν καλὸν εἶναι καὶ τὸ ἰσοδυναμεῖν τῷ καλῷ τὸ ἀγαθόν, ὅπερ ἴσον ἐστὶ τούτῳ. ἐπεὶ γάρ ἐστιν ἀγαθόν, καλόν ἐστιν· ἔστι δὲ καλόν· ἀγαθὸν ἄρα ἐστί.

And they say that only the beautiful is good. So Hecato in his treatise *On Goods*, Book 3, and Chrysippus in his work *On Beauty*. They hold, that is, that virtue and whatever partakes of virtue consists in this: which is equivalent to saying that all that is good is beautiful, or that the term 'good' has equal force with the term 'beautiful', which comes to the same thing. 'Since a thing is good, it is beautiful; now it is beautiful, therefore, it is good.'[38]

According to Diogenes Laertius, the argument that only the beautiful is the good suggests the equivalence of the good and the beautiful. If Diogenes Laertius has recorded this accurately, then these two Stoics presented a very radical idea. The equivalence of ethical and aesthetic value implies that the good shares the properties of the beautiful, and the beautiful shares the properties of the good.[39] While the first part of this suggestion is relatively unproblematic, the second part is controversial. It is very counterintuitive to say that some objects are good by virtue of being beautiful. There does not seem to be any reason to attribute more than aesthetic value to beauty, especially if it possesses such a property merely by virtue of possessing certain formal features.[40] In fact, some philosophers have argued that it is appropriate to deny aesthetic value to an object on the basis of its lack of moral value.[41] Even though the Stoic notion of the good is not equivalent to morality in a more conventional sense due to its epistemic nature, all these considerations still apply.

It is noteworthy that Diogenes introduces the argument with the phrase 'which is equivalent to saying' (ᾧ ἐστιν ἴσον), which suggests that this interpretation is either his own comment or a comment from the source he is using for the Stoic views,[42] not a part of the doctrine proposed by Chrysippus and Hecato. It is not at all clear that these earlier Stoics proposed the equivalence of the good and the beautiful. Another reason for questioning whether this is an accurate interpretation of the KA argument is the existence of an alternative reading. At the very beginning of *Letter* 120, Seneca presents and describes the Stoic[43] claim that the good and the beautiful are distinct. After greeting Lucilius, Seneca sets out to answer the question which Lucilius had asked in the previous letter, namely, how human beings acquire the concepts of the good and the beautiful. Before answering his question in detail, Seneca briefly summarises what he calls the Stoic position in the following manner:

> *Haec duo apud alios diversa sunt, apud nos tantum divisa. Quid sit hoc dicam. Bonum putant esse aliqui id quod utile est. Itaque hoc et divitiis et equo et vino et calceo nomen inponunt; tanta fit apud illos boni vilitas et adeo in sordida usque descendit. Honestum putant cui ratio recti officii constat, tamquam pie curatam patris senectutem, adiutam amici*

The Beautiful and the Good 59

paupertatem, fortem expeditionem, prudentem moderatamque sententiam. <Nos> ista duo quidem facimus, sed ex uno. Nihil est bonum nisi quod honestum est; quod honestum, est utique bonum. Supervacuum iudico adicere quid inter ista discriminis sit, cum saepe dixerim. Hoc unum dicam, nihil nobis videri <bonum> quo quis et male uti potest; vides autem divitiis, nobilitate, viribus quam multi male utantur.

These two are, in the view of others, different; in our view they are merely distinct. I will explain. Some think that the good is that which is useful. Therefore they apply this term to wealth, to a horse, to wine, and to a shoe. That is how cheap they think the good is and how utterly they think it descends into vulgarity. They think that *honestum* is that which is characterised by a reasoning out of one's correct responsibility; e.g., the faithful care of one's father in old age, relief of a friend's poverty, courageous behaviour on campaign, the utterance of sensible and moderate views [in the Senate]. We contend that these are indeed two things, but that they are rooted in one. Nothing is good except what is *honestum*; what is *honestum* is certainly good. I think it unnecessary to add what distinguishes them, since I have said it often. I will say just this one thing, that we believe that nothing is <good> which someone can also use badly; however, you see how many people make bad use of wealth, high birth, and strength.[44]

Seneca's interpretation of this argument might appear very similar to the one presented by Diogenes Laertius at first sight, but there is an important difference. Although Seneca stated that 'nothing is good except what is beautiful; what is beautiful is certainly good', he also wrote that the good and the beautiful are 'distinct' properties rooted 'in one'. In his reading, the good and the beautiful are not tied by identity, but only related by their origin.

The syllogism

The mere fact that Seneca and Diogenes Laertius present different versions of the argument raises an interesting question. It is possible that Diogenes Laertius, a doxographer, misrepresented the ideas of

Chrysippus and Hecato, but it is equally possible that Seneca had his own original interpretation of the argument which differed from the earlier versions. The simplest way of answering this question is by comparing the two versions with the other available evidence. One piece of evidence comes from Plutarch, who also records Chrysippus' argument that only the beautiful is the good. In his *On Stoic Self-Contradictions*, Plutarch extensively criticises Chrysippus' beliefs by juxtaposing them. In order to do that, Plutarch typically quotes extracts from various treatises written by Chrysippus and tries to show that they contradict each other. In one specific passage, Plutarch quotes Chrysippus as saying that although actions performed in accordance with virtue are congenial, some of them (such as extending one's finger courageously) are not examples of virtuous behaviour.[45] Subsequently, Plutarch cites Chrysippus' KA argument and claims that Chrysippus is contradicting himself, because in one of his treatises he says that certain actions performed in accordance with virtue are examples of great behaviour, while in another treatise he states that all good is praiseworthy.[46] Then he adds the following:

> καὶ μὴν ἐν τῷ Περὶ καλοῦ πρὸς ἀπόδειξιν τοῦ μόνον τὸ καλὸν ἀγαθὸν εἶναι τοιούτοις λόγοις κέχρηται· 'τὸ ἀγαθὸν αἱρετόν, τὸ δ' αἱρετὸν ἀρεστόν, τὸ δ' ἀρεστὸν ἐπαινετόν, τὸ δ' ἐπαινετὸν καλόν' καὶ πάλιν· 'τὸ ἀγαθὸν χαρτόν, τὸ δὲ χαρτὸν σεμνόν, τὸ δὲ σεμνὸν καλόν.'

Moreover, in the treatise *On Beauty* to demonstrate that only the beautiful is good he has employed arguments like this: 'what is good is chosen, what is chosen is approved, what is approved is admired, what is admired is beautiful' and again 'what is good is gratifying, what is gratifying is grand, what is grand is beautiful'.[47]

Plutarch's version shows that the KA argument was supported by a syllogism. This is a very useful piece of evidence for the following reason. In order to determine whether Diogenes Laertius or Seneca presents a more accurate commentary on the KA argument, it is sufficient to discover what this syllogism implies. The

The Beautiful and the Good   61

argument in its syllogistic form is found not only in Plutarch, but also in Cicero. In fact, Cicero records it several times in slightly different forms. Two versions of this argument can be found in a single paragraph in Book 3 of the *On Ends*, in which the Stoic spokesman Cato expounds the Stoic[48] view regarding the τέλος of human life. Although Cato does not ascribe the KA argument to any particular Stoic, it can be plausibly treated as belonging to the group of arguments which Plutarch ascribed to Chrysippus and Hecato.[49] The argument itself is presented as a rhetorical support for the proposition that living in agreement with nature is the τέλος of human beings and, therefore, all wise men lead happy and fortunate lives.[50] The KA syllogism is one of the auxiliary logical proofs[51] reinforcing this belief. Cato presents two versions, and the first, the shorter one, goes as follows:

Quod est bonum, omne laudabile est; quod autem laudabile est, omne est honestum; bonum igitur quod est, honestum est.

Whatever is good is praiseworthy; whatever is praiseworthy is *honestum*; therefore whatever is good is *honestum*.[52]

Cicero also records a refutation of this argument. The refutation consists in denying the premise that everything that is good is praiseworthy.[53] In order to address this criticism, Cato presents the following argument:

Illud autem perabsurdum, bonum esse aliquid quod non expetendum sit, aut expetendum quod non placens, aut si id, non etiam diligendum; ergo et probandum; ita etiam laudabile; id autem honestum. Ita fit ut quod bonum sit id etiam honestum sit.

But it would be the height of absurdity for there to be a good that should not be sought; or something to be sought which was not pleasing, or pleasing but not worthy of choice, and so also commendable, and so also praiseworthy; but then it is *honestum*. So it is the case that whatever is good is also *honestum*.[54]

Although their length is different, both arguments share certain notions: the good, the praiseworthy and the beautiful. This suggests that the elongation of the argument does not change its meaning; it simply refines its form, possibly in order to make it more resistant to criticism. This version replaces the problematic premise with a more acceptable one while reaching exactly the same conclusion.

Cicero also records the third version of the KA argument in his *Tusculan Disputations*. Once again, the intermediate stages differ but the conclusion of the argument remains the same. Just as in the *On Moral Ends*, the context is a discussion of the nature of the happy life. After stating that strong emotions (regardless of whether they are positive or negative) are the opposite of wisdom and reason, Cicero concludes that the wise man is always happy because he is free from disturbances caused by emotions. Then this version of the KA argument follows:

> *Atque etiam omne bonum laetabile est; quod autem laetabile, id praedicandum et prae se ferendum; quod tale autem, id etiam gloriosum; si vero glorosium, certe laudabile; quod laudabile autem, profecto etiam honestum: quod bonum igitur, id honestum.*

> Again, every good is a source of joy. What is a source of joy should be proclaimed and displayed; such a thing is also glorious but if glorious, it is certainly praiseworthy; but what is praiseworthy is surely also *honestum*, so what is good is *honestum*.[55]

An interesting part of this particular passage is the changing mood of the propositions. Some of the propositions are affirmative and some are conditional statements. This might be a clue to the original form of the syllogism. Bearing in mind that indemonstrables, the fundamentals of Stoic logic, were hypothetical syllogisms,[56] it is quite likely that originally this argument was a hypothetical *modus ponens* type of syllogism as well.

In addition to this, there are several other questions to be raised about the form of this argument. The first is whether the multiple versions of this syllogism ought to be treated as one argument or as several arguments. On the one hand, it might seem appropriate to treat these arguments as different, because every version has different intermediate stages. On the other hand, the only difference between all the arguments is the number of middle stages, while the first term (the good), the last term (the beautiful), one of the middle stages (the praiseworthy) and the title-conclusion (only the beautiful is the good) are the same in every version. This is clearly the skeleton of the argument and the additional stages present in some versions expand the argument without changing its meaning.

There are two possible explanations why this argument has a flexible form. The first is suggested by the Stoic spokesperson Cato in Cicero's *On Ends*, where he explicitly states that the longer version of the KA argument is meant to refute those critics who deny that the good is praiseworthy. This indicates that the Stoic philosophers modified the same idea in order to make it more convincing or appropriate for their needs. The most likely reasons for adapting the argument by modifying its form are either to accommodate criticism or to fit the argument into a specific context.

The second possible explanation is suggested by Plutarch. When Plutarch introduces the KA argument cited above, he refers to it in the plural (τοιούτοις λόγοις κέχρηται). This phrase indicates that the argument might have come in different forms from its early development.[57] These two suggestions are not mutually exclusive, but regardless of whether Chrysippus intended this argument to come in different forms or not, it ended up developing in this way, with the conceptual unity preserved by the skeleton of the argument.[58]

Against Diogenes Laertius

Having discussed some basic issues about the form of the syllogism, I move on to discuss its meaning and whether Seneca's or Diogenes Laertius' reading represents its implications more accurately. There are two possible ways of interpreting the meaning of the KA argument. It can be read as (i) an equivalency statement (or Diogenes Laertius' interpretation); (ii) an attributive statement (or Seneca's interpretation).[59]

Diogenes Laertius comments that the good and the beautiful

are tied by identity – to be the beautiful is to be the good, and to be the good is to be the beautiful. This conclusion, however, does not follow from the KA argument. In order for Diogenes Laertius' commentary to be correct, the copula 'is' should be an identity statement. This would not only be an unusual type of logic, but also would not reflect the content of the evidence accurately. In a typical syllogism, a proposition 'all As are Bs' distributes terms from subjects to predicate (similarly, in a conditional, terms are distributed from antecedent to consequent), but not the other way around. As a syllogism, the argument that the good is the beautiful only proves the proposition stated in its conclusion – it does not imply that the beautiful is also the good, in the same way that the statement 'all cats are animals' does not imply that all animals are cats.

Another reason to reject this interpretation is the presence of the word 'only' in the title of the argument. Without 'only', the title and the conclusion of this argument would be proposing opposite results. The title would state that the beautiful is the good (B is G), while the body of the argument would reach the conclusion that the good is the beautiful (G is B). If, however, 'only' is added to the title, then the title matches the conclusion of the argument. The context of the argument shows that this argument was intended to support the claim that virtue is the only good, that is, that the only type of good – virtue – is the true good. The title of the argument reflects this idea as well. The statement that *only* the beautiful is the good indicates that the true good is that which is also the beautiful and, consequently, that which is not the beautiful is not the good (¬B is ¬G).

This argument does not simply state that the good is the beautiful and the beautiful is the good, as if they shared identity. It suggests that beauty is a special attribute of the true good which distinguishes it from all the other, only apparent, goods.

The succession of terms which constitutes the body of the argument can be understood as follows: the good falls into the area of the praiseworthy; the praiseworthy falls into the area of the beautiful; therefore, the good falls into the area of the beautiful and thus the good is the beautiful. It shows that the good and the beautiful are connected not by identity, but by a set and subset relationship.

It can be rephrased as claiming that of all the possible sets of the good, only that good which is a subset of the beautiful is actually the good. Consequently, the phrasing of the argument suggests that the possession of an attribute of beauty distinguishes the true goods from all other types of goods.[60] This shows that Diogenes Laertius represents this argument not quite accurately.

Attribution

The reading of the KA argument as a statement of attribution is exemplified by Seneca's suggestion that beauty and the good are distinct.[61] In fact, Seneca's description of the relationship between the good and the beautiful is closer to the implications of the KA syllogism (found, according to our sources, in Chrysippus' *On Beauty*) than any other interpretation of this argument analysed so far.

The question of what the 'distinction' between the good and *honestum* consist in is crucial for determining the meaning of the argument precisely, and Seneca's other letters are quite informative in respect to this. When concluding the passage cited above, Seneca claims that he has discussed the difference between the good and the beautiful elsewhere.[62] Brad Inwood suggests that this is a reference to *Letter* 118. In this letter, Seneca discusses happiness and how those who have the wrong conception of what is the good cannot live tranquil and happy lives. Then he provides the standard Stoic definition of the good as life in accordance with nature,[63] and states that this good is *honestum*. This leads him to elaborate on the relationship between the good and *honestum* in the following manner:

> Locus ipse me admonet ut quid intersit inter bonum honestumque dicam. Aliquid inter se mixtum habent et inseparabile: nec potest bonum esse nisi cui aliquid honesti inest, et honestum utique bonum est. Quid ergo inter duo interest? Honestum est perfectum bonum, quo beata vita completur, cuius contactu alia quoque bona fiunt. Quod dico talest: sunt quaedam neque bona neque mala, tamquam militia, legatio, iurisdictio. Haec cum honeste administrata sunt, bona esse incipiunt et ex dubio in bonum transeunt. Bonum societate honesti fit, honestum per se bonum est; bonum

ex honesto fluit, honestum ex se est. Quod bonum est malum esse potuit; quod honestum est nisi bonum esse non potuit.

This point reminds me to mention the difference between the good and *honestum*. They do share something with each other which is inseparable from them. Only what has something *honestum* in it can be good, and the *honestum* is certainly good. So what is the difference between them? The *honestum* is the perfected good, by which the happy life is made complete and by contact with which other things are also made good. Here is the kind of thing I mean. There are certain things which are neither good nor bad, like military service, diplomatic service, and service as a judge. When they are conducted with *honestum*, they start to be good and make the transition from being uncertain to being good. Alliance with *honestum* makes something good, but *honestum* is good all on its own. Good flows from *honestum*; *honestum* depends only on itself. What is good could have been bad. What is *honestum* couldn't have been otherwise than good.[64]

This passage spells out what is implied by the KA argument. The *honestum* is the perfected good, and when indifferent activities are performed with the *honestum*, they become the good. Since *honestum* does not change the activities themselves, but only the way in which they are carried out, it must affect change by structuring those activities. It is a structured good. The actual, the Stoic, good is the good that contains certain formal properties. The actual good is a subset of *honestum* and hence certain formal properties that are inherent in *honestum* are an attribute of the true good. As an attribute, it distinguishes the actual good from only seeming goods. The formal properties, which are also aesthetic properties, are the indications of the actual good.[65]

Seneca also says that the *honestum* is in the sphere of the good, but presumably this is to prevent the counter-example of something with the property of the *honestum* which is in some way bad. To have *honestum* is necessary and sufficient for having the good in the particular Stoic notion of the good. Yet in terms of the general notion of the good, the Stoics recognise a distinction between the good and the *honestum*, as they recognise only the latter as the actual good.

This leaves us with the conclusion that Seneca commented on the meaning of the KA argument more accurately than Diogenes Laertius. The difference lies in the nuance, however. Diogenes Laertius' account simply abbreviates the same argument, but omits a rather significant nuance, that is, that τὸ καλόν and the good are left conceptually distinct by the Stoic syllogism. Neither the logical form of this argument nor other Stoic commentaries imply the identity of the good and the beautiful, as Diogenes Laertius suggests. Seneca's more nuanced reading presents a more accurate discussion of the relationship between τὸ καλόν/*honestum* and the good.

Theoretical virtue

So far I have argued that the beauty of the good in the syllogism titled μόνον τὸ καλὸν ἀγαθὸν εἶναι is best understood as an attribute of the good. This leaves the question of why the Stoics were interested in attributing aesthetic properties to the good. The easiest way of answering this question is by breaking it down into two parts: first, why were the Stoics motivated to assign formal values to the good and, second, what would they gain by focusing on the aesthetic aspect of those values?

The answer to the first question has already been discussed in the scholarship on Stoicism. When discussing the Stoic claim that virtue is that which ultimately confers benefits, Chris Gill notes the following:

> Goodness is defined by the conferring of benefit or the beneficial. It is also manifested in the wholeness, structure, cohesion, and in this sense the 'perfection', of a whole series of types of entities. The link between these two strands is, by inference at least, that goodness benefits by the very fact that it provides or constitutes the cohesion or structure of entities as unified wholes. Similar points can be made about virtue. Virtue is that element or factor that *consistently and invariably* benefits, as distinct from providing localized or intermittent benefits. The virtues, in themselves, constitute a structured and unified whole or set. They also confer structure and unity on the entities in which they

are present, and thus enable the perfection of them as wholes. The benefit or goodness which virtue confers – or, in another sense, which it consists in – derives from its character of being structured whole and from its role of conferring structure on entities considered as wholes.[66]

This way of interpreting the Stoic notion of virtues shows that formal properties are important for understanding how virtues affect their possessors. They confer benefit by ordering one's behaviour, beliefs and so on. Although Gill does not use an aesthetic vocabulary in this interpretation, his work is enlightening for thinking about the Stoic connection between virtue and the beautiful. If something, let's say an act, has formal properties and thus a structure, it can also be well structured or poorly structured. In the former case, formal aesthetic properties become present. Virtue, of course, can only manifest itself in the case of exceptionally good order and structure. Interest in aesthetic properties and the questions pertinent to them, therefore, naturally emerge from the Stoic conceptualisation of virtue and ethical commitments. The claims that acting virtuously is in accordance with human nature and leads to happiness, the τέλος of human life, are central to Stoic ethics. Presumably, virtue confers benefits not because it has simply any kind of structuring capacity, but because it structures in accordance with what is best in human beings. Virtue organises beliefs and behaviour in the most rational way so that a person lives her life in the way which is dictated by her nature and is most beneficial. Claiming that virtues are beautiful, therefore, is a natural consequence of the Stoic ethics.

This raises an interesting issue regarding the differences between ethical goodness and moral beauty, because they appear to be very similar or even identical. Virtues confer benefit in respect to their structuring capacity, but they themselves also have a certain structure which gives them aesthetic value. It seems that at least to some extent, Chrysippus was aiming to show that there is a significant overlap between ethical good and aesthetic value.

It is possible to draw an analogy between the Stoic use of aesthetic properties as special attributes of the good and the use of aesthetic properties by scientists as special attributes of especially apt scientific theories.[67] This analogy is intended to illustrate more generally the motivation for attributing aesthetic properties to objects excelling at their function, which is useful for understanding the Stoic position as well. In the case of especially apt, 'beautiful' theories, beauty is typically called a 'theoretical virtue'. The term 'theoretical virtue' is given to special properties that are not related to the content of a scientific theory, yet they make that theory preferable. Simplicity, coherence, elegance and sometimes beauty are examples of such properties. When a scientist is faced with two theories with equal truth value and she prefers the one which she considers to be, for instance, the more elegant, she makes the judgement based on the theoretical virtue – elegance – possessed by one of the theories. Although the question of how scientific theories acquire aesthetic values is very complex in its own right,[68] the notion of a theoretical virtue, nonetheless, might help to shed some light on the motivation for attributing aesthetic value to the good.

In the cases of both scientific theories and the Stoic concept of the good, beauty is what could be called a secondary-level value. It is clear that those who attribute beauty to either the good or especially apt scientific theories think that the fundamental value lies in the goodness or the correctness of the theory. Beauty supervenes as a kind of secondary value on properties that are intrinsically valuable themselves. The advantage of attributing this secondary value is its distinguishing aspect – it helps to create a hierarchy of values. This is especially clear in Seneca's passage cited above in which he states that although there are many goods, the Stoics consider as truly good only those that are also καλόν. Similarly, beautiful scientific explanations are preferable to non-beautiful explanations when all the other parameters are equal. It seems that some Stoics, just like some contemporary scientists and philosophers of science, claim that certain propositions will unfailingly produce in us a sensation of beauty as a mark of the superiority of these propositions.

Concluding remarks

An interesting question which follows from this discussion is how objective the attribution of the property of beauty is. Does beauty originate in the mind of a perceiver or do certain properties, originating in an object itself, render them beautiful to a perceiver? Those who analyse the beauty of scientific theories often choose the former option;[69] the Stoic argument, however, implies the latter option. These approaches differ on account of their agendas. The difference between investigating the role of beauty in scientific theories and in the KA argument lies in the fact that whereas the former aims to *explain* why some scientists experience beauty when faced with certain scientific explanations, this Stoic argument aims to *convince* us that the true good is the beautiful. Thus, for those Stoics who propose this argument, beauty is a property built into the world.

This, in its turn, raises the question of what renders virtues or especially apt scientific explanations beautiful. In the case of Stoicism, there is good reason to suspect that it is a kind of ordering. But what kind of ordering, exactly? The next section is dedicated to the examination of some particular cases of virtues in action, which will bring us closer to determining the central concepts and claims in the Stoic theory of beauty.

Notes

1. Ross (1907: 189).
2. The reasons for translating τὸ καλόν as an aesthetic term are discussed in detail below.
3. Cicero *Fin.* 3.26.
4. It is not clear whether the copula represents a set–subset type of relationship or is an equivalency statement. This problem constitutes a large part of my argument below.
5. See Broadie (2007: esp. 141–8).
6. Diogenes Laertius 7.98 (ἁπλοῦν δ' ἐστὶν ἀγαθὸν ἐπιστήμη).
7. See, for instance, Stobaeus 2.77, 16–27 W=*SVF* 3.16=LS 63A.
8. The Stoic definition of the good as that which benefits can be found in Sextus Empiricus *M* 11.22=*SVF* 3.75=LS 60G.
9. Sextus Empiricus *M* 11.99–100=*SVF* 3.38, tr. R. Bury, slightly amended replacing 'fair' with 'beautiful'.
10. Diogenes Laertius 7.85–86=*SVF* 3.178=LS 57A. See the previous chapter for the discussion of the Stoic treatment of pleasure.

11. King (1945) translates *honestum* as 'right' in the *Tusculan Disputations*, while Douglas (1990) uses the term 'morally right'. Rackham (1931) translates *honestum* in *On Ends* as 'morally beautiful', while Woolf (2001) translates the same passage using the term 'moral'. Cherniss (1976) translates τὸ καλόν as 'fair' in the passage from Plutarch's *Moralia*. Hicks (1924) uses the term 'morally good' in his translation of Diogenes Laertius. Inwood (2007) translates *honestum* in Seneca's *Letters* as 'honourable'.

12. The argument below interprets the term in a very specific context of Stoic ethics. This reading is consistent with the extant evidence in other sub-fields of Stoic philosophy as well, as the rest of this work shows. For this reason, the term τὸ καλόν is treated here as a specific Stoic term or, to be more precise, the underlying assumption is that when the Stoics employed the term in their works, they invested it with specific nuanced meaning. This is not to say that they purposefully introduced a new meaning to the common word just for the sake of doing so, but that their philosophical commitments inevitably lead to a distinct, 'Stoic' τὸ καλόν. This is also supported by the fact that the overall Stoic approach to aesthetic phenomena was fairly original and distinct from the approaches of their predecessors or their contemporaries, as the argument in Chapter 7 shows.

13. See Bychkov (2010: 176); Bychkov (2011) for a more general case for translating τὸ καλόν and *honestum* as aesthetic terms on philological grounds.

14. Diogenes Laertius 7.100, tr. Hicks, slightly amended replacing 'factors' with 'measures'.

15. See, for instance, Arius Didymus 5b4–5b5 (Pomeroy)=Stobaeus 2.62 W=*SVF* 3.278.

16. Stobaeus 2.93, 14–18 W=*SVF* 3.500=LS 59K, tr. Long and Sedley: κατόρθωμα δ' εἶναι λέγουσι καθῆκον πάντας ἀπέχον τοὺς ἀριθμούς.

17. It is not uncommon to find descriptions of virtue as 'a consistent character' which helps to achieve consistency in one's life, see Diogenes Laertius 7.89=*SVF* 3.39=LS 61A (τήν τ' ἀρετὴν διάθεσιν εἶναι ὁμολογουμένην).

18. Frede (1999: 79). Frede's primary focus is Cicero's *Fin.* 3.20–1, but the doctrine discussed is the very same one.

19. Frede (1999: 82).
20. This term is one of the fundamental notions within modern aesthetics, but it is very useful for discussing ancient views as well. The term by itself does not imply any theoretical commitments (although it does play an important role in the debates on formalism) and it is an apt description of, in this case, structural features that are responsible for aesthetic properties.
21. Frede (1999: 89).
22. Arguably, Plato's *Republic* is one of the best known examples here, as the text approaches justice as a certain kind of arrangement either in a person or a *polis* (in the case of the latter, the justice would consist of the arrangement of political roles, see *Resp.* 368E–371E for the set-up of this argument); See Aristotle *M* 13.1078a30–b6, where Aristotle explicitly says that the good has formal features. This passage is cited and discussed in Chapter 7.
23. See the section on theoretical virtues at the end of this chapter.
24. This is not an argument that τὸ καλόν ought to be always translated as an aesthetic term. In the context of the argument μόνον τὸ καλὸν ἀγαθὸν εἶναι, however, such a translation (or another one that shows that τὸ καλόν has formal properties) is important. Arguably, the aesthetic translation here is the most appropriate given the reference to *summetria*, which is undoubtedly an aesthetic concept. It helps to emphasise that by calling the perfect good καλόν, the Stoics draw attention to the idea that the true good has a certain inherent attractiveness similar to – or indeed the same as – the one found in beauty. Virtue is not just something we must pursue, but also something we are naturally inclined to pursue, because of its attractive features.
25. It would also assume more than it ought to about the nature of morality; a good example of the complex nature of Chrysippean ethics is the claim that a wise man's extending a finger is not an excellent behaviour, even though it is done with all the requirements for moral action (Plutarch *Mor.* 1038F). A less complex example is a situation in which a driver stops her car abruptly because a child runs out into the road. Her action is moral, but it is not likely to be admired. One could admire her good driving skills or quick reaction, but not the fact that she chose not to harm another human being. Morality, for this reason, is not necessarily admirable in every case.

The Beautiful and the Good 73

26. See Frede (1999: 87).
27. See Chapter 4 for an analysis of these texts.
28. It has already been mentioned that Cicero presented this argument as an auxiliary technical proof, so this interpretation of the argument follows the sources.
29. For instance, Hecato (active around 100 BC) and Diogenes of Babylon (230–150/140 BC).
30. Cicero *Fin.* 3.29; *Tusc.* 5.44.
31. See Philo *de post. Caini* 133=*SVF* 3.31.
32. Diogenes Laertius 7.99: καλὸν δ' ὅτι συμμέτρως ἔχει πρὸς τὴν ἑαυτοῦ χρείαν.
33. Diogenes Laertius 7.100.
34. λέγεσθαι δὲ τὸ καλὸν μοναχῶς μὲν τὸ ἐπαινετοὺς παρεχόμενον τοὺς ἔχοντας <ἢ> ἀγαθὸν ἐπαίνου ἄξιον. Ibid.
35. ἑτέρως δὲ τὸ εὖ πεφυκέναι πρὸς τὸ ἴδιον ἔργον. Ibid.
36. ἄλλως δὲ τὸ ἐπικοσμοῦν, ὅταν λέγωμεν μόνον τὸν σοφὸν ἀγαθὸν <καὶ> καλὸν εἶναι. Ibid. This claim will be discussed in the following chapter.
37. These definitions seem to me to come from different works and to denote very different ideas. For this reason, I do not discuss them together as a coherent whole, but use them in different chapters with appropriate topics. See Mansfeld (1999: 23) for a suggestion that Diogenes used an *eisagoge*, introductory treatises written by the members of the Stoa. See also the case of Diogenes' sources for the honorary decree issued to Zeno of Citium in Haake (2004: 482–3).
38. Diogenes Laertius 7.101, tr. Hicks.
39. An alternative reading of Diogenes Laertius' comment would be as a remark on the vocabulary. That is, to say that some object is beautiful is the same as to say that it is good. I would argue that this is problematic, because the context suggests that the issue at stake is the relationship between properties, not their nomenclature.
40. The theories inspired by Platonism might suggest that beauty leads to acquiring the goods (for instance, knowledge), but even such theories do not state that beauty itself is the good.
41. The relationship between the moral good and beauty, especially beauty in art, is a question discussed by many philosophers and thinkers. Gaut (2009) provides a comprehensive summary of the

contemporary debates. One of the most historically important expositions of the relationship between the good, beauty and art in the modern period is Tolstoy's critique of nineteenth-century attitudes. He effectively denies the relation between beauty and moral goodness in art. According to him, the theory of art, founded on beauty, sets up beauty (beauty being that which pleases certain people) as goodness, and art ought to be concerned with the latter, not the former ('Art is not, as the metaphysicians say, the manifestation of some mysterious idea, beauty, God; not, as the aesthetician– physiologists say, a form of play in which man releases a surplus of stored-up energy; not the manifestation of emotions through external signs; not the production of pleasing objects; not, above all, pleasure, but it is a means of human communion, necessary for life and for the movement towards the good of the individual man and of mankind, uniting them in the same feeling' (*What is Art?*, tr. Pevear and Volokhonsky ([original Russian edn 1897] 1995: section 5). Possibly more complex is Plato's attitude towards the good, the beautiful and the arts outlined in the *Republic 10*. The literature on Plato's views is vast. Some of the most recent studies include Denham (2012), Barney (2010) and Hyland (2008), to name only a few.

42. For Diogenes' sources, see the note 37. If Diogenes' sources for the Stoics were the introductory treatises, this phrasing might have originated from a Stoic source. Given the current state of evidence, it is not possible to determine this with certainty.
43. Seneca does this in the first person plural, which could be taken to suggest that, at least in Seneca's view, there is a consensus about this idea amongst all the Stoics. Of course, this also could be just a rhetorical device to create an appearance that this belief was a product of consensus and thus to strengthen his own view.
44. Seneca *Ep.* 120.1–3, tr. Inwood, slightly changed to leave the term *honestum* untranslated, for the reasons outlined earlier in this chapter.
45. Plutarch *Mor.* 1038F.
46. Whether Plutarch's observation is a reasonable criticism of Chrysippus' views is an interesting question. At first sight, Plutarch's observation appears to have some basis. However, his method of picking out unrelated passages from different treatises and juxtaposing them is questionable. It seems likely that originally these propositions came

from entirely different contexts and they were used to make different points, and thus they do not genuinely contradict each other.
47. Plutarch *Mor.* 1039C–D, tr. Cherniss, slightly amended replacing 'fair' with 'beautiful'.
48. Although Cato does not mention the Stoic to whom this argument belonged originally, Rackham suggests that Diogenes of Babylon might have been the author of the philosophical views found in Book 3 of the *On Ends* (Rackham (1931: 17)). Diogenes of Babylon is indeed mentioned by name twice in this dialogue (at 3.33 and 49), but this does not seem to be sufficient evidence to establish his authorship, because a number of other Stoics are also mentioned in this text. For instance, at 3.57, both Chrysippus and Diogenes are recorded as asserting views about what attitude one ought to have towards fame (the view in question is that apart from practical use, fame is not worthy of stretching out a finger for, see *Fin*. 3. 57). For this reason, Rackham's suggestion does not seem plausible.
49. I am not suggesting that Diogenes of Babylon definitely did not use this argument. I do not think that he could have been the author of this argument, although he could be added to the list of the Stoics who employed this argument just like Chrysippus and Hecato did. Unfortunately, this does not come across very clearly from the available evidence.
50. Cicero *Fin*. 3.26. Although the mentioning of the wise man might lead one to suppose that 'the beautiful' and 'the good' here refer to characteristics of a person, the issue at stake is not properties of the wise man *per se*, but the relationship between abstract values. The wise man is an instantiation of this relationship.
51. The second proof considers what a happy life consists of, and although it does have the term *honestate*, it is not a syllogistic proof (3.28). The same is true for the third proof, which establishes that an admirable wise man would not act basely (3.29).
52. Cicero *Fin*. 3.27, tr. Woolf, slightly revised by leaving *honestum* untranslated.
53. *Fin*. 3.27: *Duorum autem e quibus effecta conclusio est contra superius dici solet non omne bonum esse laudabile.*
54. Cicero *Fin*. 3.27, tr. Woolf, slightly revised leaving *honestum* untranslated.

55. Cicero *Tusc.* 5.43, tr. Douglas, slightly revised leaving *honestum* untranslated.
56. For a thorough discussion of Stoic indemonstrables, see Bobzien (1996).
57. This suggestion is dependent on the reading of 'λόγοις' as 'arguments'. It would be, however, also possible to translate this as 'words'. In that case, the implication of the plurality of the arguments is not present in this text. For this reason, the interpretation presented above is tentative. Given the context and the fact that the citation that follows is an argument, the translation as 'arguments' seems likely, but it is not possible to establish beyond a doubt that this was the intended meaning.
58. This remark only concerns the form, however. As we have seen from two distinct interpretations of Diogenes Laertius and Seneca, the argument could have been read as representing different content. The survival of the syllogism which supports the belief that only the beautiful is the good improves this situation a great deal, because it is possible to analyse whether the implications of this syllogism are compatible with Seneca's or Diogenes Laertius' interpretations.
59. Strictly speaking, there is a third possibility. Cicero calls this a sorites argument (Cicero *Fin.* 4.50=*SVF* 3.37; cf. King's notes for his translation of Cicero's *Tusculan Disputations* (1945: 468)). This is most likely a generic criticism, because previously sorites was described as 'a particularly fallacious form of argument' (tr. Woolf). Although both arguments contain chain-like linked premises, their purpose is different, as KA does not establish vagueness. Also, some extant evidence shows Chrysippus finding solutions to sorites (Sextus Empiricus *M* 7.416=LS 37F; Cicero *Acad.* 2.93=LS 37H. See Williamson (1994: 16) for an explanation of why Chrysippus might have proposed to stop answering questions of the sorites paradox rather than to say 'I do not know'.
60. It is noteworthy that this type of argument fits in very well with the better-known Stoic beliefs in ethics, and the argument that only the beautiful is good can plausibly support the belief that the only good is virtue. Both of them aim to differentiate the goods and to posit one type of good as the true good; the former argument supports the latter belief by indicating that the true good has special properties which distinguish it from all the other, only apparent, goods.

61. See Cicero *Off.* 1.95, for the Panaetian account of τὸ πρέπον/*decorum* (an aesthetic term, cf. Dyck (1996: 241)), which also theoretically distinguishes the aesthetic and the moral.
62. Seneca *Ep.* 120.3.
63. To be more precise, Seneca provided two definitions. He rejected the first one as insufficient and then provided the second one, which is the standard Stoic definition of the good; see Seneca *Ep.* 118.8.
64. Seneca *Ep.* 118.10–11, tr. Inwood, slightly revised leaving *honestum* untranslated.
65. See Frede (1999: 89).
66. Gill (2006: 150).
67. See McAllister (1996: 90): 'One of the most remarkable features of modern science is the conviction of many scientists that their aesthetic sense can lead them to the truth.' An example of such conviction can be found in Dirac (1963: 47): 'It is more important to have beauty in one's equations than to have them fit experiment. . . . It seems that if one is working from the point of view of getting beauty in one's equations, and if one has really a sound insight, one is on a sure line of progress.'
68. Breitenbach (2012); Engler (1990); McAllister (1996).
69. The most prominent example is McAllister's monograph *Beauty and Revolution in Science* (1996: esp. 61–104).

4

'The wise man is no true Scotsman': The Stoics on Human Beauty

> 'The critique of beauty is never a critique of beautiful objects but always of ideas, ideologies, social practices and cultural hierarchies.'
>
> Dave Beech, 'Art and the Politics of Beauty'[1]

The previous section was dedicated to exploring the role of beauty in the Stoic value system. Virtue, it was established, has formal features that pave the way for it having aesthetic properties. This chapter develops the enquiry into Stoic aesthetics by focusing on the evidence that reports the idiosyncratic Stoic views of human beauty, primarily the claim that only the wise man is beautiful. It also addresses the related question of the Stoic manner of theorising love. Although the main evidence comes from a single passage, a highly critical report of Stoic views composed by Plutarch, there are two distinct points of interest here. First is the question of what the claim that only the wise man is beautiful tells us about the Stoic conception of beauty. The second question of interest is the nature of the love relationship. The latter is a far more important question than it might appear at first sight, because in the previous chapters it was argued that beauty acts as an important attribute of virtue. Given that love is defined as a response to beauty by the Stoics,[2] the question of what kind of relationship this response is and how it relates to the natural attraction of virtue naturally follows. The enquiry into the passages that deal with the wise man and his love of youths, therefore, ought to shed more light on the Stoic view that virtue is inherently attractive.

Plutarch's attack

There are several extant passages on the Stoic account of love, beauty and their relationship, but none of them are quite as vivid and extensive as Plutarch's critique of this account. In his *Conspectus of the Essay 'The Stoics Talk More Paradoxically than the Poets'*, Plutarch criticises various Stoic claims about the wise man. His starting point is the following group of claims:

Ὁ Εὐριπίδου Ἰόλαος ἐξ ἀδρανοῦς καὶ παρήλικος εὐχῇ τινι νέος καὶ ἰσχυρὸς ἐπὶ τὴν μάχην ἄφνω γέγονεν· ὁ δὲ τῶν Στωικῶν σοφὸς χθὲς μὲν ἦν αἴσχιστος ἅμα καὶ κάκιστος, τήμερον δ' ἄφνω μεταβέβληκεν εἰς ἀρετὴν καὶ γέγονεν ἐκ ῥυσοῦ καὶ ὠχροῦ καὶ κατ' Αἰσχύλον 'ἐξ ὀσφυαλγοῦς καὶ ὀδυνοσπάδος λυγροῦ γέροντος' εὐπρεπὴς θεοειδὴς καλλίμορφος. καὶ τοῦ Ὀδυσσέως ἡ Ἀθηνᾶ τὴν ῥυσότητα καὶ φαλακρότητα καὶ ἀμορφίαν ἀφῄρηκεν, ὅπως φανείη καλός· ὁ δὲ τούτων σοφός, οὐκ ἀπολιπόντος τὸ σῶμα τοῦ γήρως ἀλλὰ καὶ <κακὰ> προσεπιθέντος καὶ προσεπιχώσαντος, μένων κυρτός, ἂν οὕτω τύχῃ, νωδὸς ἑτερόφθαλμος οὔτ' αἰσχρὸς οὔτε δύσμορφος οὔτε κακοπρόσωπός ἐστιν. ὁ γὰρ Στωικὸς ἔρως, ὥσπερ οἱ κάνθαροι λέγονται τὸ μὲν μύρον ἀπολείπειν τὰ δὲ δυσώδη διώκειν, οὕτως τοῖς αἰσχίστοις καὶ ἀμορφοτάτοις ὁμιλῶν, ὅταν εἰς εὐμορφίαν καὶ κάλλος ὑπὸ σοφίας μεταβάλωσιν, ἀποτρέπεται.

Euripides' Iolaus has changed suddenly from being feeble and elderly to being youthful and strong by means of a prayer; but the Stoic wise man, who yesterday was most ugly and, at the same time, most vicious, today suddenly becomes virtuous and changes from being wrinkled, sallow and, as Aeschylus says 'from a wretched old man with a sore back, racked by pain', to being good-looking, godlike and beautiful. Athena has removed Odysseus' wrinkles, baldness and ugliness, so that he would appear beautiful, but the body of the Stoic wise man not only remains old, but also acquires bad things and gets burdened by them. And while he remains – if he happened to be such – hunchbacked, toothless and one-eyed, he is neither ugly nor misshapen nor ugly-faced. For the Stoic love consorts with the ugliest and most unshapely and turns away from them whenever they change into shapeliness and beauty by means of wisdom in the same way that dung beetles are said to avoid perfume and seek foul-smelling things.[3]

In a manner typical of Plutarch when he writes about the Hellenistic schools, several distinct groups of claims are jumbled together in this passage: i) the claim that the change from ignorance to wisdom is sudden and instantaneous; ii) the claim that only the wise man is beautiful; iii) the claim that the wise man might pursue promising youths as love interests. The confusing picture that Plutarch draws in this passage is the result of his applying the implications of one claim to another. Thus, for instance, the claim that Stoic love seeks the foul is the result, according to Plutarch, of claims ii) and iii). Plutarch's reading is hardly fair because he takes the three Stoic claims out of their respective contexts.

In order to interpret the Stoic claims more charitably, it is necessary to examine the claims on the wise man and the claims on love separately, with their respective contexts in view. Only then will it be possible to say how – or if – these claims are related.

No true Scotsman

Plutarch's vivid criticism ridicules the idea that an ugly man who is supposed to be beautiful will fall in love with a beautiful youth who is supposed to be ugly. Although Plutarch's text is quite rhetorical, there is more than rhetoric at stake. His remarks suggest a substantial criticism of this Stoic claim, that is, Plutarch suggests that the Stoic statement about the beauty of the wise man is a kind of a fallacy. This is for the following reason: if I provide an argument which claims that a young boy who is conventionally perceived as beautiful is not beautiful, but an old man who is conventionally perceived as not beautiful is actually beautiful, then all I am doing is redefining the term 'beautiful'. Such a statement does not offer any explanation of the problematic term; it simply changes its definition. This move is comparable to the so-called No

True Scotsman fallacy.[4] It might be the case that Plutarch's criticism is fair. A harsh critic of Stoicism such as Plutarch, however, is not necessarily the most reliable source for detailing the nuances of Stoic beliefs and presenting them in the best light. It is useful, therefore, to approach this question of the relationship between wisdom and beauty, as well as the question of whether Plutarch's critique is accurate, by looking at some additional evidence. The nature of the Stoic paradoxes about the wise man in general is revealing background information for interpreting the claims about the wise man's beauty.

Paradoxes: what kind of a claim is this?

Plutarch describes the Stoic beliefs about the wise man as 'paradoxes', which seems to be intended to convey a critical view of these claims, but there is evidence to suggest that the Stoics themselves called their views 'paradoxes' (παράδοξα).[5] The reason the Stoics chose this name is not in the extant evidence. The term seems to have distinguished a certain class of auxiliary statements that supported the central Stoic tenet that only virtue is the good. Perhaps by giving a special name to these claims, the Stoics signified their awareness that these ideas would challenge the conventional opinions on what the good was.

In Plutarch's texts, the term appears to be critical, and it is noteworthy that there are other cases of the adjective 'paradoxical' (παράδοξος) being used to denote something strange, extraordinary or surprising.[6] Although one might expect that, in a philosophical context, the term would refer to a logical paradox, such as the Liar, the paradoxicality in this case does not seem to amount to much more than idiosyncrasy. The Stoic paradoxes typically state that only the wise man is x, where x is some property commonly deemed to be desirable, such as being wealthy, free, beautiful, happy and in possession of various kinds of knowledge. Although certainly strange, there is no contradiction in these claims; at most, they require an explanation. There is, furthermore, no evidence to suggest that Stoic logic produced logical puzzles for any purpose (unlike Zeno of Elea, for instance). On the contrary, there is evidence that Chrysippus, a noted logician of his times,[7] offered solutions to known paradoxes. He suggested to stop answering the questions that constitute the sorites paradox when they become tricky and one can no longer answer with certainty.[8] It is also worth noting that Plutarch is not focused on criticising the argumentation itself, but only its conclusion, namely, that only the wise man is beautiful. This shows that the idiosyncrasy of the claim is the target of his criticism.

The context suggests the same. Throughout the *Conspectus of the Essay 'The Stoics Talk More Paradoxically than the Poets'*, Plutarch makes parallel comparisons of Stoic beliefs and poets' tales. The wise man's transformation into beauty while remaining in the same state physically is compared to the episode in the *Odyssey* in which Athena rejuvenated Odysseus. Plutarch writes that while Athena actually enhanced the physical features of Odysseus,[9] the Stoic wise man remains in the same state and, therefore, the Stoics speak more paradoxically, that is, they make a more counterintuitive claim than Homer, who was telling a story involving magical elements.

Hypothetical scenarios

The question that naturally follows is why the Stoics posited such a claim, the oddity of which they themselves appear to acknowledge. The central notion in all of the Stoic paradoxes is the wise man. What is so special about wise men that allows them – and only them! – to own all the conventional good?

Arguably, the starting point ought to be the claim that all the beliefs that the wise man holds are true, because he assents to true impressions only.[10] The existence of such a person is an intriguing possibility philosophically, and examining the case of a person who only holds true beliefs can be used in arguments in various ways. Positing the notion of the wise man is especially useful for exploring the motivations and implications of various philosophical positions. It is relatively common to use the notion of a perfectly rational person to argue that such a person would act in a certain way and, therefore, this course of behaviour is normative. Philosophers also examine the hypothetical mental content of a perfectly rational person and on that basis draw general conclusions about metaphysical or epistemological features of the world.[11]

In the case of the Stoic wise man, the assertions that only the wise man is happy, free, wealthy and so on are used to defend the Stoic idea that the only good is virtue, arguably the central Stoic ethical doctrine. The Stoics also employ the notion of the wise man to investigate how his special cognitive state enables him to act in problematic situations. Since the wise man has a superior kind of understanding of when to assent and when to withhold his assent to impressions, he is also able to make judgements of how one ought to act in any given situation. Determining what the wise man would do when faced with a decision either about one's lifestyle or a course of action in a difficult situation shows how one ought to act in such a case. When read this way, the Stoic claims about the wise man are hypothetical explorations. An interesting consequence of this reading is that the issue at stake is not whether the wise man exists, but how such a person would act if he existed.

The hypothetical reading sheds some light on the motivation for the wise man paradoxes. To be precise, by saying that only the wise man is in possession of what is generally deemed to be the good, the Stoics aim to explore the necessary and sufficient conditions for various goods, with the conclusion that their conception of the good, although restrictive from a conventional point of view, fits those conditions the best.

The claims about the goods that only the wise man has are many and various. Only the wise man, for instance, is said to be free,[12] happy[13] and beautiful.[14] Cicero's *Stoic Paradoxes* is an important source in this case because it contains not only the paradoxes but also lengthy explanations of why the Stoics made these claims. The claim that only the wise man is free, for instance, is related to the claim that the wise man never does anything against his will in the following manner:

> *Quid est enim libertas? Potestas vivendi, ut velis. Quis igitur vivit, ut volt, nisi qui recte vivit? qui gaudet officio, cui vivendi via considerata atque provisa est, qui ne legibus quidem propter metum paret, sed eas sequitur et colit, quia id salutare esse maxime iudicat, qui nihil dicit, nihil facit,*

> *nihil cogitat denique nisi libenter ac libere, cuius omnia consilia resque omnes, quas gerit, ab ipso proficiscuntur eodemque referuntur, nec est ulla res, quae plus apud eum polleat quam ipsius voluntas atque iudicium . . . Soli igitur hoc contingit sapienti, ut nihil faciat invitus, nihil dolens, nihil coactus.*
>
> For what is freedom? The power to live as you will. Who then lives as he wills except one who follows the things that are right, who delights in his duty, who has a well-considered path of life mapped out before him, who does not obey even the laws because of fear but follows and respects them because he judges that to be conducive to health, whose every utterance and action and even thought is voluntary and free, whose enterprises and courses of conduct all take their start from himself and likewise have their end in himself, there being no other thing that has more influence with him than his own will and judgement? . . . It therefore befalls the wise man alone that he does nothing against his will nor with regret nor by compulsion.[15]

This passage shows that, according to the Stoics, conventional notions of freedom are conceptually inadequate, because a person who is said to be free conventionally is still often compelled to act against his will and by virtue of this he is not truly free. The meaningful and coherent attribute of freedom can only be found in a perfectly rational person because only such a person acts without any restrictions on his will. Although this argument might seem to be just a sophistic move which replaces the meaning of terms – the so-called No True Scotsman fallacy – it is important to note that it contains an element of conceptual analysis which renders the argument more rigorous than it might appear at first sight. The Stoics do not merely change the meaning of the term 'free', because the argument supplied with the paradoxical claim shows that the conventional use of this term is inconsistent with its actual meaning. The Stoic doctrine that posits rationality as the foundation of any good provides a better account of what it means to possess the good.

A similar strategy is used to establish that only the wise man is rich,[16] happy[17] and beautiful.[18] In all of these cases, the notion of the wise man is used to analyse such concepts as freedom, happiness and wealth. The wise man is compared with those people who are thought to have these desirable properties in order to show that only the former can truly be said to possess the good. Interestingly, the Stoic claims aim to show that the Stoic paradoxes are the reasonable option on the table, while the conventional understanding of such properties as freedom or wealth have flaws that contradict the very meaning of those properties. It is inappropriate and incorrect, for instance, to call a man who is compelled to act in certain ways free. In the same way, a person who is conventionally free, wealthy and beautiful is still in some sense not free, not wealthy and not beautiful. Only rationality genuinely grounds these properties. A description of the wise man as someone who has all the goods, therefore, is an exploration of how being perfectly rational is the foundation of having all the other goods.

It is also worth noting that the wise man paradoxes apply not only to properties, but also to activities. Diogenes Laertius records the Stoic claim that the wise man would engage in dialectic, because dialectic would enable him to distinguish between true and false, plausibility and ambiguity,[19] followed by the claim that only the wise man is a dialectician.[20] In Stobaeus, the Stoics are reported as claiming that only the wise man can be a lover of music and literature.[21] Only wise men are also said to be priests, for they study and engage in all things relevant to religion.[22] According to Chrysippus, only wise men are kings because only they have the knowledge of good and evil necessary for the ruler, and only they are fit to be magistrates, judges and orators.[23]

Presumably, these paradoxes are also motivated by the view that only wise men are able to engage in these activities in a proper sense, because only wise men have a rationality-based approach which guarantees that any act they undertake is performed in the way that genuinely fulfils the description of the act. Arguably, it is very important to interpret these claims in a hypothetical manner in order to make sense of them. The message here is not that people who typically perform these activities are, in some sense, frauds, or that they ought to be replaced by philosopher priests and philosopher kings.[24] The Stoics, as far as it is possible to tell from the extant evidence, did not have a utopian political programme with a philosopher king as the proper ruler.[25] Instead, these claims explore hypothetically the significance of being rational. It is only rationality, according to the Stoics, that guarantees the possession of the goods in a genuine way, regardless of whether those goods are certain properties, expertises or professions.[26] For this reason, the wise man's case is best understood as an exploration of what it takes to possess the good, rather than a prescriptive doctrine or an explicit critique of standard cultural practices. If we take the Stoic paradoxes to be nuanced explorations of value in the manner proposed, then the meaning of the claims about the wise man's beauty become clearer as well.

Where does the wise man's beauty come from?

So far, it has been argued that the claims about the wise man can be understood as the Stoic conceptual analysis of the good. This is an especially important point when it comes to beauty, because this interpretation suggests that there is more at stake than a mere redefinition of beauty terms in the claim that only the wise man is beautiful. It is, in other words, not the case that the Stoics committed the so-called No True Scotsman fallacy. The paradox stating that only the wise man is beautiful does not simply redefine beauty. Instead, it is – just like the other wise man paradoxes – a hypothetical argument motivated by an attempt to analyse the foundations of any good and to prove that the fundamental condition of gaining even the conventional goods is virtue.

The paradox is also not simply equating beauty with wisdom, despite the fact that the appearance of the latter is immediately followed by the former.[27] In his *Stoic Paradoxes*, Cicero records the Stoic explanation of why only the wise man is free or wealthy. I have argued that this explanation shows that statements of the form 'only the wise man is x' indicate that virtue is a necessary and sufficient condition for gaining any good. By analysing conceptually what it means to have a particular good, the Stoics argued that it is impossible to have a coherent concept of that good without including virtue as a necessary and sufficient condition. This is not the same kind of move as the replacement of the good with virtue. It is clear that the claim that only the wise man is wealthy, for instance, does not imply that wisdom is true wealth, but that one cannot be said to be genuinely wealthy without also possessing wisdom. Wisdom grounds the goods, rather than replaces them. It is not plausible, for this reason, to assume that the claim that only the wise man is beautiful redefines beauty as wisdom.

At the very end of Book 3 of Cicero's *On Ends*, the Stoic spokesperson Cato talks about the Stoic paradoxes, including the one about the beauty of the wise man, as follows:

> *Recte eius omnia dicentur, qui scit uti solus omnibus, recte etiam pulcher appellabitur-animi enim liniamenta sunt pulchriora quam corporis-, recte solus liber nec dominationi cuiusquam parens nec oboediens cupiditati, recte invictus . . .*

> The one who alone knows how properly to use all things is the owner of all things. Such a person will rightly be called beautiful too, since the soul's features are more beautiful than those of the body; and uniquely free, the servant of no master, the slave of no appetite, truly unconquerable.[28]

In this passage, the wise man is said to be simply more beautiful than a physically attractive person. There is no claim that the latter is ugly, as Plutarch extrapolates in his criticism of the Stoic paradoxes. Instead, the beauty of the wise man is said to be greater because the beauty of the soul is greater than that of the body. Just as in the case of professions and expertises, the point here is not to deny that conventionally attractive people are attractive, but that this attractiveness pales in comparison with the beauty of the soul and, effectively, only wise people are beautiful. This raises the question of what it is about the beauty of the soul that makes it so much greater than the beauty of the body.

An important passage to consider here is a short definition of beauty cited by Diogenes Laertius amongst other Stoic claims employing aesthetic vocabulary.[29] This definition is presented as follows:

> . . . ἄλλως δὲ τὸ ἐπικοσμοῦν, ὅταν λέγωμεν μόνον τὸν σοφὸν ἀγαθὸν καὶ καλὸν εἶναι.
>
> . . . while in yet another sense the beautiful is that which lends new grace to anything, as when we say of the wise man that he alone is good and beautiful.[30]

This very short passage shows that the claim about the wise man's beauty is not made on the basis of merely proclaiming the superiority of the soul over the body. The beauty of the wise man is a kind of embellishment. Beauty, therefore, is a property that the wise man acquires on account of becoming wise, but it is not synonymous with it, since the Stoic virtue is certainly not an embellishment. This raises the question of what changes when one moves from ignorance to wisdom. The passage from Arius Didymus' *Epitome* is a useful source for answering this question, as it contains the same claim about the superiority of the soul over the body, but with the following details:

> τῆς δὲ ψυχῆς οὔσης κυριωτέρας τοῦ σώματος καὶ πρὸς τὸ κατὰ φύσιν ζῆν φασὶ τὰ περὶ τὴν ψυχὴν κατὰ φύσιν ὄντα καὶ προηγμένα πλείονα τὴν ἀξίαν ἔχειν τῶν περὶ σῶμα καὶ τῶν ἐκτός, οἷον εὐφυΐαν ψυχῆς πρὸς ἀρετὴν ὑπεράγειν τῆς τοῦ σώματος εὐφυΐας καὶ ὁμοίως ἐπὶ τῶν ἄλλων ἔχειν.
>
> Since the soul is more in control than the body, they say that, with respect to living in accord with nature, things concerning the soul which are in accord with nature and preferable also have more value than things concerning the body and externals. Thus, in relation to virtue, natural ability of the mind surpasses the natural ability of the body and they say that the same holds for the other things.[31]

This passage explains that the superiority of the soul over the body refers to being in accord with nature, which is a crucial point. The accord with nature is a central notion in Stoic philosophy, as it features prominently in the definitions of happiness and virtue.[32] In Stoic epistemology, acting in accordance with nature means assenting to cognitive impressions only and thus achieving the state of pure rationality.[33] The Stoics are known for stating that the nature of human beings is to be rational, and rationality is a very important – if not the most important – part of being a human.[34] The claim that the wise man is the only one who is beautiful, therefore, can be unpacked as the claim that the wise man alone has the type of beauty which is important and appropriate for human beings.

This would also resolve the supposed self-contradiction regarding the simultaneous beauty and ugliness of a youth, which is pointed out by Plutarch in his critique of the Stoic claims about human beauty. It is likely that the Stoics did recognise that the young man does possesses bodily beauty in a conventional way.[35] When compared to the wise man, however, his beauty is lesser, because it is not of the kind that is truly significant for human beings, given the kind of beings they are. The beauty of the soul possessed by the wise man is both different and, in a sense, more relevant for a human being than bodily beauty. Bodily beauty only concerns the proportion of limbs and, therefore, it concerns only a fairly small part of being human. The wise man's beauty, by contrast, concerns what is peculiarly human, that is, the rationality which is the very foundation of human nature. The extent of such a person's beauty, therefore, is naturally greater.

This introduces a conceptualisation of beauty not mentioned previously. Beauty is conceptualised as a property that arises when an object fulfils its function or a person fulfils her role perfectly. In this study, this type of conceptualisation of beauty will be called the functional theory of beauty. The detailed analysis of this theory is presented in Chapter 6, but for now, it is enough to note that this is the kind of explanation that emerges from the claim that only the wise man is beautiful.

There is, furthermore, another layer to the wise man's beauty. In the previous chapter it was shown that virtues possess aesthetic properties because they possess formal properties or, to put it simply, because they are well structured. This, however, differs from the functional explanation of the wise man's beauty. There is a passage in Cicero which draws an explicit parallel between the beauty of the body and the beauty of the soul in terms of formal properties. When discussing the notions of health and disease in his *Tusculan Disputations*,[36] Cicero states that, according to the Stoics, good proportion is responsible for both the beauty of the body and the beauty of the soul in the following way:

> *Et ut corporis est quaedam apta figura membrorum cum coloris quadam suavitate eaque dicitur pulchritudo, sic in animo opinionum iudiciorumque aequabilitas et constantia cum firmitate quadam et stabilitate virtutem subsequens aut virtutis vim ipsam continens pulchritudo vocatur.*

And as in the body a certain proportionate shape of the limbs combined with a certain charm of colouring is described as beauty; so in the soul the name of beauty is given to an equipoise and consistency of beliefs and judgements, combined with a certain steadiness and stability, following upon virtue and comprising the true essence of virtue.[37]

The wise man and a conventionally handsome youth possess two distinct, yet not genuinely different, kinds of beauty. Both types can be reduced to the same principle, that is, a certain proportionality. What distinguishes the beauty of the soul from the bodily beauty is the fact that the former is more 'functional'.[38] Given the kind of beings human beings are, this is the more profound beauty, as it arises from perfectly fulfilling one's role as a human being. The formal and the functional ways of accounting for the presence of aesthetic properties, then, are not mutually exclusive. The way in which they contribute to the Stoic theory of beauty more generally is discussed in Chapter 6. For the purposes of the current chapter, it is enough to note that such an account of beauty quite aptly explains the meaning of the Stoic paradox that only the wise man is beautiful.

Love

There still remains the problem of the Stoic account of love. A few pertinent testimonials are preserved in Arius Didymus' *Epitome*, including the following definition of love:

διὸ καί φασιν ἐρασθήσεσθαι τὸν νοῦν ἔχοντα. τὸ δὲ ἐρᾶν αὐτὸ μόνον ἀδιάφορον εἶναι, ἐπειδὴ γίνεταί ποτε καὶ περὶ φαύλους. τὸν δὲ ἔρωτα οὔτε ἐπιθυμίαν εἶναι οὔτε τινὸς φαύλου πράγματος, ἀλλ' ἐπιβολὴν φιλοποιίας διὰ κάλλους ἔμφασιν.

Hence they also say that the person who has good sense will fall in love. To love by itself is merely indifferent, since it sometimes occurs in the case of the worthless as well. But erotic love is not an appetite nor is it directed at any worthless thing; rather it is an inclination to forming an attachment arising from the impression of beauty.[39]

According to this definition – also preserved by Diogenes Laertius – love is a response to aesthetic features. This text puts a strong emphasis on the claim that proper erotic love is not an appetite (ἐπιθυμία), which implicitly suggests it is not pursued for the sake of pleasure.[40] Instead, it is a response to an impression of beauty. This claim is a bit vague, and one might wonder whether appetite cannot arise from the impression of beauty as well. Arguably, this passage suggests that an appetite is a response to the pleasure and pleasure alone. The impression of beauty must be a different type of reaction. It seems likely that this passage establishes a dichotomy between love as a psychological response and love as an epistemic response. This passage does not make clear what would be the epistemic contents of this impression of beauty, but one might argue that it is the apt ordering,[41] on the basis of another piece of evidence. Here, the Stoic claim that the wise man falls in love is explained as follows:

τὸν δὲ ἔρωτά φασιν ἐπιβολὴν εἶναι φιλοποιίας διὰ κάλλος ἐμφαινόμενον νέων ὡραίων· δι' ὃ καὶ ἐρωτικὸν εἶναι τὸν σοφὸν καὶ ἐρασθήσεσθαι τῶν ἀξιεράστων, εὐγενῶν ὄντων καὶ εὐφυῶν.

They say that erotic love is an inclination to forming an attachment resulting from the beauty displayed by young men in their prime. As a result the wise man is erotic and falls in love with those worthy of erotic love, the well-bred and naturally suitable.[42]

Those worthy of erotic love are well-bred and naturally suitable (εὐφυῶν). By itself, the meaning of this statement is not very clear and raises the question of what this aptitude consists of. The following passage containing Zeno's description of a desirable youth cited in Clement's *The Instructor*, however, illustrates what such statements might refer to:

καλήν τινα καὶ ἀξιέραστον ὑπογράφειν ὁ Κιτιεὺς ἔοικε Ζήνων εἰκόνα νεανίου καὶ οὕτως αὐτὸν ἀνδριαντουργεῖ· ἔστω, φησί, καθαρὸν τὸ πρόσωπον, ὀφρὺς μὴ καθειμένη μηδὲ ὄμμα ἀναπεπταμένον μηδὲ ἀνακεκλασμένον, μὴ ὕπτιος ὁ τράχηλος μηδὲ ἀνιέμενα τὰ τοῦ σώματος μέλη, ἀλλὰ [τὰ] μετέωρα ἐντόνοις ὅμοια, ὀρθόν οὖς πρὸς τὸν λόγον [ὀξύτης καὶ κατοκωχὴ τῶν ὀρθῶς εἰρημένων] καὶ σχηματισμοὶ καὶ κινήσεις μηδὲν ἐνδιδοῦσα τοῖς ἀκολάστοις ἐλπίδος αἰδὼς μὲν ἐπανθείτω καὶ ἀρρενωπία, ἀπέστω δὲ καὶ ὁ ἀπὸ τῶν μυροπωλίων καὶ χρυσοχοείων καὶ ἐριοπωλίων ἄλυς καὶ ὁ ἀπὸ τῶν ἄλλων ἐργαστηρίων, ἔνθα ἑταιρικῶς κεκοσμημέναι, ὥσπερ ἐπὶ τέγους καθεζόμεναι διημερεύουσιν.

Zeno of Citium seems to sketch a beautiful and properly loveable image of a young man. He sculpts him like this:

Let his countenance be pure; his brow not relaxed; his eye not wide open nor half-closed; his neck not thrown back; nor the limbs of his body relaxed, but keyed up like strings under tension; his ear cocked for the *logos*; and his bearing and movement giving no hope to the licentious. Let modesty and a manly look flower upon him, but away with the excitement of perfumers' shops and goldsmiths and wool shops – and indeed all the other shops, where women spend the whole day adorned like courtesans, as though they were sitting in a brothel.[43]

There are no actual physical features on the list. No, for example, description of the facial features or the shape of the body parts is provided.[44] Indeed, the description seems to be formulated in such a way as to emphasise the good receptive qualities of the youth. Everything about this youth, from his behaviour to the way he stands, shows him to be good material to impart philosophical teachings to. The passive demeanour of the youth does not mean that he is not keen on wisdom or that he is indifferent to the type of education he receives. It seems reasonable to suppose that once Zeno's youth was persuaded to pursue philosophy, his ears became cocked for the *logos*. The word ὀξύτης usually indicates the sharpness of hearing, but here, paired with the *logos*, this word must be describing not so much hearing itself as a directed effort to hear something, listening, or paying attention. The youth, thus, is an attentive listener to the *logos*.[45] Zeno, therefore, describes not just any youth one might happen to see, but someone who has proven himself to be worthy of philosophical teaching by following instructions and exhibiting keenness for learning philosophy.[46] A short fragment preserved by Diogenes Laertius supports this reading because it explains the affection of the wise man towards the youth as arising from the latter's endowment for virtue.[47]

Such a description, I would argue, is best explained in terms of functionality, that is, what is appropriate for the youth given the kind of being he is. The nature of human beings is to be rational, and beauty manifests in a young man who shows by his bearing an inclination to learning and virtue.[48] This kind of beauty is, of course, not as significant as the mature intellectual beauty of the wise man, but it can also be understood as a legitimate kind of beauty in the Stoic aesthetic framework. This, in turn, elicits love in the wise man for the youth. In this way, the notion of functionality – in the sense of actions and properties that are appropriate for the kind of being that someone is – allows us to interpret this difficult material on human beauty in a rather elegant way.

One small problematic point remains, namely Plutarch's claim that the Stoic notion of love is comparable to the pursuit of foul things by beetles, because the wise man stops loving the young men (who are not yet wise and hence not beautiful according to the Stoics' own understanding) once they turn wise, and hence, beautiful. This critique is presumably based on Plutarch's extrapolation from the Stoic definition of love as the response to beauty in youths who are 'in bloom'.[49] If that is the case, then Plutarch represents the Stoic position correctly, but whether it is a fair criticism is not so clear. The latter depends on what motivated the Stoic claim. There are two, not mutually exclusive, possibilities here, both of them arising from the fact that it is quite evident that love in the Stoic fragments is strongly associated with patronage and guidance.[50]

First, the format of the claim resembles other claims about the wise man in which certain common practices are tested by the rational agent. The statement that the wise man would fall in love is comparable to, for instance, the statement that the wise man would get married.[51] According to this reading, the Stoics are simply referring to ancient Greek notions of love as a cultural practice. Their claim amounts to saying that it is not irrational to engage in such a relationship of love as long as the youth shows the promise of virtue. In the case of this reading, the notion of love would not be philosophically motivated at all; instead, what we find in the extant evidence is the philosophically motivated approach to a common phenomenon.

The second option is a more philosophically motivated reading. As was mentioned above, love in the extant Stoic fragments is strongly associated with tutelage.[52] As such, it is an appropriate response to the kind of beauty which originates in the inclination to virtue requiring nourishing and tutelage. The love for a fully wise person, however, does not have such a purpose. It is, therefore, reasonable that such love would cease once its object fully develops rationally and no longer requires further guidance.[53] To many thinkers, this account of love might undoubtedly appear unsatisfactorily pragmatic, but it is not entirely surprising to find such ideas in Stoic texts. In the hands of the Stoics, the devoted theorists of rationality, love is just another opportunity to develop and promote what is the best in human beings.

Concluding remarks

The Stoic account of human beauty indicates that there is a functional aspect of the phenomenon that proper aesthetic judgements ought to depict. It is necessary to investigate another case of beauty, that of the world, before drawing any conclusions about how formal properties and functionality are combined by the Stoic understanding of aesthetic properties. These texts will be addressed in the following chapter. For now, it is worth noting that, from a more general philosophical point of view, the interesting point that the Stoic account makes is showing that a formal account of aesthetic properties can be 'contextualised', that is, one could claim that the formal features have a reference point. One could argue that the reference point 'human nature' is as vague a notion as can be. But a parallel could be found in evolutionary aesthetics. This is not to say, of course, that the Stoics were even remotely committed to something like evolution; quite the opposite. The common ground is the idea that humans find beautiful what they are made – either intentionally or unintentionally, by a designer or by evolution – to find attractive.[54] The design of the world and the role of beauty in this design are explored in the following chapter.

Notes

1. Beech (2009: 12).
2. This is not to say such a view is unique. Such an association is drawn both in antiquity (Plato *Symp.* 204C–205A) and in later philosophy; see, for example, Mothersill (2009: 167), who lists this as one of the common observances about beauty in philosophy.
3. Plutarch *Mor.* 1057E–1058A; the translation is mine, after Cherniss. Aeschylus' fr. 361 translated by Sommerstein.
4. Flew (1975: 47–8): 'Imagine some Scottish chauvinist settled down one Sunday morning with his customary copy of *The News of the World*. He reads the story under the headline, "Sidcup Sex Maniac Strikes Again". Our reader is, as he confidently expected, agreeably shocked: "No Scot would do such a thing!" Yet the very next Sunday he finds in that same favourite source a report of the even more scandalous ongoings of Mr Angus MacSporran in Aberdeen. This clearly constitutes a counter example, which definitely falsifies the universal proposition originally put forward. Allowing that this is indeed such a counter example, he ought to withdraw; retreating perhaps to a rather weaker claim about most or some. But even an imaginary Scot is, like the rest of us, human; and we none of us always do what we ought to do. So what in fact he says is: 'No true Scotsman would do such a thing!' . . . it is immediately obvious what is going on, and

wrong. A bold, indeed reckless, claim about all those who happen to be members of a certain group is being surreptitiously replaced by an utterance which is, in effect, made true by an arbitrary redefinition.'
5. Origen *in evang. Ioan.* 2.10=*SVF* 3.544.
6. See Plutarch *Pomp.* 14.6. Plato *Resp.* 472A. When Diogenes Laertius writes about Eubulides (Diogenes Laertius 2.108), the author of many famous logical paradoxes, he describes Eubulides as someone who propounded arguments in dialectic. There is no mention of the term παράδοξος at all: τῆς δ' Εὐκλείδου διαδοχῆς ἐστι καὶ Εὐβουλίδης ὁ Μιλήσιος, ὃς καὶ πολλοὺς ἐν διαλεκτικῇ λόγους ἠρώτησε, τόν τε ψευδόμενον καὶ τὸν διαλανθάνοντα καὶ Ἠλέκτραν καὶ ἐγκεκαλυμμένον καὶ σωρίτην καὶ κερατίνην καὶ φαλακρόν.
7. See Diogenes Laertius 7.180=*SVF* 2.1-LS 31Q, where it is said that if gods had dialectic, it would not differ from that of Chrysippus.
8. Chrysippus *Log. Quest.* 3, 9.7–12=*SVF* 2.298=LS 37G; Sextus Empiricus *M* 7.416=LS 37F; Cicero *Acad.* 2.93=LS 37H.
9. Plutarch *Mor.* 1058A.
10. While everybody can assent to cognitive impressions, the ability to assent to cognitive impressions only is the distinguishing feature of the wise man; see Plutarch *Mor.* 1057A–B=*SVF* 3.177=LS 41F.
11. A famous example would be the case of Mary the super-scientist put forth by Frank Jackson (1982), although cf. Ierodiakonou (2005a) for the discussion of issues concerning what could be called ancient thought experiments.
12. Diogenes Laertius 7.121–2=LS 67M; Cicero *Parad.* 5.33–4.
13. Cicero *Fin.* 3.26=*SVF* 3.582.
14. Diogenes Laertius 7.100; Cicero *Fin.* 3.74; Philo *Gen.* 4.99=*SVF* 3.592.
15. Cicero *Parad.* 5.34–5, tr. Rackham.
16. Cicero *Parad.* 6.52.
17. Cicero *Parad.* 2.17–18.
18. See note 14 above.
19. Diogenes Laertius 7.46–8=*SVF* 2.130=LS 31B.
20. Diogenes Laertius 7.83=*SVF* 2.130=LS 31C.
21. Stobaeus 2.67, 5–12=*SVF* 3.295=LS 26H. A passage from Seneca shows a less controversial explanation of how the wise man's knowledge differs from an expert's knowledge. Seneca wrote that the wise man

would study arithmetic just like a mathematician or a geometer, but while a mathematician calculates and measures heavenly bodies, the wise man 'knows the rationale of the heavenly bodies, their power and their nature' (*qua ratione constent caelestia, quae illis sit vis quaeve natura sapiens scit*), Seneca *Ep.* 88.25–28=LS 26F, tr. Long and Sedley.
22. Origen *in evang. Ioan.* 2.10=*SVF* 3.544; Diogenes Laertius 7.119.
23. Diogenes Laertius 7.122=*SVF* 3.612, 3.617; cf. Cicero *Fin.* 3.75.
24. See Vogt (2008: 126–30), who argues that these are revisionist claims about knowledge.
25. See Obbink and Waerdt (1991: 389), who interpret the notion of a city of wise men in the fragments attributed to Diogenes of Babylon (who follows Chrysippus at least to some extent) and conclude that the Stoic political programme was not intended for actual cities such as Athens or Sparta, but for the city of wise men. See also Schofield (1999: 97).
26. See Vogt (2008: 60–3), who argues that the infamous Stoic claims about cannibalism and incest are also best understood not as prescriptive, but as reflections of Stoic thought on appropriate action.
27. In the passage cited above (*Mor.* 1057E–1058A), Plutarch emphasised how unusual the idea of the suddenness of the transition from ignorance to wisdom (and from ugliness to beauty) is by writing that while the Stoic wise man was ugly and vicious yesterday, today he is both virtuous and beautiful (ὁ δὲ τῶν Στωικῶν σοφὸς χθὲς μὲν ἦν αἴσχιστος ἅμα καὶ κάκιστος, τήμερον δ' ἄφνω μεταβέβληκεν εἰς ἀρετὴν καὶ γέγονεν ἐκ ῥυσοῦ καὶ ὠχροῦ).
28. Cicero *Fin.* 3.75, tr. Woolf.
29. Diogenes Laertius 7.100.
30. Diogenes Laertius 7.100, tr. Hicks.
31. Arius Didymus 7b (Pomeroy), Stobaeus 2.81–82W, tr. Pomeroy.
32. Diogenes Laertius 7.87–9=LS 63C.
33. Sextus Empiricus *M* 7.151–7=LS 41C.
34. See, for instance, Seneca *Ep.* 76.9–10=*SVF* 3.200a=LS 63D.
35. See Epictetus *Disc.* 2.23.30–35, discussed in the previous chapter. Epictetus argues that only an ignorant and boorish person would be terrified of preferred indifferents enough not to recognise that Achilles was more beautiful than Thersites. The correct way of action is to recognise the actual value of every object and to treat them

appropriately, rather than to deny that the preferred indifferents are valuable in some sense.

36. Earlier in book 4, Cicero describes at length, following the Stoics, various analogies between ills in the body and the soul. Just before this passage starts, he notes that the body and the soul are comparable both with respect to their bad states and their good ones. He then turns to the topic of health which he calls a balanced condition, both mental and physical. Such a condition is found either in the wise man or in a non-wise person who is sedated by medicine. He then abruptly changes the topic to mental and physical beauty. On the possible connection between health and beauty in Stoicism, see note 11 on page 165.
37. Cicero *Tusc.* 4.31=*SVF* 3.279, tr. King, slightly amended by replacing 'symmetrical' with 'proportionate'. See also Arius Didymus 5b4–5b5 (Pomeroy)= Stobaeus 2.62–3W=*SVF* 1.563.
38. See Boys-Stones (2019: 109–10).
39. Arius Didymus 5b9 (Pomeroy)=Stobaeus 2.66W=*SVF* 3.717, tr. Pomeroy.
40. This is stated more explicitly in Diogenes Laertius 7.130: Εἶναι δὲ τὸν ἔρωτα ἐπιβολὴν φιλοποιίας διὰ κάλλος ἐμφαινόμενον: καὶ μὴ εἶναι συνουσίας, ἀλλὰ φιλίας.
41. My reading somewhat differs from Nussbaum (1995: 259), who interprets this Stoic tenet as follows: 'the wise man will reason that what he finds so moving is not really the bodily beauty, but the signs of the soul within that make their way into his presence through the body. He can fairly claim that his object is really the soul, not the body, and that the young really are not truly beautiful until they have become educated.'
42. Arius Didymus 11s (Pomeroy)=Stobaeus 2.115W=*SVF* 3.650, tr. Pomeroy.
43. Clement *Paed.* 3.11.74 (after Schofield (1999: 115–116))=*SVF* 1.246, tr. Schofield.
44. See Boys-Stones (2007: 79); Nussbaum (1995: 259).
45. An interesting parallel can be found in Epictetus' *Disc.* 4.11.25–6. Epictetus states that given the choice between two potential students, one of whom took too much care of his appearance while the other did not even take care of his hygiene, he would prefer the former,

because such a student would already be a keen pursuer of the beautiful and would only need to be pointed to the right kind of beauty, that is, the beauty of the soul. See Stephens (1996) for an argument that, according to Epictetus, the wise man's love consists in sharing his wisdom.
46. See Schofield (1999: 117) who suggests that Zeno's description of the youth was an encouragement to aim for particular physical bearing.
47. Diogenes Laertius 7.129, tr. Hicks: 'The wise man will feel affection for the youths who by their countenance show a natural endowment for virtue' (καὶ ἐρασθήσεσθαι δὲ τὸν σοφὸν τῶν νέων τῶν ἐμφαινόντων διὰ τοῦ εἴδους τὴν πρὸς ἀρετὴν εὐφυΐαν). According to Diogenes, this view was found in both Zeno's *Republic* and Chrysippus' *On Modes of Life*.
48. See Price (2002: 187), who argues as follows: 'We must suppose that the Stoics conceived of visual and visible beauties as uniting, within the person of a promising adolescent, in a blend that is only apparent to the man who is at once an actual sage and a potential lover . . . If there is a mystery here in the chemistry of eyes and heart, it may be one that is not invented but revealed.'
49. Diogenes Laertius 7.130, this 'bloom' is of virtue: εἶναι δὲ καὶ τὴν ὥραν ἄνθος ἀρετῆς.
50. A very similar idea is espoused by Pausanias in Plato's *Symp.* 184D–185B, cf. Dover (1978: 91). See also Laurand (2007).
51. Cicero *Fin.* 3.62=*SVF* 3.68=LS 57F.
52. Also in the context of the cosmic order, see Boys-Stones (1998).
53. Konstan (1997: 114) argues that 'the definition of *eros*, attributed to the Stoic founders Zeno and Chrysippus . . . looks to eliminating the sexual component of pederasty in favour of a disinterested and educative affection identified as *philia*. Perhaps the effect of such virtuous passion is to convert the beloved intro a Stoic friend.' Vogt (2008: 159–60) also makes a similar suggestion. It is noteworthy that no extant evidence explicitly suggests that the relationship between a youth and his teacher would naturally move from love to friendship, but it is plausible that some Stoics might have held this view. The Stoic definition of friendship is a complicated notion in its own right, because they claimed that only wise men were friends (Diogenes Laertius 7.124). Glenn Lesses (1993) presents a comprehensive analysis of this claim.

54. For evolutionary aesthetics, see, for example, Rusch and Voland (2013) and Dutton (2009). See also Sedley (2017: 34–42) for an argument connecting ancient ideas about functional beauty and the evolutionary accounts of the beauty of nature.

5

Beauty in Stoic Theological Arguments

'... adaptation of means to an end will find itself recognised as one of the implements or elements of beauty. But it will not be the manifestation of means to any end or service outside of themselves, as a machine is adapted to do a certain work; it will be rather the adaptation of means to an end within themselves, as life manifests itself by the structure and activity of the living body. The more perfectly this body is fitted to manifest life, the more beautiful will it be.'

Charles Carroll Everett, *The Science of Thought: A System of Logic*[1]

Beauty vocabulary features rather prominently in Stoic theological arguments. Beauty terms are attested to in at least three such arguments. Cicero's *On the Nature of the Gods* contains two of them: Cleanthes' statement that the beauty of the world is one of the proofs for the existence of god[2] and Chrysippus' claim that if one saw a beautiful house, one would know that it was built by human beings rather than by mice.[3] Plutarch also cites Chrysippus as saying that the peacock was created for the beauty of its tail.[4] In these extant fragments, beauty is 'reverse engineered' in order to make inferences about the underlying generative process. The inference typically takes the form of a material entailment, and the very nature of beauty is used as evidence. For this reason, these arguments are useful evidence for the Stoic theorisation of aesthetic properties. They are also useful for answering the question of what is it that we perceive when we perceive beauty, and thus building on the conclusions reached in the previous chapters.

The beautiful world and its design

In Cicero's *On the Nature of the Gods,* Balbus, the Stoic spokesperson, states that if Posidonius' sphere were brought to barbarian lands such as Scythia or Britain, no one in these lands would think that this mechanism was not a product of reason.[5] Posidonius' sphere is a mechanism consisting of a revolving sun, a moon and five planets.[6] When moving, it exhibits the effects of night and day. In the same work, an Academic philosopher, Cotta, attributes to Chrysippus the following argument:

> Et 'Si domus pulchra sit, intellegamus eam dominis' inquit 'aedificatam esse non muribus; sic igitur mundum deorum domum existimare debemus'. Ita prorsus existimarem, si illum aedificatum, non quem ad modum docebo a natura conformatum putarem.

Chrysippus also states: 'If a beautiful house appeared before our eyes, we would realise that it had been built by the owners, and not by mice; so we must likewise realise that the universe is the home of the gods.' I should certainly agree, if I thought that the universe had been built, rather than, as I shall show, fashioned by nature.[7]

Posidonius' sphere and Chrysippus' house are two different examples underpinned by the same argument. In the first case, the complexity of the structure makes it evident that it is a product of reason. In the second case, Chrysippus' analogy between a beautiful house and the universe could be interpreted as saying that just as a house cannot be built by mice, so the world cannot be generated by atoms, the smallest, indivisible particles that can be found in the world. The existence of the world, therefore, requires intentional design which, in its own turn, requires an intelligent creator.

It has been pointed out that these arguments appear to be predecessors to the intelligent design arguments. One of the most recent interpretations of this kind is found in David Sedley's monograph

Creationism and its Critics in Antiquity. Sedley points out the resemblance of the Stoic Posidonius' sphere argument to one of the best-known versions of the argument from design, that is, Paley's watch analogy.[8] Paley's argument states that an examination of a watch leads one to discover that the parts of a watch fit together in such a way as to indicate intentional design and, subsequently, the conclusion that the watch had a maker. According to Paley, the same inference can be drawn for organic objects, for example, plants, animals and human beings, in order to conclude that they were designed by god.[9] Sedley suggests that Posidonius' sphere is a Stoic version of an argument from design,[10] defining this type of argument as belonging to 'a family of arguments aimed at demonstrating the existence of a creator god'.[11]

The similarity between this Stoic argument and Paley's argument is, as Sedley points out, remarkable. Yet in addition to positing a creator god, these arguments presuppose a certain conceptualisation of that deity. To be more precise, according to Paley's watchmaker analogy, god created the world intentionally and *ab initio*, which is consistent with the monotheistic theological view. Merely stating that the world was generated rationally by a rational creator, however, does not constitute a typical creationist view, because the latter is more narrow. The Stoics are part of the tradition which used the notion of god in diverse ways, often in scientific and philosophical enquiries.[12] In fact, the early Christian thinkers, genuine creationists, emphasise the difference between their own views of genesis and the account of world-generation proposed by Greek philosophers.[13] The presence of matter means the world creation is not truly *ab initio*, since there is another primal element involved. It makes god not the sole creator, but only a partner in creation. This shows that the mere presence of matter in the process of world creation complicates the creationist interpretation of Stoic thought.

More importantly, the argument about the beautiful house does not commit the Stoics to very much. It is certainly true that the world according to this and similar arguments is made in some rational manner, but such a claim still leaves a number of possibilities about world creation open. The context of this quotation and the demarcation of the exact words of Chrysippus are worth noting here. The passage consists of a citation and a comment, and while the citation ('If a beautiful house appeared before our eyes, we would realise that it had been built by the owners, and not by mice; so we must likewise realise that the universe is the home of the gods')[14] can be assumed to be Chrysippus', the text indicates that the comment which states that the universe was created rather than fashioned by nature belongs to Cotta, an Academic spokesperson. Cotta, of course, is not necessarily committed to representing Chrysippus' meaning accurately and therefore it is possible to question whether it was Chrysippus himself who claimed that the analogy showed that the world had been built rather than 'fashioned by nature'. If Cotta's commentary is bracketed off, a subtly different interpretation of the passage becomes possible. When read on its own, Chrysippus' argument only seeks to establish that a rational process, rather than an irrational and accidental one, is responsible for the creation of the world. The formulation is parallel to Paley's argument from design, but the context of this argument suggests that the purpose of Chrysippus' claim might differ in some respects.

Chrysippus' argument is most likely an attack on Epicurean physics.[15] If this argument is read as indicating Chrysippus' commitment to downward causation, then Chrysippus was criticising the Epicureans for claiming that atomic particles rather than an intelligent designer were the causes of generation. In this case, Chrysippus' argument would equate mice with atoms, but this does not seem to be a coherent point. Houses, after all, are not made of mice. Chrysippus must have been making a point about the method of generation, rather than the components of generation. The Epicureans held that the principle which generates the world is the properties of atoms.[16] Thus in Chrysippus' argument, mice are comparable to atoms in the sense that just as the irrational nature of mice does not allow them to be builders of houses, so the nature of atomic motion does not allow them to be the principle of generation. The properties of atoms are too limited and therefore insufficient to make them the generative principle of the world. Chrysippus was clearly interested in showing that the world could not have come into existence by the mechanical[17] and sometimes even random[18] motion of atoms, but this passage only shows that he thought there must be a rational generative principle, not that the world was designed intentionally *ab initio*. The Stoic spokesman Balbus makes it quite explicit that the Stoic argument is designed to refute the Epicurean doctrine of atomic motion when he states that, according to the Epicurean way of reasoning, it is just as plausible to believe that if numerous copies of the alphabet's twenty-one letters made of gold or similar material were shaken together and thrown on the ground, they would produce a copy of Ennius' *Annals*.[19] Although there is a striking resemblance to the arguments from design, these Stoic claims are only concerned with rejecting the Epicurean idea that arbitrary motion was partly responsible for the world's generation.

This, of course, does not rule out the possibility that the Stoics might be creationists of some kind – depending how one defines creationism and its branches – but such a question is outside the scope of this work. For the purposes of this study, the only pertinent issue is that the Stoic claim about the presence of beauty in the world cannot be explained in quite the same way as the claims by the early moderns. In order to examine the peculiarities of the Stoic account, it is necessary to focus on the specific description of the Stoic god. According to the Stoics, the principle which generates the world, often called god/intelligence/fate/Zeus[20] as well as nature and fire,[21] is an entity that is constantly present in the world. The immanence of the god in the world raises the question of how the god designs the world in such a way, and how exactly aesthetic properties are imparted into the world so that they can be used for forming inferences about the generation of the world.

Timaeus

Before examining the extant Stoic evidence further, it is necessary to discuss the significant background role that Plato's *Timaeus* plays here. It is often noted in the scholarship that the *Timaeus* was one of the most important influences on Stoic physics.[22] Beauty, as well as the cosmic creator's intention to create beauty, are found in the Platonic account of the generation of the world as well, and it is worth noting their significance for the Stoics.

According to Timaeus, the main spokesperson in the dialogue, the creator of the world of becoming generated the world because he was good (and thus not envious), and therefore wanted everything to become as much like himself as possible.[23] Then Timaeus describes the elemental generation with a reference to geometrical principles and the generation of the world from the elements, including the spherical shape of the world. But it is the description of the making of the soul of the world which is the most relevant part of the Platonic account for present purposes. First, the cosmic creator mixes the components of 'being', 'identity' and 'difference'.[24] This mixture is then divided by the creator according to a series of proportions. The constituents of the mixture enable the world soul to be cognisant,[25] while the proportions introduce bodily motion of the heavenly bodies and time.[26] This ordering, however, is also responsible for the aesthetic properties inherent in the world, because it is not permissible for the best (τῷ ἀρίστῳ) to produce anything but the most beautiful (τὸ κάλλιστον).[27] This indicates that aesthetic properties originate from the formal divisions of the world. In this respect, the Stoic account resembles the one found in the *Timaeus*.[28]

In Plato's dialogue, however, the creator uses the pattern of Being to construct the world (as opposed to Becoming).[29] The Platonic account, thus, involves the forms, the existence of which the Stoics deny.[30] If the pattern of the proportion that generates the structure of the world (and, at the same time, its beauty) is not copied from anything outside of the universe, then it must come from the god or the active principle inherent in the world. The most obvious solution is to claim that the pattern of proportion comes from god's mind. Some extant evidence shows that the Stoics claimed the forms only exist in the mind.[31] This, however, leads to the possibly even more complex question of how the god's thought translates into a creative act. This question is addressed in the following section, and it will lead, in its turn, to a further question especially pertinent to aesthetics, a kind of aesthetic version of the problem of theodicy. In the Platonic universe, the patterns responsible for beauty are set in place at the genesis. The Stoic god, however, is ever-present in the world. This leads to the problem of theodicy and the question of whether god shapes every object that is beautiful, as well as, for example, gnats and mud.

The activities of the Stoic god

In Sextus Empiricus' *Against the Professors*, the Stoic metaphysical belief that 'the substance of what exists . . . needs to be set in motion and shaped by some cause' is immediately followed by an analogy which compares the world with a sculpture in the following manner:

. . . ὡς χαλκούργημα περικαλλὲς θεασάμενοι ποθοῦμεν μαθεῖν τὸν τεχνίτην ἅτε καθ' αὑτὴν τῆς ὕλης ἀκινήτου καθεστώσης, οὕτω καὶ τὴν τῶν ὅλων ὕλην θεωροῦντες κινουμένην καὶ ἐν μορφῇ τε καὶ διακοσμήσει τυγχάνουσαν εὐλόγως ἂν σκεπτοίμεθα τὸ κινοῦν αὐτὴν καὶ πολυειδῶς μορφοῦν αἴτιον.

. . . when we look at a very beautiful bronze we want to know the artist (since in itself the matter is in an immobile condition), so when we see the matter of the universe moving and possessing form and structure we might reasonably enquire into the cause which moves and shapes it into many forms.[32]

Then the argument concludes that it is an all-pervading, fundamental power which shapes the world and is analogous to the human soul pervading the body.[33] At first sight, this analogy seems to suggest the idea that god creates like a craftsman and the work generated is the product of an outside designer. At the same time, the notion of pervasiveness makes such an interpretation a little bit more difficult, because it invites us to think of god as the soul of the world rather than its external creator.[34] The way in which a human soul 'works' on the human body is very different from the way in which a craftsman works on bronze. The soul not only shapes a human being in premeditated and intentional ways, it also *is* the human being. The properties and the acts of the soul are, presumably, determined by its nature. The rational soul renders human beings rational not because it designs them, but because its nature renders any object in which it is present to possess the property of being rational. The passage, therefore, seems to present two different accounts of the generation of the world. It might be the case that the analogy with a sculptor is not a citation from a Stoic source but Sextus' own addition intended to illustrate the Stoic claims, yet it is not clear whether that could have been the case. This chapter offers a different way of reconciling these two apparently contradictory conceptualisations of divine generation by investigating the meaning of the notion τέχνη, a term typically associated with the activities of a craftsman, and determining what kind of activity it presupposes.

Mixtures

The standard answer to the question of how the Stoic god affects the world is by means of pervading it, which is a rather vague description. Chrysippus' doctrine of mixtures,[35] however, provides information about the technical aspects of the Stoic god's activity. The Chrysippean notion of mixture can be understood as following from materialist commitments. According to the Stoics, the world is generated by two entities: matter (or the passive principle) and god (also called fire, the active principle and by other names).[36] Any philosopher who commits to the claim that there is a single principle underlying the whole of existence has to give an account explaining why phenomenally different objects exist. The Stoics were not strong ontological monists, because they held that there are two fundamental generative principles, but they still had to answer the question of how the plurality of phenomenal objects is produced by only two entities. In his work *On Mixture*, Alexander of Aphrodisias, a Peripatetic commentator, records that Chrysippus presented three kinds of mixtures as a solution to this problem.[37] Alexander elaborately criticises Chrysippus' views in favour of Aristotle's account of mixtures and, in the process, provides a fairly detailed account of the mixtures, including an explanation of the significance of the difference between the mixtures. Alexander cites Chrysippus as arguing that 'we could not have this difference in presentations if bodies had been juxtaposed by juncture whatever way they were mixed',[38] which suggests two points. First, Chrysippus held that mixtures can provide an account of how a plurality of objects can be produced by a limited number of base principles. Second, different types of mixtures produce different properties. Chrysippus held that juxtaposition, for instance, the most basic form of mixture in which constituents are simply put together without interacting with each other in a substantive way, does not account for the great variety of observable phenomenal objects. Amongst the arguments which Alexander presents in order to refute Chrysippus, there is one which directly addresses the problem of the role of god in the process of generation and maintenance of the world in the following way:

πῶς δ' οὐκ ἀνάξια τῆς θείας προλήψεως τό τε τὸν θεὸν διὰ πάσης τῆς ὑποκειμένης πᾶσιν ὕλης κεχωρηκέναι λέγειν καὶ μένειν ἐν αὐτῇ, ὁποία ποτ' ἂν ᾖ, καὶ τὸ προηγούμενον ἔχειν ἔργον, τὸ ἀεί τι γεννᾶν τε καὶ διαπλάσσειν τῶν ἐξ αὐτῆς γενέσθαι δυναμένων, καὶ ποιεῖν τὸν θεὸν δημιουργὸν σκωλήκων τε καὶ ἐμπίδων, ἀτέχνως ὥσπερ κοροπλαθόν τινα τῷ πηλῷ σχολάζοντα καὶ πᾶν τὸ δυνάμενον ἐξ αὐτοῦ γενέσθαι τοῦτο ποιοῦντα;

Surely it demeans our preconception of the deity to say that God pervades the whole of the matter underlying everything and remains in it, whatever it might be like, and has as its premeditated task the perpetual generation and moulding of anything that can come to be from it; and for them to make God a craftsman of grubs and gnats, simply devoting himself like a modeller to clay, and making everything that can be created from it?[39]

In this passage, the Stoic view that god pervades everything and remains in everything is criticised by Alexander because it contradicts a common preconception of gods as lofty beings above mundane things. Alexander raises a serious theological problem about the presence of god in mundane objects, and the way in which Chrysippus tackled the problem of theodicy is discussed below. In order to understand Chrysippus' position, it is necessary to determine the manner in which the Stoic god is present in the world.

The explanation of what this idea entails can be found in the Stoic theory of mixtures criticised by Alexander. According to him, Chrysippus recognised three kinds of mixtures: juxtaposition, fusion and blending.[40] Juxtaposition (παράθεσις) occurs when the components of a mixture are juxtaposed 'by juncture' (καθ' ἁρμήν), and each constituent preserves its surface and properties. The example given for this type of a mixture is a pile of beans and wheat grains. During the process of fusion (σύγχυσις), meanwhile, both the substances and the properties of constituents are completely destroyed. Such a process occurs when medical drugs and a disease are jointly destroyed and a new entity is produced. The third type of mixing is blending (κρᾶσις). This occurs when the substances and qualities of the entities that are mixed coextend mutually, while preserving their own identity. An important characteristic of this mixture is that the blended bodies are able to be separated again.[41]

Unfortunately, it is not spelled out very clearly in the *On Mixture* by means of which type of mixture god pervades matter. An informative passage comes immediately after Alexander has described each of the mixtures. In this passage, Alexander discusses the application of the Stoic mixture theory in the following way:

> καὶ τῶν στοιχείων δέ φασι τῶν τεσσάρων τὰ δύο, τό τε πῦρ καὶ τὸν ἀέρα, λεπτομερῆ τε καὶ κοῦφα καὶ εὔτονα ὄντα, διὰ τῶν δύο, γῆς τε καὶ ὕδατος, παχυμερῶν καὶ βαρέων καὶ ἀτόνων ὄντων διαπεφοιτηκέναι ὅλα δι' ὅλων, σώζοντα τὴν οἰκείαν φύσιν καὶ συνέχειαν αὐτά τε καὶ ἐκεῖνα. δηλητήριά τε τὰ φθείροντα καὶ τὰς ὀσμάς, ὅσαι τοιαῦται, ἡγοῦνται κιρνᾶσθαι τοῖς ὑπ' αὐτῶν πάσχουσιν, ὅλα δι' ὅλων παρατιθέμενα. καὶ τὸ φῶς δὲ τῷ ἀέρι ὁ Χρύσιππος κιρνᾶσθαι λέγει. καὶ αὕτη μὲν ἡ περὶ κράσεως δόξα Χρυσίππου τε καὶ τῶν κατ' αὐτὸν φιλοσοφούντων.

> And they say that two of the four elements, Fire and Air, being rare, light, and having tension, completely pervade Earth and Water which

Beauty in Stoic Theological Arguments   111

are dense, heavy and lack tension; and that each pair preserves its own nature and continuity. They think that drugs that are deleterious, and all such odours, are mixed with the bodies affected by them in a total juxtaposition. Chrysippus also thinks that light is mixed with air. This is Chrysippus' theory of blending and that of the philosophers who follow him.[42]

On the one hand, the language of this passage is not very illuminating. It is not very clear whether Alexander is presenting a collection of distinct beliefs, some examples of different mixtures or a group of Stoic beliefs. This lack of clarity is increased by inconsistent terminology. Instead of using the same terms as he did in the definitions of mixtures, Alexander uses the term διαπεφοιτηκέναι for pervasion. Similarly, although at the end of the passage he says that this is Chrysippus' theory of κρᾶσις, a term which he used to describe blending earlier, we cannot be certain that Alexander actually intended to say that all of the instances of mixture described above were blending, because he uses the term κρᾶσις very loosely throughout this treatise.[43]

On the other hand, it is possible to compare the passage above with the descriptions of three kinds of mixtures and to determine which one of the mixtures fits most accurately the description of how god pervades matter. The very first sentence states that fire and air (which are synonymous with the active principle in Stoicism)[44] completely pervade earth and water (which are synonymous with matter),[45] while preserving their own natures. This statement suggests that god pervades matter in the manner of blending.

A similar conclusion can be reached by investigating the detailed descriptions of all the mixtures. The mixture by juxtaposition clearly produces the kind of properties that are sometimes called mechanical or summative.[46] When the constituents of a mixture correspond to each other by juxtaposition, they simply exist in combination; there is no binding activity between them. To use the example given by Chrysippus, the property of being a pile of wheat grains and beans is reducible to the properties of beans and grains. This kind of mixture cannot be involved in the generation of the world, because if god just juxtaposed with matter, the world as we know it, with a plurality of objects, would not exist. This mixture does, however, produce some objects in the world.

Fusion (σύγχυσις)[47] is defined as a process by means of which the constituents are jointly destroyed and transformed into a new entity. An example of such a phenomenon is a medicine and a disease when they are jointly destroyed (συμφθειρομένων), and a new object comes into existence. Claiming that god's substance is in some sense destroyed in the process of creating new substances would contradict another Stoic claim, that is, that the god is constantly present throughout the world. It is likely, therefore, that fusion was used to explain the origin of various substances but it did not apply to the process of god's pervading the world.[48]

Blending, meanwhile, is a highly suitable option. According to Alexander, an example of this type of mixture is the smell of incense spreading across large expanses of air while preserving its peculiar quality, that is, its smell.[49] Chrysippus' notorious claim that a drop of wine mixed in the sea spreads throughout the whole sea is another example of this mixture.[50] The most important aspect of blending is that the new compounds inherit the qualities of their constituents. Although the constituents combine thoroughly in this type of mixture, they do not lose their original properties. At the same time, the resulting mixture has to be productive of new properties, otherwise this type of mixture would not differ from juxtaposition. When the smell of incense spreads through air and mixes with it, the resulting properties of smell supervene on the properties of pure incense smell and air.

The advantage of describing the mixture of god and matter as blending is the fact that this type of mixture would preserve the properties of god. God's properties must be in some way prominent throughout the existence of the world if god is the active principle that maintains the world.[51] By means of blending, the property of rationality spreads throughout matter. This is the manner in which the active principle is able to order the world. Thus the property of rationality in the construction of the world is due to the fact that one part of that compound that is the world is rational.

Blending, therefore, is in some sense the most significant mixture for explaining how the world is generated, but in order to understand how the Stoics conceptualised the ontology of the world, it is important to take into account all three mixtures. On the most fundamental level, there is blending of the god and matter. That is the process which accounts for the existence of the world as it is. It is not, however, necessary for explaining absolutely everything. Health in a recovering patient is best explained by fusion; the properties of a pile of beans and grains are best explained as resulting from juxtaposition. God's pervasion of the world does not necessarily play a role in every single explanation of why some particular object is the way it is. In some cases, it is more appropriate to explain the existence of some property in reference to the underlying mechanical processes.

The force which enables those processes to take place is, of course, the rationally designing god, but it designs on a grounding level, producing a framework for other processes to occur in. The fragments which suggest that god is concentrated in aether also confirm this interpretation to the extent that it shows that god's pervasion of the world refers to generating cosmic principles which pervade the world from a specific central point.[52] This suggests that the description of the Stoic god as operating like the soul is preferable to the description of the god as a sculptor. Yet it is certainly the case that the acts of the Stoic god are often described as *techne*, which suggests craftsman-like acts. This leads to the central question of the nature of god's acts, that is, god's *techne*.

God's τέχνη

Although not all the relevant evidence compares god to a craftsman, it is not uncommon to find a fragment which describes the generation of god as τέχνη. When Diogenes Laertius reports Stoic theological views, for instance, he presents the following definition of the active generative principle which in this case is called φύσις:

δοκεῖ δ' αὐτοῖς τὴν μὲν φύσιν εἶναι πῦρ τεχνικόν, ὁδῷ βαδίζον εἰς γένεσιν, ὅπερ ἐστὶ πνεῦμα πυροειδὲς καὶ τεχνοειδές·

Nature in their view is a τεχνικόν fire going on its way to create; which is equivalent to a fiery, τεχνοειδές breath.[53]

This passage shows that the Stoic god generates and maintains the world in a way which can be described as τέχνη, but it also raises the question of what the notion of τέχνη entails. What does it mean for god to be τεχνικόν? The term τέχνη is widely used by the Stoics in various arguments,[54] yet, arguably, especially illuminating for this purpose is Olympiodorus' *On Plato's Gorgias*, the work dedicated to the investigation of the relationship between rhetoric and τέχνη. As part of his analysis, Olympiodorus surveys various accounts of τέχνη, including a discussion of the ways in which the first three heads of the Stoa defined τέχνη. He records the views of the early Stoics as follows:

> Κλεάνθης τοίνυν λέγει ὅτι 'τέχνη ἐστὶν ἕξις ὁδῷ πάντα ἀνύουσα'. ἀτελὴς δ' ἐστὶν οὗτος ὁ ὅρος, καὶ γὰρ ἡ φύσις ἕξις τίς ἐστιν ὁδῷ πάντα ποιοῦσα· ὅθεν ὁ Χρύσιππος προσθεὶς τὸ 'μετὰ φαντασιῶν' εἶπεν ὅτι 'τέχνη ἐστὶν ἕξις ὁδῷ προϊοῦσα μετὰ φαντασιῶν' ... Ζήνων δέ φησιν ὅτι 'τέχνη ἐστὶ σύστημα ἐκ καταλήψεων συγγεγυμνασμένον πρός τι τέλος εὔχρηστον τῶν ἐν τῷ βίῳ.

Cleanthes says that τέχνη is a tenor which achieves everything methodically. This definition is incomplete. After all, nature also is a tenor which does everything methodically. That is why Chrysippus added 'with impressions', and said that τέχνη is a tenor which advances methodically with impressions ... Zeno says that τέχνη is a systematic collection of cognitions unified by practice for some goal advantageous in life.[55]

All these definitions are intended to explain the nature of τέχνη, a skill-based activity. Three Stoic definitions of τέχνη share the notion that the fundamental aspect of τέχνη is the employment of a method. The Stoics presumably take τέχνη to be an alternative to ignorance and accident.[56] This suggests that in order to perform an action with τέχνη, one must be capable of reasoning about means and ends as well as understanding what sort of action would result in a desired outcome. In other words, one must have a grasp of the functionality of certain actions.

It is important, however, to note the difference between the terms used in Zeno's definition on the one hand and by Cleanthes and Chrysippus on the other. According to Zeno, τέχνη works towards τέλος. This suggests that an action produced by τέχνη is intentionally aimed at achieving a certain goal and thus such an action is teleological. Cleanthes' and Chrysippus' definitions of τέχνη, by contrast, do not use teleological language as explicitly as Zeno's. In these definitions, the prominent term is ὁδός which implies systematicity or methodical action. Zeno clearly thought that actions produced by τέχνη were necessarily goal-directed; the same cannot be said with certainty about Chrysippus and Cleanthes. It is probable that Zeno's definition with its strong teleological emphasis was found to be problematic.[57] Zeno's definition could be criticised by pointing out, for example, that it does not account for the expertise required for skill-based activity. This definition cannot rule out the following scenario. A woman decides that she wants to make statues. She inspects many statues (thus gaining σύστημα ἐκ καταλήψεων) and then simply makes a statue herself. By doing this, she achieves τέλος and, at the same time, having fulfilled all of Zeno's conditions, she immediately comes to possess the τέχνη of a sculptor. This example illustrates that Zeno's definition does not distinguish sufficiently between expert and amateur. It does not account for the necessary condition of being a skilled shoemaker – namely, a consistent success in producing shoes whenever she makes shoes.

Cleanthes' and Chrysippus' definitions, which state that τέχνη is a tenor which achieves everything methodically, address the gap left by Zeno's definition. According to these definitions, expertise (τέχνη) consists of an ability to perform an action in a methodical manner. Systematicity is an important addition, because it accounts for expert knowledge which an amateur lacks. A skill-based action is determined by the properties inherent in the skill rather than the intentions of an agent. By virtue of having a skill, an expert has a method of acting which allows her to perform a task in an appropriate and a successful manner while following relevant impressions. This slight change in the way in which the early Stoics defined τέχνη is extremely significant. The definitions of τέχνη in early Stoic thought clearly indicate that τέχνη is a functional activity, yet the concept of functionality changed between Zeno and Cleanthes from intentional functionality to methodical functionality. The latter is motivated by the requirements imposed by a system in which an object functions or by the nature of an object itself.

This distinction has important consequences for the conceptualisation of the divine activity. As Olympiodorus notes in the passage cited above, the definition of τέχνη and the definition of the generation of nature (φύσις) are identical in Cleanthes' work, and they are only slightly different in the works of Chrysippus who adds that τέχνη, unlike φύσις, proceeds methodically 'with impressions'. This might strike one as a somewhat surprising distinction. In Diogenes Laertius' passage, nature is described as generative fire which is τεχνικός. It is, therefore, odd to find a distinction between the activities of nature and τέχνη. If we assume that the definition of τέχνη preserved by Olympiodorus primarily refers to τέχνη manifesting in human beings, however, the apparent inconsistency disappears. The need to follow impressions is primarily applicable to human beings because humans, unlike god, are prone to epistemic errors.[58] Humans can only reach the methodical consistency of nature's generation when they act methodically with their impressions. Given the fact that god is perfectly rational and never irrational, the condition of following impressions does not apply to him in a meaningful way.

This provides enough evidence for answering the question of how the mental content of the Stoic god translates into generative action. God's τέχνη is a know-how. God is the kind of entity that has the ability to produce in a certain way, and it is entirely defined by that ability as it is the active principle. An interesting subsequent question is whether this activity is intentional. An analogy with craftwork suggests that intention is necessary to trigger the action which is then directed by the know-how. In the case of god, however, the ability to generate is the definitive feature. It does nothing but generate the world because it is the kind of entity that does this.

In either case, this clarifies how the Stoic god can be compared to the world soul and the sculptor at the same time. In terms of the constitution of the world, god is the ever-present fundamental generative principle. Its generative powers, however, are a kind of divine know-how, and in this respect god is the methodically working force which orders the world in a systematic way, just like a craftsman. One point of especially great interest is the question of the extent to which god sculpts the object in the world directly. Arguably, there is no need for such a sculpting entity, because the world is shaped by the processes set in motion by the fundamental rational ordering of the active principle.[59] These processes constitute such phenomena as piles of grain and wheat, or health and disease. This reading implies a certain non-transitivity of explanation in the Stoic theoretical framework. The case of theodicy shows more clearly than the evidence discussed so far how the Stoics address the issue of the scope of god's creative activity.

Theodicy

In the passage cited earlier in this chapter, Alexander of Aphrodisias objects to the Stoic belief that god is constantly present in the world by saying that god could not possibly be present in mundane objects, such as grubs and gnats.[60] This criticism is based not only on the fact that the Stoic concept of god does not conform to more conventional beliefs; it also contains a substantial philosophical objection. It is not at all clear what the presence of divine rationality accomplishes in such an object as for example, a puddle. It is neither manifest nor does there seem to be a reason for it to be there. It seems, therefore, that it is a mistake to envisage divine rationality as being directly present in every object it generates. Yet it is uncharitable to conclude that Chrysippus missed such an important drawback of his own theory without considering how he might have avoided making such a problematic assertion.

The theory of mixtures would have been a useful theoretical device to address this problem. The Stoic god blends with matter thus producing elements which can then further blend and perhaps even fuse[61] to create the substance of a gnat. Divine rationality can be present at the mixture level of a gnat by ordering matter without being manifest directly, that is, without making a gnat rational, only originating from a rationally designed system.[62]

An especially interesting case of a theodicean argument is recorded by Plutarch. This Stoic argument uses the presence of beauty to form a very peculiar inference about the functional role of a particular object in the world. Plutarch's *On Stoic Self-Contradictions* contains a brief argument about the beauty of the peacock's tail, which is grouped with a number of other Chrysippean arguments dealing with theodicy. According to Plutarch, after arguing that mice and bed-bugs are not vicious, but beneficial for human beings – because they force people to wake up on time and be hygienic – Chrysippus states that beauty is the reason for the existence of many animals in the world in the following way:[63]

γράψας τοίνυν ἐν τοῖς Περὶ φύσεως, [ὡς] ὅτι πολλὰ τῶν ζῴων ἕνεκα κάλλους ἡ φύσις ἐνήνοχε φιλοκαλοῦσα καὶ χαίρουσα τῇ ποικιλίᾳ, καὶ λόγον ἐπειπὼν παραλογώτατον ὡς ὁ ταὼς ἕνεκα τῆς οὐρᾶς γέγονε διὰ τὸ κάλλος αὐτῆς, αὖθις ἐν τῷ Περὶ πολιτείας νεανικῶς ἐπιτετίμηκε τοῖς ταὼς τρέφουσι καὶ ἀηδόνας, ὥσπερ ἀντινομοθετῶν τῷ τοῦ κόσμου νομοθέτῃ καὶ τῆς φύσεως καταγελῶν φιλοκαλούσης περὶ τὰ τοιαῦτα τῶν ζῴων, οἷς ὁ σοφὸς ἐν τῇ πόλει τόπον οὐ δίδωσι. πῶς γὰρ οὐκ ἄτοπον ἐγκαλεῖν τοῖς τρέφουσιν ἃ γεννῶσαν ἐπαινεῖ τὴν πρόνοιαν; ἐν μὲν οὖν τῷ πέμπτῳ Περὶ φύσεως εἰπὼν ὅτι 'οἱ κόρεις εὐχρήστως ἐξυπνίζουσιν ἡμᾶς καὶ οἱ μύες ἐπιστρέφουσιν ἡμᾶς μὴ ἀμελῶς ἕκαστα τιθέναι, φιλοκαλεῖν δὲ τὴν φύσιν τῇ ποικιλίᾳ χαίρουσαν εἰκός ἐστι', ταῦτα κατὰ λέξιν εἴρηκε· 'γένοιτο δ' ἂν μάλιστα τούτου ἔμφασις ἐπὶ τῆς κέρκου τοῦ ταώ. ἐνταῦθα γὰρ ἐπιφαίνει τὸ ζῷον γεγονέναι ἕνεκα τῆς κέρκου καὶ οὐκ ἀνάπαλιν, τῷ <δ'> ἄρρενι γενομένῳ οὕτως τὸ θῆλυ συνηκολούθηκεν.'

Furthermore, after he had written in the books *On Nature* that beauty is the purpose for which many of the animals have been produced by nature, since she loves the beautiful and delights in diversity, and had appended a most irrational argument, namely that the peacock's tail on account of its beauty is the purpose for which the peacock has come to be, in his work *On Commonwealth* again he has vehemently censured people who keep peacocks and nightingales. It is as if he were legislating competition with the lawgiver of the universe and deriding nature for bestowing her love of the beautiful upon animals of a kind to which the sage denies room in the city. Is it not clearly absurd to object to those who keep the creatures that he praises providence for creating? Well, in the fifth book *On Nature* after having said that bugs are useful in waking us up and mice in making us attentive about putting things away carefully and that nature probably loves the beautiful as she delights in diversity he has stated the following in so many words: 'The tail of the peacock would be an especially impressive example of this, for here nature makes it evident that the creature has come to be for the sake of the tail and not contrariwise, <and> the existence of the male, which had this origin, implied the existence of the female.[64]

Although the citations of Chrysippus are very tangled in this passage, they clearly contain the very peculiar claim that peacocks come into existence for the sake of the beauty of their tails. To be precise, not only peacocks, but also peahens exist so that peacock tails are present in the world. The beauty of a peacock's tail necessitates the existence of a whole species of peafowl. This suggests that god's activity is in some respect constrained. Beautiful tails do not exist just by themselves; the existence of beauty requires a whole system of other properties to support it. While the generativity of the Stoic god is grounded in its rationality, it is also constrained by it. The outcomes of a generative process are dictated not by the will of god in the sense that it can will anything at all, but by rational constraints. It is possible to rephrase this in a way which does not involve the language of constraint, as such terms might seem to be an inappropriate way to describe the Stoic god. The Stoics would probably say that rationality is the will of god in the sense that god would not and cannot will anything irrational. This, however, amounts to the same result – god's activity is determined and limited by its rationality in the same way as the properties of a skill determine how and what a skill-based action produces.

If Plutarch is reporting correctly and the argument about the usefulness of mice and bed-bugs was followed by the argument about peacocks in Chrysippus' *On Nature*, then the latter argument ought to be interpreted as explaining the role of evil in the world. The role of evil in the case of the peacock argument is played by peahens and even peacocks themselves minus their tails, while the good for the sake of which peahens and peacocks exist is the beauty of the tails. Of course, peahens and peacocks are not evil *per se*, so it is unlikely that this is a straightforward theodicean argument. Arguably, Chrysippus used the peacock argument to complement a more counterintuitive argument about the usefulness of mice and bed-bugs, and Plutarch records it in order to present Chrysippus' views in a more unfavourable light. Chrysippus' claim about peafowl might have been based on the following reasoning: we might say that the only point in the existence of peafowl is the beauty of a peacock's tail, but it would not follow that peacocks themselves and peahens are bad or useless. There is a use not only for the best part of a species, but also for the rest that constitutes a supporting system. We cannot conclude that some objects or creatures are not useful.[65]

This or a similar line of reasoning is consistent with the stronger and more specific claim that mice and bed-bugs come into existence for the sake of the utility and overall well-being of humankind, even if it might not seem so at first sight. The point of this argument is not to convince the critics of the Stoics that certain things are necessary evils; rather, it aims to show that seeming evils are not actually such. Later Stoics, for instance Seneca, employ the idea that the world is diverse – and ought to be accepted as such – for their moral teachings.[66] The moral lesson of these arguments is that human beings ought to learn to understand what is actually good for them, and then they would not find conventional evils to be bad.[67]

Poikilia and proportion

Interestingly, the diversity of the world is associated with aesthetics in the Stoic theoretical framework. The passage from Plutarch cited above contains a quote of Chrysippus saying that nature is beauty-loving and delights in *poikilia* (φιλοκαλεῖν δὲ τὴν φύσιν τῇ ποικιλίᾳ χαίρουσαν εἰκός ἐστι).[68] Although this fragment is a very small piece of evidence by itself, additional evidence for the Stoic use of *poikilia* can be found in Latin texts, especially in Cicero's *On the Nature of the Gods*.

Before looking closely into how the Stoic spokesperson Balbus applies the notion of *poikilia* to Stoic theology, it is important to acknowledge that there are at least two ways of conceptualising beauty in this treatise. The first and arguably more prominent one is the understanding of beauty as arising from a certain structure or order. When discussing the intelligence of stars Balbus states the following:

> Sensum autem astrorum atque intellegentiam maxume declarat ordo eorum atque constantia; nihil est enim quod ratione et numero moveri possit sine consilio, in quo nihil est temerarium nihil varium nihil fortuitum.
>
> What especially denotes that the stars are conscious and intelligent is their consistent regularity and the absence of random or fortuitous variation, for no such rational, ordered movement can be conducted without planning.[69]

The argument here is simple: the ordered motion would not be possible without a premeditated rational action. The rationality of an action here refers to acting not arbitrarily but for the sake of a certain goal – in this case, order. Without this, the motion is random and, thus, irrational. This passage suggests that rationality manifests as order, and order ought to be understood as a matter of proportion, and it follows that beauty can be denoted numerically. This indicates that beauty is a formal property. In addition to this, it is a formal property underpinned by design. Beautiful objects are beautiful because their structure is skilfully executed. The skilful execution imparts the properties of rationality and, arguably, functionality to these structures so that no act of theirs, as the text says, is an accident without a purpose.

The second aesthetic concept that comes from the Stoic theological fragments is the above-mentioned notion of *poikilia*. Having given the four reasons why the Stoics maintain the existence of the gods (the last of them being the beauty in the motions of the heavenly bodies), Balbus distinguishes the three aims of providence for the world as follows:

> *Talis igitur mens mundi cum sit ob eamque causam vel prudentia vel providential appellari recte possit (Graece enim πρόνοια dicitur), haec potissimum providet et in is maxime est occupata, primum ut mundus quam aptissimus sit ad permanendum, deinde ut nulla re egeat, maxume autem ut in eo eximia pulchritudo sit atque omnis ornatus.*

Such, then, is the mind of the universe, and for this reason it can be justly termed 'Prudence' or 'Providence' (for its name in Greek is *pronoia*); hence its chief provision and preoccupation is to ensure first, that the universe is most suitably ordered for survival; secondly, that it is deficient in no respect; and above all, that its beauty is outstanding in its universal adornment.[70]

The very last word in this passage, *ornatus*, indicates that there might be more to the beauty of the world than proportion. The word indicates the property of being embellished, ornate, decorated; in short, the aesthetic property that cannot be reduced to proportionality, as in the case of the heavenly bodies. This is not the only instance of this notion occurring in this treatise. In the context of discussing how well-designed human bodies are, Balbus states that the human eye is an adept judge of art, including paintings, sculptures and engravings, and then adds that 'our eyes assess beauty and order and the propriety, so to say, of colours and shapes'.[71] The eye, according to this passage, judges not only the arrangement but also the colour when determining beauty. Beauty, then, consists of certain ornateness that involves colours and shapes. This is quite likely the same kind of beauty as that found in the citation of Chrysippus.

In Chrysippus' citation, this understanding of beauty is denoted by the word *poikilia*. *Poikilia* is not a Stoic term, as it is a prominent aesthetic concept in Greek literary texts. It is often associated with material culture, but this adjective can be applied to a wide variety of objects, including the natural world and even Odysseus' *metis*.[72] In the context of material culture, *poikilia* is the result of craftsmanship and the skill of inlaying varied materials.[73] An important aspect of the concept of *poikilia* is the implication of a fairly specific process of production of an object that is ποικίλος.

As Grand-Clement explains, 'the process of creation lies in bringing heterogeneous elements together, as a unified whole, while they retain their own nature and keep interacting in a dynamic fashion'.[74] The fact that *poikilos* can refer to a positive intellectual value is also pertinent here.[75] The reference to craftsmanship implied in the concept of *poikilia* arguably explains why this term is adopted in philosophical texts, especially in the context of divine generation. In Plato's *Timaeus*, the term *poikilia* is employed in describing the revolutions of the wondrous heavenly bodies that signify time[76] as well as the way in which the demiurge intervenes in the race of heavenly gods (οὐράνιον θεῶν γένος) throughout all of the heavens (περὶ πάντα κύκλῳ τὸν οὐρανόν).[77]

It might seem that there is a significant overlap between beauty as a proportion and beauty as *poikilia* in the philosophical tradition. There is, however, a difference that emerges more clearly in Cicero's texts. Arguably, Cicero uses the term *varietas* to denote a certain aesthetic phenomenon that has close ties to the Greek *poikilia*.[78] The *On Ends* contains a definition of *varietas* that claims this notion primarily refers to colours as follows: '"Variation" is certainly a word in our language, and in its strict sense is applied to differences in colour, though it may be used derivatively for many kinds of difference.'[79] This definition of *varietas* is followed by the examples of other objects to which the term may be applied including a poem, a speech, behaviour, fortune and pleasure.

In the Stoic theological texts, variety as an aesthetic phenomenon primarily applies to the natural world. In Seneca's *Letter* 113 and Cicero's *On the Nature of the Gods*, it denotes the awe-inspiring diversity of natural life, in terms of colours, shapes and sizes. It seems that the basis of this aesthetic phenomenon is the sheer range of the differences, but arguably, the issue at stake is subtler. The world is awe-inspiring not only because there are many different kinds of objects and, furthermore, many variations within each kind, but also because it manifests all of this variety as a single piece of creation. The existence of multiple colours in general does not constitute an aesthetic phenomenon. By contrast, the existence of a particular artefact, such as a piece of textile, that cleverly combines multiple colours does constitute an aesthetic phenomenon.

To put it briefly, when it comes to judging an object as possessing *poikilia/varietas*, the issue at stake is combination. It is not, however, numerically the expressible combination that one can see in the case of the limbs, but a harmonious combination of colours or textures and shapes.[80] It is, therefore, possible to distinguish two accounts of beauty in Balbus' speech, both of them relying on the notion of harmony: the harmony of parts which can be accounted for numerically and the harmony of colours and textures, which cannot be expressed numerically.[81] Although by no means interchangeable, both concepts share something in common, as a harmonious relationship between the elements is the basis for both of them. This means that the world, as an object of craftsmanship and design, can manifest both *poikilia* and numerical proportion without any contradiction as they refer to different aspects of the harmonious structure of the world.[82]

Perceiving beauty

In regard to the beliefs underlying Chrysippus' theodicean arguments, the core idea is the rational systematicity of the world which renders everything in the world functional and hence ultimately good and beneficial. This leaves the question of the purpose of beauty, and especially the beauty of particular objects, such as birds. It might be tempting to answer this question by taking a Platonic route and suggesting that perhaps Chrysippus thought that contemplating beautiful objects would lead to metaphysical knowledge.[83] If Chrysippus had similar ideas, the peacock argument would have been an ideal place to expound them, because he could have shown that certain beautiful objects lead us to metaphysical knowledge, and conventional evils are a small price to pay for the existence of such easy access to knowledge. There is, however, no evidence to support such an interpretation.[84] In fact, such a line of reasoning is more in line with the Platonic tradition. Plotinus, the founder of the Neoplatonist school and a harsh critic of the Stoic conceptualisation of aesthetic properties, theorises aesthetic properties in this way.

Plotinus starts his *On the Intellectual Beauty* (*Ennead* 5.8) by stating that beauty originates from the Form.[85] Later in the treatise, Plotinus compares perfect philosophical wisdom to the non-discursive[86] perception of beauty and even claims that such wisdom consists of *seeing* beauty. When describing god-like contemplation, Plotinus states that such a life is 'wisdom not acquired by reasonings, because it was always all present, without any failing which would make it need to be searched for; but it is the first, not derived from any other wisdom'.[87] Plotinus' statement clearly shows that such wisdom is fundamental and not derivative from any other concepts. In the same treatise, he suggests that wise men in Egypt understood this, because they used images rather than letters and words to signify ideas.[88] In another section, Plotinus adds that Zeus, as well as any person who is his fellow-lover (συνεραστής), 'sees' by participating in intelligible beauty.[89]

Some contemporary philosophers pick up the idea that the Neoplatonists posited an account of the perception of beauty as non-conceptual experience that is revelatory of important theological or ethical truths as well. James Kirwan, for instance, has suggested that the Neoplatonic account of beauty, broadly construed, has marked advantages over other theories of beauty, such as radical subjectivism (beauty is in the eye of the beholder) or what Kirwan calls synaesthetic theories.[90] Kirwan argues that the perception of beauty is 'aconceptual'.[91] He explains his view as follows: 'Beauty is one thing we do "know" absolutely, its being is to be perceived, and thus it guarantees its own reality. The inscrutability of beauty, its traditional grounding in the "I-know-not-what", simply signifies that the perception of beauty is so immediate as to leave no room for enquiry.'[92] Kirwan uses Neoplatonic ideas as an inspiration and justification for his claims. According to him, the Neoplatonic texts contain some very important insights into aesthetic experience as follows:

> ... what distinguishes them from other forms of discourse is that, in them, the God that will complete us is not hidden within a love of humanity, or life, or justice, or integrity, or even truth; they are explicit on the impossibility of conceiving of the in-itself, and, in being so, can account for the positive pole of beauty. Indeed everything associated

with the experience of beauty, both the sensation itself and the resistance of that sensation to logical definition, points to beauty being a yearning not for any individual end or object but rather for that object which is the goal of being itself, that perfection of the self towards which every action aims and which every pleasure registers.[93]

There is some ground to suspect that the Stoics very likely held the opposite view. Plotinus criticises the Stoic definition of beauty as *summetria*,[94] and his attempt to posit non-conceptual perception as the best form of philosophical knowledge can be understood as the answer to the deflationist views of such thinkers as Chrysippus. These two ways of thinking about the perception of beauty are polar opposites, because they explore distinct ways in which beauty can contribute to the acquisition of knowledge. Whereas in Plotinus' account, the non-conceptual perception of beauty is the key for developing an advanced understanding of metaphysics, in the Stoic account, the perception of beauty is not marked at all.

Chrysippus' concept of beauty seems pretty prosaic. So far, all the evidence has shown that the Stoics account for beauty in terms of formal and in certain cases functional properties. Beauty, it follows, is a sign of good composition. Good composition can be an important aspect of some objects. The beauty of astronomical objects and their motion, for instance, shows that they are functioning well according to rational principle. The beauty of ordinary objects, meanwhile, is much less significant. The beauty of a peacock's tail indicates that it is a well-composed object (and, in this case, has a nice colouring), but it does not imply much more than that. If my suggested reconstruction of Chrysippus' argument is correct, the beauty of a tail cannot even be read as a sign of rational functioning of the world as a whole, because it would imply that peacocks without their tails – and, to a certain extent, peahens – are signs that god fails, that is, the products of its creation could have been better and therefore they are not in the perfect state. Chrysippus' point is precisely that we ought not to concentrate on the excellences or deficiencies of particular objects, but take a holistic view of the world. On the whole, the world is good, useful and providential.

The physical beauty of particular objects, moreover, is not an indication of value that ought to be pursued. In one extant fragment, Chrysippus warns that people who are overly enthusiastic about pursuing beautiful objects were 'close to painting their privies'.[95] This is consistent with the doctrine of indifferents presented in Chapter 2.[96] At the same time, such arguments as Posidonius' sphere and Chrysippus' beautiful house appear to use the presence of beauty as a kind of inference that indicates that beauty can be revelatory in some sense. Arguably, despite the fact that there is no insight to be gained from merely perceiving beauty, beauty can be analysed to learn more about its composition and components. The Stoic epistemology is an important background. After stating that the Stoics apply the term αἴσθησις to *pneuma* passing from the leading part of the soul to the senses, sense-perception and the apparatus of sense organs, Diogenes Laertius records the following Stoic claim:

ἡ δὲ κατάληψις γίνεται κατ' αὐτοὺς αἰσθήσει μὲν λευκῶν καὶ μελάνων καὶ τραχέων καὶ λείων, λόγῳ δὲ τῶν δι' ἀποδείξεως συναγομένων, ὥσπερ τὸ θεοὺς εἶναι, καὶ προνοεῖν τούτους.

It is by sense-perception, they [the Stoics] hold, that we get cognition of white and black, rough and smooth, but it is by reason that we get cognition of conclusions reached through demonstrations, such as the gods' existence and their providence.[97]

This passage shows that the Stoics distinguish between the sense perception which directly conveys data about the perceived object and the perception by inference. It explicitly states, moreover, that important theological and metaphysical beliefs are, according to the Stoics, established by inferences.[98] Diogenes Laertius even specifies that these kinds of inference are demonstrations. The demonstrations are specific types of argument that reveal non-evident conclusions. These arguments are governed by logic, and they are revelatory not in the sense of conveying their conclusions in a non-conceptual manner, but in the sense of combining the premises in a way which leads to the conclusion which is not evident in the premises themselves.

128 The Stoic Theory of Beauty

This is not to say, however, that beauty cannot be used for the acquisition of knowledge at all. The Stoic belief that only the beautiful is the good (proved by the fact that even irrational animals take the beautiful to be choice-worthy) indicates that aesthetic properties can be analytical tools in Stoic arguments. If the presence of beauty in certain actions renders them choice-worthy, then choice-worthiness can be explained in terms of beauty, and consequently, beauty has an explanatory role to play. Beauty, therefore, can be analysed by means of concepts, and it can be used for forming inferences. This is especially evident in the case of theological arguments which suggest that the beauty of the world helps to establish the conclusion that the world was generated rationally. In the second book of Cicero's *The Nature of The Gods*, the Stoic spokesperson Balbus criticises the Epicurean idea that atoms rather than gods are responsible for the physical processes that generate and maintain the world. He presents the Stoic arguments supporting their belief that the world is generated and maintained by a rational god as follows:

> *Dico igitur providentia deorum mundum et omnes mundi partes et initio constitutas esse et omni tempore administrari. Eamque disputationem tris in partes nostri fere dividunt . . . secunda est autem quae docet omnes res subiectas esse naturae sentienti ab eaque omnia pulcherrume geri; quo constituto sequitur ab animantibus principiis eam esse generatam.*

I therefore assert that it is by the providence of the gods that the world and all its parts were first compounded and have been governed for all time. The defence of that thesis is usually divided into three parts by our school . . . Second is the part which proves that all things are under the control of a sentient nature, and that nature's works are all of the utmost beauty: once this is established, it follows that they are generated from animate origins.[99]

This passage illustrates how the Stoics use the concept of beauty in an argument to establish a very important metaphysical conclusion.[100] The passage describes an inference which can be made on the basis of the presence of beauty, and this indicates that beauty is conceptually analysable, that is, it is a property which can be broken down and explained by using underlying concepts. The Stoics use the term 'sign' (σημεῖον) to denote phenomena which are indicatory of non-evident information. The theorisation of signs helps to explain what kind of explanatory role aesthetic properties can have.

The signs

It is important to note that signs played a prominent role in Hellenistic philosophy in general. There was a continuous debate between the Epicureans, the Sceptics and the Stoics regarding the existence and the classification of signs,[101] therefore it is unsurprising to find the notion of a sign featuring fairly prominently in Stoic epistemology and logic. The ability to make inferences by means of signs distinguishes human beings from irrational animals. Although animals also receive simple impressions, they are unable to use them as signs, that is, to infer what follows from them.[102] The main evidence for the Stoic definition of a sign comes from Sextus Empiricus' *The Outlines of Pyrrhonism*. While attempting to prove that the dogmatic philosophers' notion of a sign is untenable, he records the Stoic definition of a sign as follows:

αὐτίκα γοῦν οἱ ἀκριβῶς περὶ αὐτοῦ διειληφέναι δοκοῦντες, οἱ Στωικοί, βουλόμενοι παραστῆσαι τὴν ἔννοιαν τοῦ σημείου, φασὶ σημεῖον εἶναι ἀξίωμα ἐν ὑγιεῖ συνημμένῳ προκαθηγούμενον, ἐκκαλυπτικὸν τοῦ λήγοντος . . . προκαθηγούμενον δὲ λέγουσι τὸ ἐν συνημμένῳ ἀρχομένῳ ἀπὸ ἀληθοῦς καὶ λήγοντι ἐπὶ ἀληθὲς ἡγούμενον. ἐκκαλυπτικὸν δέ ἐστι τοῦ λήγοντος, ἐπεὶ τὸ 'γάλα ἔχει αὕτη' τοῦ 'κεκύηκεν αὕτη' δηλωτικὸν εἶναι δοκεῖ ἐν τούτῳ τῷ συνημμένῳ 'εἰ γάλα ἔχει αὕτη, κεκύηκεν αὕτη.'

For example, those who are thought to have made accurate distinctions about the sign, the Stoics, when they wish to establish the conception of the sign, say that a sign is a leading proposition in a sound conditional, revelatory of the consequent . . . By 'leading' proposition they mean the antecedent in a conditional with true antecedent and true consequent. It is 'revelatory' of the consequent, since in the conditional

'If this woman has milk, this woman has conceived', 'This woman has milk' seems to be indicative of 'This woman has conceived.'[103]

Certain objects or properties can be revelatory according to the Stoics in the sense that they disclose a piece of information that can be conceptually constructed into an inference about non-evident facts. The example recorded by Sextus – a woman's having milk is a sign that she has conceived – shows this very clearly. The argument that the beauty of the *kosmos* is evidence of the rational generation of the world could plausibly illustrate the Stoic notion of a sign, even though the text does not contain the term 'sign'. The way in which the beauty terms are used in those passages resonates with the definition of a sign cited by Sextus Empiricus.

It is noteworthy, however, that a phenomenon is a sign not by virtue of some special characteristic, but by virtue of having a role to play in a specific inference. The passage of Diogenes Laertius quoted above recording the Stoic distinction between sense impressions and impressions reached by inference calls the latter kind of impression a demonstration (ἀπόδειξις). Diogenes Laertius presented no more information about what a demonstration entails, but Sextus Empiricus' refutation of dogmatic epistemology in *The Outlines of Pyrrhonism* contains a more detailed description of the Stoic notion of a demonstration. According to Sextus, the Stoics distinguished demonstrations from progressive arguments that lead to a conclusion by means of trust and memory[104] as follows:

οἱ δὲ οὐ μόνον ἐφοδευτικῶς ἀλλὰ καὶ ἐκκαλυπτικῶς ἄγουσιν ἡμᾶς ἐπὶ τὸ συμπέρασμα, ὡς ὁ τοιοῦτος 'εἰ ῥέουσι διὰ τῆς ἐπιφανείας ἱδρῶτες, εἰσὶ νοητοὶ πόροι. ἀλλὰ μὴν τὸ πρῶτον· τὸ δεύτερον ἄρα·' τὸ γὰρ ῥεῖν τοὺς ἱδρῶτας ἐκκαλυπτικόν ἐστι τοῦ πόρους εἶναι, διὰ τὸ προειλῆφθαι ὅτι διὰ ναστοῦ σώματος ὑγρὸν οὐ δύναται φέρεσθαι. ἡ οὖν ἀπόδειξις καὶ λόγος εἶναι ὀφείλει καὶ συνακτικὸς καὶ ἀληθὴς καὶ ἄδηλον ἔχων συμπέρασμα [καὶ] ἐκκαλυπτόμενον ὑπὸ τῆς δυνάμεως τῶν λημμάτων, καὶ διὰ τοῦτο εἶναι λέγεται ἀπόδειξις λόγος δι' ὁμολογουμένων λημμάτων κατὰ συναγωγὴν ἐπιφορὰν ἐκκαλύπτων ἄδηλον.

Those which lead us to the conclusion in a not only progressive but also revelatory way are ones like this: 'If sweat flows through the surface, there are ducts discoverable by thought. But the first, therefore the second. For the proposition that sweat flows is revelatory of the proposition that there are ducts, thanks to our preconception that liquid cannot penetrate a solid body. Thus a demonstration must be an argument, and deductive, and true, and with a conclusion which is non-evident and revealed by the force of the premises. That is why a demonstration is said to be an argument which through agreed premises by means of deduction reveals a non-evident conclusion.[105]

This passage elaborates on what demonstrations are. It is noteworthy that although demonstrations can be described accurately as 'revelatory', they are not channels of non-conceptual knowledge. 'Revelation' in this case denotes a disclosure of non-evident facts by means of an inference. Demonstrations can be described as reasoning about entailment, as the example of sweat ducts indicates. The presence of sweat on skin entails the existence of sweat ducts, because liquid cannot permeate a solid body. This mundane example illustrates the same epistemological mechanism that can be applied to discovering loftier propositions. The beauty of the world, for instance, is revelatory of its rational generation by the same thought process that discovers the existence of sweat ducts on the basis of the presence of sweat on skin. The theological argument stating that beauty is indicative of the rational generation of the world preserved by Cicero, for instance, implies roughly the following line of thought: if the world is beautiful, then it has a certain formal structure; this structure is a product of rationality, which does not come into existence by means of arbitrary motion. The beauty of the world, therefore, indicates the rational nature of its generation.

The Stoic account of the perception of beauty is best described as deflationist. In the Stoic fragments, the property of being beautiful is no different for the process of knowing than the property of being sweaty or lactating. As the object of a sense impression, beauty is not special. An impression of beauty by itself does not have any additional information attached to it. As a 'sign', it can have an interesting role to play in certain arguments, but no more so than any other property. There is, therefore, no specific Stoic theory of beauty that differs from the Stoic account of perception in general. The fact that beauty can be a sign, however, shows us that it is the kind of phenomenon that can be unpacked logically. The unpacking of beauty reveals that certain formal and functional properties underlie aesthetic phenomena. This finding is consistent with the conclusions about how the Stoics theorised in the previous chapters.

Concluding remarks

The conclusion above has some bearing on how we understand the role that beauty plays in the context of Stoic theological arguments. Overall, it does not have an especially significant role to play; it is unlikely that the Stoics considered ordinary objects indicative of anything very important theologically. At the same time, they drew the conclusion about the manner in which the world is generated based on the beauty of that world. These two ideas are not at odds if we bear in mind that beauty, according to the Stoics, originates from functional structures. In the case of an ordinary object, such as the tail of a bird, beauty indicates that the underlying parts are functionally well arranged and this conclusion, while an interesting explanation, does not have many consequences. In the case of the world, however, its beauty suggests that the world is generated in functionally structural way and, moreover, that there is a principle responsible for that structuring. The Epicureans, according to the Stoics, could not be right in saying that random atomic motion generated the world, because the world, by virtue of being beautiful, exhibits a rational, non-random structure. If we want to understand what principles govern the generation of the world, we ought to start by considering the functional structure that the world possesses rather than by considering how atomic movement could produce an entire world.

The theological arguments are arguably some of the most important tenets of Stoic cosmology and the fact that they contain inferences from beauty suggests that the conceptualisation of beauty was firmly intertwined with more familiar Stoic views. They also reveal certain Stoic commitments regarding not only the epistemology but also the metaphysics of aesthetic properties. By now, certain elements of the Stoic account of beauty are evident as they emerge consistently in different arguments that employ aesthetic terms. The following section is dedicated to discussing these elements as a single and coherent Stoic theory of beauty.

Notes

1. Everett (1882: 224).
2. Cicero *Nat. D.* 2.12–15=LS 54C.
3. Cicero *Nat. D.* 3.26=*SVF* 2.1011.
4. Plutarch *Mor.* 1044C–E.
5. Cicero *Nat. D.* 2.88=LS 54L.
6. For an in-depth study of these types of mechanisms in antiquity, see Jones (2017).
7. Cicero *Nat. D.* 3.26=*SVF* 2.1011, tr. Walsh.
8. Sedley (2007: 207). See also Mansfeld (1999a: 460), who calls Chrysippus' argument at *Nat. D.* 2.16 (which claims that the orderliness of the world and the regularity of astronomical phenomena cannot be brought about by anything else but god) an argument from design.
9. One of his most often-cited claims is that a human eye alone is sufficient evidence that organic objects show signs of intelligent design; cf. Paley (1802: 37ff.).
10. Sedley (2007: 207): 'The Stoics' appeal to contemporary astronomical mechanisms makes their version of the Argument from Design even more powerful than Paley's watch. In an age of geocentric astronomy, such as theirs, the structural resemblance of state-of-the-art planetary mechanisms to the celestial globe as we see it around us was much greater and more direct than in Paley's heliocentric age.'
11. Sedley (2007: 205). For different interpretations of the Stoic notions of god, see Gerson (1990: 159); Baltzly (2003).
12. See Broadie (1999) for a survey of rational theology in early Greek philosophy and Algra (2003: 156–7). See also Classen (1962), who investigates numerous early philosophical and literary sources in

order to argue that the notion of god as a craftsman can only be properly found in Plato, and even in Plato it was probably metaphorical.

13. Athenagoras *Leg. Supp. Chris.* 4.1. Interestingly, Galen makes the same distinction; see *UP* 11.14 (3.905K).
14. Cicero *Nat. D.* 3.26=*SVF* 2.1011, tr. Walsh.
15. See Hankinson (2001: 263–4).
16. Epicurus *Ep. Hdt.* 45=LS 13A; Lucretius 1.543–50.
17. Epicurus argued that atomic movement is determined by the weight of atoms, collisions between atoms and so on; see Epicurus *Ep. Hdt.*, especially 43–4=LS 11A and 61–2=LS 11E.
18. Lucretius 2.216–50=LS 11H.
19. Cicero *Nat. D.* 2.93=LS 54M.
20. Diogenes Laertius 7.135–6=*SVF* 1.102=LS 46B.
21. Diogenes Laertius 7.156 (I cite and discuss this passage later in this chapter) and Aetius 1.7.33=*SVF* 2.1027=LS46A. See also Diogenes Laertius 7.135–6=*SVF* 1.102=LS 46B, which contains a list of names the Stoics used for the active principle, such as 'god', 'intelligence', 'fate' and 'Zeus', amongst others (ἕν τ' εἶναι θεὸν καὶ νοῦν καὶ εἱμαρμένην καὶ Δία· πολλαῖς τ' ἑτέραις ὀνομασίαις προσονομάζεσθαι).
22. See Salles (2018) for the connection between the Stoic proofs of the intelligibility of the world and Plato's *Philebus*.
23. *Ti.* 29E.
24. *Ti.* 35A–B.
25. *Ti.* 37B–C.
26. *Ti.* 37D–38B, cf. O'Meara (2014: 29)
27. *Ti.* 30A: θέμις δ' οὔτ' ἦν οὔτ' ἔστιν τῷ ἀρίστῳ δρᾶν ἄλλο πλὴν τὸ κάλλιστον.
28. See Scade (2010: 144–5; 163–7). Although it is worth noting that accounting for beauty in terms of formal properties certainly was not invented by Plato; this way of theorising aesthetic properties is part of a much older Greek tradition. See the next chapter on this.
29. *Ti.* 28C–29A.
30. Stobaeus 1.136, 21–137, 6 W=*SVF* 1.65=LS 30A.
31. Syrianus *In Ar. Met.* 105, 21–5=*SVF* 2.364=LS 30H; Aetius 1.10.5=*SVF* 1.65=LS 30B.

32. Sextus Empiricus *M* 9.75=*SVF* 2.311=LS 44C, tr. Long and Sedley.
33. Sextus Empiricus *M* 9.75–6=*SVF* 2.311=LS 44C.
34. See Marcus Aurelius 4.40.
35. In his work, Alexander often attributes various beliefs to 'the Stoics'. As he noted in *Mix*. 216.7–9, however, most Stoics followed Chrysippus' version. Others were committed to the Peripatetic theory of mixture (216.9–11).
36. See Diogenes Laertius 7.134=*SVF* 2.300=LS44B. See also Sedley (2002) for an argument that the Stoics derived the model of the generation of the world through two principles from Plato's *Timaeus*. Although cf. Reydams-Schils (2013).
37. See Lewis (2010: 84–5). Notably, there are parallels in modern philosophy. The philosophers who favour emergence address the very same problem by pointing out the difficulty of explaining plausibly how a variety of objects exists by using the model with mechanical properties alone. C. D. Broad, for instance, contrasts mechanism and emergence thus: 'Mechanism gives a neat, tidy account of the way the world is: everything boils down to one single constituent. . . . But it has no trace of self-evidence; it cannot be the whole truth about the external world, since it cannot deal with the existence or the appearance of "secondary qualities" until it is supplemented by laws of the emergent type which assert that under such and such conditions such and such groups of elementary particles moving in certain ways have, or seem to human beings to have, such and such secondary qualities; and it is certain that considerable scientific progress can be made without assuming it to be true' (Broad (1925: 76–7)). Both mechanism and the Stoic juxtaposition cannot plausibly account for the variety of phenomenon in existence. Fusion and blending are the necessary additional types of mixtures in the Stoic account.
38. Alexander of Aphrodisias *Mix*. 217.7–9, tr. Todd: ἣν διαφορὰν φαντασιῶν οὐκ ἂν εἴχομεν, εἰ πάντα τὰ ὁπωσοῦν μιγνύμενα παρέκειτο ἀλλήλοις καθ᾽ ἁρμήν.
39. Alexander of Aphrodisias *Mix*. 226.24–9, tr. Todd.
40. Alexander of Aphrodisias *Mix*. 216.14–217.1.
41. The same idea is recorded by Stobaeus 1.155,5-11 W=LS 48D.
42. Alexander *Mix*. 217.32–218.6, tr. Todd, slightly amended replacing 'blended' with 'mixed' in the second sentence for the sake of clarity.

136   The Stoic Theory of Beauty

Alexander used the term κρᾶσις with different senses throughout his work (see n. 43 below for details), but in this case, it only makes sense to read κρᾶσις as a general term for mixing rather than the much more specific 'blending', because otherwise he would be describing the process as being both blending and juxtaposition, while they are clearly supposed to be different kinds of mixtures.

43. When introducing three types of mixtures, Alexander described the pervasion of matter by *pneuma* as blending (κρᾶσις) (*Mix.* 216.14: ἔστι δὲ ἡ Χρυσίππου δόξα περὶ κράσεως ἥδε). Later in the *On Mixture*, while describing three kinds of mixtures, Alexander specified that only the third type of mixing is blending in the strict sense of the word (*Mix.* 216.28: ἥντινα τῶν μίξεων κρᾶσιν ἰδίως εἶναι). This remark makes it clear that when Alexander quoted Chrysippus as saying that the world came about through blending, 'the blending' was probably used as a general term to refer to unspecified mixture.

44. Galen *Plen.* 7.525.9–14=*SVF* 2.439=LS 47F.

45. Ibid.

46. The term 'mechanical' was used by John Stuart Mill in his work *A System of Logic* ([1843] 1919: Book 3, chapter 6.1), while Beardsley (1958: 83–4) described this type of property as 'summative'.

47. When Alexander discussed three kinds of mixtures, he dealt with them in the following order: juxtaposition, fusion and blending. It seems that he did this for narrative purposes: he paid most attention to blending, and therefore it was more stylistically convenient to mention it last, and then to concentrate on refuting it in the rest of the treatise. However, considering what level of mixing each mixture denotes, it seems much more likely that Chrysippus himself would have listed mixtures in the following order: juxtaposition, blending and fusion. This way, the entries in the list are ordered according to the extent and the effects of mixing. Juxtaposition, in which constituents are merely put together, is followed by blending, in which constituents coextend with each other yet preserve their own substance, and blending is followed by fusion, in which constituents are destroyed and turned into something else.

48. Reesor (1954: 49), however, tentatively suggested that fusion could be a mechanism for genesis. Since fusion generates new substances,

it appears to be a good option, although it would be hard to explain in what sense god is 'jointly destroyed' in the process and why passages such as the one referred to above insist that the god blends with matter.
49. Alexander of Aphrodisias *Mix.* 217.13–19.
50. This story is reported differently. Diogenes Laertius cites it as a claim (7.151=*SVF* 2.479), while Plutarch reports it as if Chrysippus admitted that nothing prevents such a case from happening, which sounds like a logical consequence of the blending, not a claim in the original proposition of the doctrine (*Mor.* 1078E=*SVF* 2.480). Alexander of Aphrodisias also uses a wine and water mixing example, but in his report the scope of this experiment is much humbler. He mentions a cup of wine being mixed in a large quantity of water at 217.30–1.
51. That the active principle maintains the world; see Diogenes Laertius 7.147=*SVF* 2.1021=LS 54; Cicero *Nat. D.* 1.39=*SVF* 2.1077=LS 54B; Calcidius *Comm. In Plat. Tim.* 294=*SVF* 1.87.
52. Diogenes Laertius 7.138–9=*SVF* 2.634=LS 47O; Plutarch *Mor.* 1077C–E=LS 28O.
53. Diogenes Laertius 7.156, tr. Hicks, slightly revised to keep problematic terms untranslated. See also Aetius 1.7.33=*SVF* 2.1027=LS46A.
54. τέχνη has a wide range of activities falling under it. See Epictetus *Disc.* 1.20.1–5 (the right kind of living is also τέχνη). See also Bett (2010: 148).
55. Olympiodorus *In Plat. Gorg. Comm.* 12.1=LS 42A, tr. Long and Sedley. A similar definition is employed by the later Stoics as well; cf. Marcus Aurelius 6.16.
56. For instance, it is possible that a person, when faced with a mathematical equation, might guess the answer correctly or perform an inadequate calculation which, by accident, would give her the correct answer. This, however, would not be a product of τέχνη. Solving an equation would only be τέχνη if a person had experience and knowledge of how to solve equations.
57. The identity of the potential critics is left intentionally vague. It may be that Cleanthes and Chrysippus were these critics, but it seems even more likely that these critics were from outside the Stoa and Cleanthes and Chrysippus reacted to the latter, rather than aimed at

criticising Zeno himself.
58. As Diogenes Laertius records (7.147=*SVF* 2.1021=LS 54A), the Stoic god is not anthropomorphic (ἀνθρωπόμορφον). Humans might share rationality with the god, but the way in which they interact with their surroundings must be fundamentally different, including the capacity for error.
59. On the complex nature of the Stoic god, see Algra (2003: 165–70). Quite telling here are texts such as Plutarch's *Concerning the Face Which Appears in the Orb of the Moon*, in which Stoic physics, and especially the doctrine of natural places, is criticised for effectively ruling out providence; see Opsomer (2017: 87).
60. Alexander of Aphrodisias *Mix.* 226.24=*SVF* 2.1048.
61. I refer to fusion here only very tentatively. The question of what role fusion plays in organic generation is very interesting, given that substances are destroyed in this process, but this problem is outside the scope of the present work.
62. A different solution to this problem, albeit not incompatible with my interpretation, can be found in Powers' interpretation of the Stoic arguments for the rationality of the cosmos (2012). A completely different interpretation is presented in Bénatouïl (2009: 43–4). He reads Alexander's criticism in a manner which justifies it: 'Just as good soldiers do not recoil from construction work ... the Stoic god does not shy away from constantly performing analogous menial activities, because what makes an action good or bad, noble or base, free or servile is neither any of its intrinsic features nor its objects or target, but its stemming from right reason or not, namely its being coherent or not with all the other actions performed by its agent.'
63. Just like in the passage cited at the beginning of this chapter, yet it is very likely that the apparent contradiction amongst Chrysippus' claims was created by Plutarch himself juxtaposing various Stoic claims taken out of context. Chrysippus most probably criticises the ownership of peacocks because it shows excessive pursuit of decoration. In fact, a little later in the text, Plutarch cites Chrysippus' view found in the *On Commonwealth* which states that some people are on the verge of painting pictures on their privies when they decorate their farms with plants and peacocks (1044D–E). Chrysippus, therefore, is not criticising the existence of peacocks *per se*, but the

pursuit of luxury.
64. Plutarch *Mor.* 1044C–E, tr. Cherniss.
65. The Academics criticised the Stoic idea of divine providence by pointing out that there are many things harmful to human beings. The Stoics answered this criticism in several ways. Plutarch's passage cited above shows that Chrysippus suggested that some things are only apparently bad for humans, whereas in fact they are beneficial; for instance, bed-bugs help in waking up and mice encourage tidiness (Plutarch *Mor.* 1044D=*SVF* 2.1163=LS 54O). Similarly, Lactantius recorded that the Stoics answered this criticism by suggesting that there were apparently harmful things whose usefulness for humankind had not yet been discovered, but would become obvious in the future (Lactantius *IrD* 13.9–10=*SVF* 2.1172=LS 54R). Aulus Gellius cited Chrysippus as claiming that evil is necessary for understanding what the good is (Aulus Gellius 7.1.1–13=*SVF* 2.1169–70=LS 54Q). Another type of Stoic theodicean argument acknowledged that there are evil things, but suggested that these are minor flaws in an otherwise well-managed world. This seems to have been a pervasive idea, because while Plutarch attributed it to Chrysippus (Plutarch *Mor.* 1044C), it can also be found in Marcus Aurelius (*Med.* 8.50) and Seneca, who argued that human beings were in fact provided with everything they needed without being pampered (Seneca *Ep.* 119.15). On this point, cf. Frede (2002: 107–9).
66. Seneca *Ep.* 113.15–16.
67. An especially interesting example of this idea is Marcus Aurelius' exercise in learning to see beauty even in the 'secondary effects of nature's processes' (*Med.* 3.2, tr. Farquharson: τὰ ἐπιγινόμενα τοῖς φύσει γινομένοις).
68. Plut. *Mor.* 1044D.
69. Cicero *Nat. D.* 2.43, tr. Walsh.
70. *Nat. D.* 2.58, tr. Walsh.
71. *Nat. D.* 2.145, tr. Walsh: *Primum enim oculi in his artibus, quarum iudicium est oculorum, in pictis fictis caelatisque formis, in corporum etiam motione atque gestu multa cernunt subtilius, colorum etiam et figurarum [tum] venustatem atque ordinem et ut ita dicam decentiam oculi iudicant.*

72. Grand-Clement (2015: 406–7).
73. Grand-Clement (2015: 410; 413).
74. Grand-Clement (2015: 415).
75. Fitzgerald (2016: 20).
76. *Ti.* 39D.
77. *Ti.* 40A; cf. *Resp.* 529C, where the term is also applied to heavenly bodies.
78. See Fitzgerald (2016: 8–9). See also Fitzgerald (2016: 49) for a discussion of the cases in which the *varietas* can represent not only *poikilia* but also *metabole*.
79. *Fin.* 2.10, tr. Woolf: *varietas enim Latinum verbum est, idque proprie quidem in disparibus coloribus dicitur.*
80. See Grand-Clemens (2015: 410): 'As we can see, *poikilia* is more than a simple hybrid alliance of contrasting colors and substances. It is in no way a shapeless, random, or jumbled amalgamation: in the Archaic sensibility, it implies dynamics that create balance, order, beauty, and harmony.'
81. See the discussion of the Stoic definition of beauty as *summetria* in Chapter 6. Some of the sources preserve the definition as positing both proportion and colour as the conditions of beauty. See also Ierodiakonou (2005: 4) for the discussion of Empedocles' distinction between form and colour as the objects of perception.
82. In his monograph *The Origins of Aesthetic Thought in Ancient Greece: Matter, Sensation, and Experience*, James Porter has argued that there is a tension between what he calls formalist aesthetics and materialist aesthetics. The former, represented by Plato and Aristotle, 'favors clear (formal) outlines over (sensuous) colors and textures' (Porter (2010: 95); for a critical response to this classification, see Halliwell (2012: 364–6)). The latter is focused on sense perception and this is often represented by *poikilia* (cf. Porter (2010: 86–7) on Plato *Resp.* 399E). The Stoics were strongly influenced by Plato's *Timaeus* and perhaps one might cite the passages on the orderly rotations of the heavenly bodies as an example of formalism in Porter's sense of the term, but it is also evident that the Stoics embraced the *poikilia* and were happy to apply it as a positive aesthetic value to the world in general.
83. Bychkov (2010: 188–9): 'Although the Stoics tried to prove these

positions and present them in the form of arguments, their truth and validity ultimately rested on a direct and immediate intuition, or "seeing" – in Balthasarian terms – the way things really are (the order or "truth" of reality). This explanation clarifies why the Stoics, in order to ground the possibility of cognition of truth, persistently appeal to the apparent and clear (immediately evident) nature of the experience that results in cognitive impressions, which are particularly clear and manifest types of perception. Their "demonstration" of the existence of cognitive impressions, then, is based neither on empirical evidence nor on rational arguments, but solely on what we can call an "aesthetic" proof.'
84. Bett (2010: 138–9): 'It is also not unreasonable – although, as far as I know, this is not explicitly reported in the sources – to think of the various examples of physical beauty in the world as being especially vivid illustrations of the all-pervading divine reason. If the cosmic divinity is revealed in the orderliness of the world, then that divinity shines with particular intensity in the *summetria* that constitutes physical beauty. So beauty of body and beauty of soul are not merely analogous in some accidental way; they are both manifestations of rationality functioning at its best.'
85. Plotinus *En.* 5.8.1. This conclusion is also established in the *On Beauty*, *En.* 1.6.2.
86. In translations of Plotinus' text, non-conceptual perception is typically described with the English term 'non-discursive' perception, but this term has the same conceptual underpinnings as non-conceptual perception.
87. Plotinus *En.* 5.8.4, tr. Armstrong: σοφία δὲ οὐ πορισθεῖσα λογισμοῖς, ὅτι ἀεὶ ἦν πᾶσα καὶ ἐλλείπουσα οὐδενί, ἵνα ζητήσεως δεηθῇ· ἀλλ' ἔστιν ἡ πρώτη καὶ οὐκ ἀπ' ἄλλης.
88. *En.* 5.8.6. It is important to note that while discursive thought contemplates images, non-discursive thought *is* an image. See also Sorabji (1982: 310).
89. *En.* 5.8.10.
90. Synaesthetic theory, according to Kirwan, explains the presence of beauty by using concepts such as uniformity in variety or equilibrium, see Kirwan (1999: 51–5). Kirwan presents his classification of beauty theories as follows: 'There are, in effect, only three theories

of beauty. The first (that beauty is in the eye of the beholder) is not a theory at all, the second (synaesthetic in its various forms) has never been found convincing even by its proponents, and the third (the Neoplatonic) is based on premises, and proceeds by a method that places it quite beyond the bounds of sense. It is, then, this last theory, being furthest removed from that rigorous logic which abandoned beauty, which is, as might be expected, the most fruitful' (Kirwan (1999: 14)).

91. Kirwan (1999: 12–13).
92. Kirwan (1999: 5).
93. Kirwan (1999: 48).
94. See Chapter 6 for a detailed discussion of this definition.
95. Plutarch *Mor.* 1044D–E.
96. See Wynne (2012) for the discussion of the relationship between the Stoic god and the indifferents, including beauty.
97. Diogenes Laertius 7.52=LS 40P, tr. Long and Sedley.
98. See Price (2002: 182) for the same conclusion based on a slightly different set of passages.
99. Cicero *Nat. D.* 2.75–6=LS 54J.
100. This conclusion is shared with the arguments discussed earlier in this chapter. It is worth noting that, in this passage, the complexity of the world is not mentioned and so beauty alone carries the burden of proof.
101. See the in-depth study of this topic in James Allen's *Inference from Signs* (2001).
102. Sextus Empiricus *M* 8.275–6=LS 53T. It is worth noting that the genus 'sign' has several species, but the detailed study of this issue is outside the scope of the present work. See Allen (2001: 187) for more details and a suggestion of how the account might have developed.
103. Sextus Empiricus *Pyr.* 2.104–7=LS 35C, tr. Long and Sedley. See also Cicero *Acad.* 2.36=LS 42F; Philodemus *Sign.* 1.2–4.13, 6.1–14=LS 42G, H.
104. An example of such an argument would be as follows: 'If some god has told you that this man will be rich, this man will be rich. But this god (I refer demonstratively to, say, Zeus) has told you that this man will be rich. Therefore this man will be rich' ('εἴ τίς σοι <θεῶν> εἶπεν ὅτι πλουτήσει οὗτος, πλουτήσει οὗτος· οὑτοσὶ δὲ ὁ

θεός (δείκνυμι δὲ καθ' ὑπόθεσιν τὸν Δία) εἶπέ σοι ὅτι πλουτήσει οὗτος· πλουτήσει ἄρα οὗτος,' *Pyr.* 2.141–2=LS 36B, tr. Long and Sedley).

105. Sextus Empiricus *Pyr.* 2.142–3=LS 36B, tr. Long and Sedley.

6

The Stoic Definition of Beauty as *Summetria*

'Moreover, the perfection of mathematical beauty is such (as Colin Maclaurin learned of the bee), that whatsoever is most beautiful and regular is also found to be most useful and excellent.'

D'Arcy Thompson, *On Growth and Form*[1]

The Stoics employ aesthetic terms in a fairly sizeable number of their arguments that can be found in a variety of contexts. Two conceptualisations or two ways of theorising aesthetic properties underly all of these cases: the formal and the functional. This chapter is focused on the question of how these ways of theorising beauty are unified and made coherent in the Stoic definition of beauty as *summetria*, the most theory-laden aesthetic notion in the extant evidence.

Before focusing on the Stoic use of the term *summetria*, it is worth noting that it does not mean 'symmetry' in the sense of bilateral symmetry. As Giora Hon and Bernard Goldstein show in their monograph *From Summetria to Symmetry: the Making of a Revolutionary Scientific Concept*, the contemporary understanding of symmetry as either bilateralism or, in mathematics and logic, a certain stability in mathematical properties that undergo changes[2] originated in the work of the eighteenth-century French mathematician Adrien-Marie Legendre. In antiquity, *summetria* referred to, broadly speaking, a property of being well proportioned.[3] This is quite evident in, for example, Galen's anatomical account of the human body in his treatise *On the Utility of Parts*. When describing the bilateral relationship between the left and the right sides of the human body, he uses the word ἴσος, 'equal'.[4] *Summetria*, meanwhile, is more commonly found in texts that discuss beauty and art; in other words, in texts that address aesthetic issues. It is worth noting from the outset that these are diverse, and this tradition as a whole is discussed in the following chapter. In order to determine the role that the Stoic theory of *summetria* plays in the ancient tradition, it is first necessary to look closely at how the extant fragments conceptualise this term.

The evidence

The definition of beauty as *summetria* of parts with each other and with the whole is, arguably, the most fundamental piece of evidence for analysing the Stoic conceptualisation of beauty.[5] This definition, typically attributed simply to 'the Stoics', can be found in a number of texts. It is recorded by Arius Didymus, Plotinus, Galen and Cicero.[6] Galen's *On the Doctrines of Hippocrates and Plato*, however, is especially informative, as Galen attributes this definition to Chrysippus. Galen notes that Chrysippus distinguishes between the health and the beauty of the body by stating that health depends on the proportion of elements, while beauty depends on the proportion of parts. Then Galen states the following:

τὸ δὲ κάλλος οὐκ ἐν τῇ τῶν στοιχείων ἀλλ' ἐν τῇ τῶν μορίων συμμετρίᾳ συνίστασθαι νομίζει, δακτύλου πρὸς δάκτυλον δηλονότι καὶ συμπάντων αὐτῶν πρός τε μετακάρπιον καὶ καρπὸν καὶ τούτων πρὸς πῆχυν καὶ πήχεως πρὸς βραχίονα καὶ πάντων πρὸς πάντα . . .

He believes that beauty does not lie in the proportionality of the elements but in the proportionality of the parts: of finger, that is, to finger and of all the fingers to palm and wrist, of these to forearm, of forearm to shoulder, and of all to all . . .[7]

Galen's record of Chrysippus'[8] definition appears to refer to visual beauty alone, as is evident from the fact that he uses the term τὸ κάλλος for beauty as well as from the fact that he illustrates this with the example of the proportionality of limbs. Other sources, however, emphasise that *summetria* explains both visual and intellectual or moral beauty. Since ethical questions play an important role in the Stoic corpus overall, it is likely that the definition was supposed to account for both the beauty of the body and the beauty of the soul. The extended versions of the definition that include the beauty of the body and the soul, moreover, are not only more prevalent, but also more uniform.

One of the main sources for the elaborated version of the definition stating that the same phenomenon – *summetria* – accounts for the beauty of both the body and the soul is Arius Didymus.[9] This fragment is found in Stobaeus' *Eclogae*, amongst the excerpts from Arius Didymus' *Epitome of Stoic Ethics*. It is cited as follows:

ὥσπερ τε τὸ κάλλος τοῦ σώματός ἐστι συμμετρία τῶν μελῶν καθιστάντων αὐτὸ πρὸς ἄλληλά τε καὶ πρὸς τὸ ὅλον, οὕτω καὶ τὸ τῆς ψυχῆς κάλλος ἐστὶ συμμετρία τοῦ λόγου καὶ τῶν μερῶν αὐτοῦ πρὸς τὸ ὅλον τε αὐτοῦ καὶ πρὸς ἄλληλα.

Just as the beauty of a body is the proportionality of limbs when they relate to each other and to the whole, so the beauty of the soul is the proportionality of *logos* and its parts when they relate to the whole of the soul and to each other.[10]

Similarly, Cicero, when discussing notions of health and disease in his *Tusculan Disputations*,[11] states that, according to the Stoics, good proportion is responsible for both the beauty of the body and the beauty of the soul. It has been shown that Cicero's source for the *Tusculan Disputations* was very likely Chrysippus himself. More importantly, Cicero is using the *On Emotions*. The very same treatise is used by Galen in the *On the Doctrines of Hippocrates and Plato*.[12] This is possibly a significant fact to take into consideration, because Cicero's formulation of the definition includes some additional conditions not mentioned by Galen as follows:

et ut corporis est quaedam apta figura membrorum cum coloris quadam suavitate eaque dicitur pulchritudo, sic in animo opinionum iudicio-

rumque aequabilitas et constantia cum firmitate quadam et stabilitate virtutem subsequens aut virtutis vim ipsam continens pulchritudo vocatur.

When used of the body, the word 'beauty' refers to a nice configuration of the limbs together with a pleasant coloring, and similarly 'beauty' of mind means an evenness and consistency in the opinions and judgements, together with a certain toughness and stability, either following upon virtue or identical with it.[13]

Here, colour, as well as *summetria* of limbs, is said to constitute the bodily beauty of human beings. The beauty of the soul consists not only of the consistency of beliefs, but also of their stability. The requirement of steadiness or stability for the beauty of the soul, unlike the requirement of colour for bodily beauty, is found only in Cicero. It refers to a tranquil state of mind unperturbed by strong emotions and wrong beliefs. One possible reason why the condition is found here would be the context in which Cicero records the Stoic definition, namely, the Stoic treatment of emotions and mental health.[14] It is quite likely that Cicero put an emphasis on the stability of opinions and judgements for this reason.

It is hard to determine when the conditions of colour and stability were added to the Stoic definition and what role they were intended to play. It has already been mentioned above that Cicero and Galen very probably used the same treatise by Chrysippus as their source. It might be the case that the conditions present in Cicero but not Galen are due to Cicero's interpretation. It is worth noting, however, that colour is mentioned by Plotinus as well. This passage, which can be found at the beginning of Plotinus' *On Beauty*, contains the following statement:

λέγεται μὲν δὴ παρὰ πάντων, ὡς εἰπεῖν, ὡς συμμετρία τῶν μερῶν πρὸς ἄλληλα καὶ πρὸς τὸ ὅλον τό τε τῆς εὐχροίας προστεθὲν τὸ πρὸς τὴν ὄψιν κάλλος ποιεῖ καὶ ἔστιν αὐτοῖς καὶ ὅλως τοῖς ἄλλοις πᾶσι τὸ καλοῖς εἶναι τὸ συμμέτροις καὶ μεμετρημένοις ὑπάρχειν . . .

More or less everyone says that *summetria* of parts with one another and with the whole, with the addition of fine colour, produces visual beauty and that both for the objects of sight and, generally, for everything else being beautiful is a matter of being *summetros* and measured . . .[15]

Despite the fact that Plotinus claims he is criticising a view held by 'almost everyone', it is generally agreed that the target of this critique is the Stoic definition of beauty.[16] Galen's testimony shows that it was adopted by the Stoics as early as Chrysippus. The idea criticised is also not easily mistaken for the views held by any other ancient philosophical school.[17] Plotinus makes it clear that he is attacking the theory positing *summetria* as the sole explanation for the presence of beauty; in his view, *summetria* can be a part of beauty, but it cannot fully account for it. The aim of his attack is the account that suggests that *summetria* fully accounts for the existence of beauty as the only relevant factor, because according to Plotinus, beauty cannot be explained by the presence of *summetria* alone.[18]

Plotinus' record of this definition also corroborates the evidence in Cicero that the definition included the requirement of colour. Unless Plotinus used Cicero as his source, for which we do not have evidence,[19] it is unlikely that the addition of colour is simply Cicero's interpretation. It is more likely that it was added by the Stoics themselves. It is also possible that the colour requirement in visual objects might have been included in response to a criticism. In his *Ennead* 1.6, Plotinus criticises the advocates of *summetria* by arguing that this theory of beauty does not explain how colour can be beautiful.[20] This criticism is very pertinent as it is indeed difficult, if not impossible, to account for the beauty of colour by means of *summetria*, which typically refers to a certain proportionality or ratio. It is quite possible that Plotinus was not the first to point out this shortcoming, and therefore, the requirement for the 'charm' of colour was added by one of the Stoics (possibly even Chrysippus himself) as a response. In addition to this, it is worth remembering that the notion of *poikilia*, which can refer to the property of being multi-coloured, features fairly prominently in Stoic theological texts. These texts describe the world designed by god as both proportional and *poikilos*, and both of these properties are sources of beauty. It is, therefore, not surprising to find that

The Stoic Definition of Beauty as *Summetria* 149

Cicero and Plotinus include colour in their records of the Stoic definition of beauty as *summetria*. In all the cited passages, the central part of the Stoic definition is the simple statement that beauty is *summetria* or the proportionality of parts with each other and with the whole. The most straightforward and obvious interpretation of the Stoic notion of *summetria* is that it conceptualises beauty as proportionality. According to such a reading, *summetria* of parts with each other and with the whole means that all the parts have harmonious ratios with each other, such as exemplified by Polycleitus' *Doryphoros* or described in Vitruvius' *On Architecture*.[21] The harmony of beliefs and cognitive functions required for the beauty of the soul could be interpreted in a similar way.[22]

Plotinus' critique

In Plotinus' *Ennead* I.6, Stoic ideas mostly serve as a foil for presenting Plotinus' own account, yet his critique raises some significant – and possibly enlightening – questions about the Stoic definition of beauty. Plotinus starts *Ennead* I.6, traditionally labelled *On Beauty*, by raising some general questions of whether the nature of beauty is the same in different kinds of objects and what attracts the eye to beautiful things. Then he proposes that there is a principle which bestows beauty on objects and states that it is the Form of Beauty.[23] Before any further exposition of his own ideas, Plotinus presents the following critique of the alternative account:

τό τε ὅλον ἔσται καλὸν αὐτοῖς, τὰ δὲ μέρη ἕκαστα οὐχ ἕξει παρ'
ἑαυτῶν τὸ καλὰ εἶναι, πρὸς δὲ τὸ ὅλον συντελοῦντα, ἵνα καλὸν ᾖ·
καίτοι δεῖ, εἴπερ ὅλον, καὶ τὰ μέρη καλὰ εἶναι· οὐ γὰρ δὴ ἐξ αἰσχρῶν,
ἀλλὰ πάντα κατειληφέναι τὸ κάλλος ... εἰ δὲ δὴ μεταβαίνοντες καὶ
ἐπὶ τὰ ἐπιτηδεύματα καὶ τοὺς λόγους τοὺς καλοὺς τὸ σύμμετρον καὶ
ἐπ' αὐτῶν αἰτιῷντο, τίς ἂν λέγοιτο ἐν ἐπιτηδεύμασι συμμετρία καλοῖς
ἢ νόμοις ἢ μαθήμασιν ἢ ἐπιστήμαις; θεωρήματα γὰρ σύμμετρα
πρὸς ἄλληλα πῶς ἂν εἴη; εἰ δ' ὅτι σύμφωνά ἐστι, καὶ κακῶν ἔσται
ὁμολογία τε καὶ συμφωνία. τῷ γὰρ τὴν σωφροσύνην ἠλιθιότητα
εἶναι τὸ τὴν δικαιοσύνην γενναίαν εἶναι εὐήθειαν σύμφωνον καὶ

συνῳδὸν καὶ ὁμολογεῖ πρὸς ἄλληλα. κάλλος μὲν οὖν ψυχῆς ἀρετὴ πᾶσα καὶ κάλλος ἀληθινώτερον ἢ τὰ πρόσθεν· ἀλλὰ πῶς σύμμετρα; οὔτε γὰρ ὡς μεγέθη οὔτε ὡς ἀριθμὸς σύμμετρα·

The whole will be beautiful, in their view, while the individual parts will not have the quality of being beautiful in themselves but will contribute to making the whole beautiful. But if the whole is beautiful, the parts must be beautiful too; it could not be composed of ugly parts – all the parts must have beauty . . . If they move on to practices and beautiful expressions of thought and claim that here too the *summetros* is responsible for beauty, what could be meant by *summetria* in beautiful practices, or laws, or types of learning and knowledge? How could theories be *summetros* with one another? If the point is that they are in harmony, bad ideas can be consistent and in harmony with one another: the claims that 'self-control is folly' and that 'justice is noble silliness' are harmonious and in tune and consistent with each other. All virtue is beauty of soul, a truer beauty than the one mentioned earlier. How is virtue *summetros*? It is not *summetros* in the same way as magnitudes and numbers.[24]

Plotinus' critique consists of a series of cases that exemplify objects or phenomena which, according to him, the Stoic definition of beauty could not account for. One of the most significant of these objections is that nothing beautiful can be made of parts which have no beauty themselves.[25] This criticism raises the question of the metaphysics of the Stoic concept of aesthetic properties. It is an important issue that ought to be addressed in order to understand the implications of the Stoic definition of beauty.

In addition to this, Plotinus asks how *summetria* can account for the beauty of such phenomena as laws, customs, virtue and even intellect itself. He writes that his opponents cannot mean that these phenomena are beautiful by virtue of being 'in harmony', because vices and wrong beliefs can be in harmony with each other as well and therefore they ought to be beautiful too. This is a powerful critique, possibly designed to showcase the strengths of Plotinus' own theory. In *Ennead* 6.7, Plotinus states that an ugly living man is more beautiful than a statue of a beautiful man, because 'the living is more desirable; and this is because it has soul; and this is because it has more the form of good; and this means that it is somehow coloured by the light of the Good, and being so coloured wakes and rises up and lifts up that which belongs to it, as far as it can makes it good and wakes it'.[26] According to Plotinus' theory, the form helps to establish an exclusive relationship between beauty and the good. Plotinus employs the notion of Forms in order account for the phenomena that, according to him, *summetria* cannot account for.

The Stoics are indeed committed to the view that there is a connection between the good and aesthetic properties, while the vices are not able to form such a connection. Chapter 3 was dedicated to the evidence showing that Chrysippus and other Stoics employ syllogisms to prove that only the beautiful is the good.[27] These arguments show that the Stoics establish important connections between beauty and morality. There is another pertinent piece of evidence in Plutarch's *Against the Stoic on Common Conceptions*. When criticising the Stoic theodicean argument that even apparently bad things are not truly bad, Plutarch argues that the Stoics are contradicting themselves, because they also state that evils are not good or useful for human beings as follows:

πρὸς δὲ κάλλος ἡμῖν ἢ πρὸς ἰσχὺν εὔχρηστος ἡ κακία γέγονεν; οὔ φασιν.

Has vice proved to be useful to us for beauty or for strength? They deny it.[28]

The fact that the Stoics deny the assignment of beauty to vice raises the question of whether they could have defended themselves against Plotinus' accusation that their definition of beauty does not rule out the possibility of vices, as well as virtues, being beautiful. As Plotinus rightly notes, mere good composition and the fitting together of parts do not sufficiently explain why abstract and especially moral objects are beautiful,[29] and if the Stoic theory had no answer to this problem, it would constitute a serious shortcoming. Thus Plotinus raises two problematic questions: how is it possible that the whole is beautiful when the parts lack beauty, and how could the Stoics say that virtues – but not vices – possess beauty?

Supervenience

Plotinus argues that the Stoic conception of beauty implies that aesthetic properties depend on bases that are unrelated to these properties. If Plotinus' critique depicts the Stoic claims accurately and they account for beauty in this way, then they subscribe to the view that aesthetic properties supervene on non-aesthetic properties. Such a claim is not necessarily a drawback, despite the fact that it is presented as such by Plotinus. Conceptualising aesthetic properties in this way would have been not only an original stance, but also a substantial theoretical contribution to ancient aesthetics.

The verb ἐπιγίγνεσθαι, found in several sources on the Stoic views on virtue, shows how the Stoics employ the notion of supervenience.[30] Diogenes Laertius, for instance, records that one of the Stoic definitions of the good is 'the natural perfection of a rational being qua rational',[31] adding that such a thing is virtue, virtuous acts and men. Then it is added that joy and gladness supervene on virtue. Similarly, despair and moroseness supervene on everything that partakes in vice. Joy and gladness, then, are novel properties that are dependent on virtue. An even more revealing passage comes from Cicero's *On Ends*. Here, the Stoics are reported as claiming that the property of being 'artistic' is unlike the property of being 'wise', because the former is applicable only subsequently to the activity, whereas the latter is applicable from the outset. This is due to the fact that the wise act is an end in itself. Some actions are said to be bad given their consequences, while others are said to be bad in themselves, and virtuous actions can be judged right from their inception.[32] As virtuous actions are done for the sake of themselves, the virtue of such actions depends on the agent; virtue, in these cases, follows from virtue.

This is not the case with the properties that are subsequent to the action, such as the property of being 'artistic'. The fact that the example employed here is 'artistic' shows that this principle certainly (although not exclusively) applies to art objects. These prop-

The Stoic Definition of Beauty as *Summetria* 153

erties must follow from different properties. A dance, for example, is artistic because the movements of the dancer are swift, precise and so on. Swift motion in itself is not artistic, as one can see from the case of running. The aesthetic value of the dance, therefore, merely supervenes on the swift motion. Whereas virtue produces virtue, being artistic needs to be produced by different, subvening properties. There is, in addition to this, an explicit statement in Stobaeus that beauty supervenes as follows:

ταύτας ... ἀρετὰς τελείας εἶναι λέγουσι περὶ τὸν βίον καὶ συνεστηκέναι ἐκ θεωρημάτων· ἄλλας δὲ ἐπιγίνεσθαι ταύταις, οὐκ ἔτι τέχνας οὔσας, ἀλλὰ δυνάμεις τινάς, ἐκ τῆς ἀσκήσεως περιγιγνομένας, οἷον τὴν ὑγίειαν τῆς ψυχῆς καὶ τὴν ἀρτιότητα καί τὴν ἰσχὺν αὐτῆς καὶ τὸ κάλλος. ὥσπερ γὰρ τὴν τοῦ σώματος ὑγίειαν εὐκρασίαν εἶναι τῶν ἐν τῷ σώματι θερμῶν καὶ ψυχρῶν καὶ ξηρῶν καὶ ὑγρῶν, οὕτω καὶ τὴν τῆς ψυχῆς ὑγίειαν εὐκρασίαν εἶναι τῶν ἐν τῇ ψυχῇ δογμάτων.

These ... virtues, they [*sc.* the Stoics] say, are complete in the sphere of life and consist of theorems; but others supervene on these because they are no longer forms of expertise but certain powers that are acquired through training, for instance the soul's health and soundness as well as its strength and beauty. For just as bodily health is a good blend of the hot, cold, dry and wet elements in the body, so too psychic health is a good mixture of the doctrines in the soul.[33]

Although this passage is not attributed to any specific Stoic, Teun Tieleman convincingly argues that it is quite likely based on Chrysippus' *On Virtues*, with a minor variation.[34] The central argument here is the juxtaposition of power (δύναμις) and expertise (τέχνη). It is best understood as the claim that 'certain qualities of the soul cannot be directly influenced by reason, i.e. through acts of assent. Strength of character and inner harmony lend an additional quality to mental life; hence they are said to supervene on the theoretical virtues'.[35] Beauty, health and strength are 'powers' that depend on training. The passage precedes the definition of beauty as *summetria* by Arius Didymus cited above, which states that *summetria* of limbs and *summetria* of beliefs are responsible for the beauty of the body and the soul respectively. In both cases, beauty supervenes on the composition of the parts. In the case of bodily beauty, the composition or structure of the limbs renders a body beautiful. In the case of the soul, it is the structure, arguably a coherent structure, of beliefs that renders it as having a certain aesthetic property as well. If beauty is conceptualised as a kind of property that supervenes, then it can depend on non-aesthetic properties, and the Stoics could be defended against the charge of Plotinus.

The second criticism issued by Plotinus, however, presents another challenge. *Summetria*, as was shown above, is typically understood in terms of the proportionality of parts. If this is the case, Plotinus' critique suggests, then vice can be beautiful as well, since nothing prevents a vicious mind from being harmoniously vicious. I would argue, however, that the Stoic definition could be defended even against this criticism, if it is read as stating that beauty supervenes not on just any kind of proportionality of parts but on the proportionality which enables an object to perform its function well.

Functional composition

The functional theory of beauty maintains that beauty depends not only on the structural properties of an object, such as the ratio amongst its parts, but also on how those structural properties allow the object to fulfil its role as the kind of object it is.[36] Different ratios and proportions are generally considered to be beautiful in a family house and a gothic church. The properties of these two buildings differ based on their respective functions, and beauty in each case depends on not merely being well proportioned, but well proportioned in regards to what is appropriate to that kind of building. Whereas a high ceiling and good acoustics typically contribute to the beauty of gothic churches, very different properties are typically found in family houses that might be called beautiful. Beauty is functional in the sense that it depends not only on the internal structural properties of an object, but also on how well those properties enable their owner to function as an object of its kind. It is not uncommon to discuss functionality as one of the aspects of beauty in ancient Greek philosophy. Plato's *Hippias Major* contains a discussion of functional beauty, although ultimately, this account is rejected.³⁷ A similar attempt to theorise beauty can be found in Xenophon's *Memorabilia*.³⁸ Such an understanding of beauty can also be found in the theoretical underpinnings of the aesthetic vocabulary. Aristotle, for instance, uses the term τὸ καλόν when describing the teleological functionality of animals.³⁹ This notion plays an important role in the Stoic conceptualisation of beauty as well.

The notion of functional beauty can be read as a teleological claim, but arguably, in these cases, it is more appropriate to adopt the language of excellence. The concepts of τέλος and excellence are, of course, related, but excellence is a particularly useful notion for discussing aesthetic properties.⁴⁰ When writing about Aristotle's use of τὸ καλόν, Kelly Rogers notes that one of its references is 'functional excellence'. She illustrates this meaning of τὸ καλόν by citing a passage from Xenophon's *Memorabilia* in which Socrates describes the shield as beautiful because it does not impede the use of hands while protecting the vulnerable parts.⁴¹ While all shields have the same end, their excellences may vary. Both a hoplite's shield and a primitive woven shield protect their bearers, so both of them achieve their end, yet the hoplite's shield has certain advantages which make it excel at its function. Beauty, therefore, can be understood as resulting not just from achieving a certain end, but also from achieving that end particularly well, that is, having a certain excellence.

The notion of aesthetic functionality is captured by the Stoic notion of τὸ πρέπον (*decorum* in Latin), attributed to Panaetius. Possibly the best source for Panaetius' views, including this one, is Cicero's *On Duties*. It is clear that τὸ πρέπον has aesthetic, and functional, meaning in the following passage which describes τὸ πρέπον as analogous to bodily beauty:

... *natura doceat non neglegere, quem admodum nos adversus homines*

> *geramus, efficitur, ut et illud, quod ad omnem honestatem pertinet, decorum quam late fusum sit appareat et hoc, quod spectatur in uno quoque genere virtutis. Ut enim pulchritudo corporis apta compositione membrorum movet oculos et delectat hoc ipso, quod inter se omnes partes cum quodam lepore consentiunt, sic hoc decorum, quod elucet in vita, movet adprobationem eorum, quibuscum vivitur, ordine et constantia et moderatione dictorum omnium atque factorum.*

> . . . nature teaches us to be mindful of the way we behave towards other men, it becomes apparent how widespread is not only that seemliness (*decorum*) which extends over all that is honourable, but also that which is seen in one part of virtue. For just as the eye is aroused by the beauty of a body, because of the appropriate arrangement of the limbs, and is delighted just because all its parts are in graceful harmony, so this seemliness (*decorum*), shining out in one's life, arouses the approval of one's fellows, because of the order and constancy and moderation of every word and action.[42]

The analogy with visual beauty indicates that τὸ πρέπον is an equivalent of bodily proportionality ('appropriate arrangement of limbs', to be precise), but it belongs to the sphere of action. Human beings delight in τὸ πρέπον of actions in the same way as they delight in the arrangement of limbs. It is not very easy to pinpoint what exactly τὸ πρέπον is. A useful definition is offered by Andrew Dyck, who suggests that it 'is a concept without a content of its own; it merely sets up a proportional relationship between two terms'.[43] In addition to this, I would argue that this relationship can be described as functionality, in the sense that an act which exhibits τὸ πρέπον is in accordance with the agent's nature or function. The passage cited above as well as a number of other remarks in the *On Duties* indicate that the notion of τὸ πρέπον is tied to what is natural or in accordance with the nature of human beings. The source of τὸ πρέπον – regardless of whether the issue is a human body or mind – are nature's laws.[44]

The functional aspect of τὸ πρέπον is also evident in the comparison of the appropriate character in poetry and real life. The poets are said to observe seemliness 'when what is said and done is worthy of the role'.⁴⁵ When some immoral phrase or speech fits the character of the immoral person in a play, it is applauded and admired because of τὸ πρέπον (yet this would not be the case if the same was uttered by a noble character). This claim is immediately succeeded by a further clarification stating that in poetry, unlike in real life, τὸ πρέπον can apply to various characters, including the bad ones. In real life, τὸ πρέπον applies only to virtues, because 'our parts have been given to us by nature: since they are the ones of constancy, of moderation, of restraint, of a sense of shame'.⁴⁶ The beauty of the soul, when denoted by τὸ πρέπον, derives from achieving our τέλος – or fulfilling our 'function' – of living in accordance with our nature as rational virtuous agents.⁴⁷

One might raise the question of whether it is permissible to use this notion to interpret the definition of beauty, typically denoted by another term (*summetria*). These two concepts are treated as separate by some scholars. Giovanni Lombardo in his *L'Estetica Antica*, for instance, reserves functional connotations to the term τὸ πρέπον and suggests that *summetria* refers to internal structural properties alone.⁴⁸ In addition to this, the fact that τὸ πρέπον is often associated with Panaetius, whereas *summetria* can be attributed to the earlier Stoics, especially Chrysippus, might constitute an obstacle to such an interpretation. Yet the connection between the two concepts is discussed in Cicero's *On Duties*, or to be more precise, the text contains a comparison between τὸ πρέπον and *honestum*.⁴⁹

It is necessary to consider the relation between *honestum* and τὸ πρέπον in order to determine whether the functional connotations of the latter also apply to the former. In the *On Duties*, *honestum* and τὸ πρέπον are described as distinct,⁵⁰ but the difference between τὸ πρέπον and *honestum* is hard to outline clearly. The difference between them is said to be more easily grasped than explained.⁵¹ There is also a strong connection between them, because what is τὸ πρέπον is *honestum* and what is *honestum* is τὸ πρέπον. Moreover, everything just is πρέπον, but what is unjust is lacking in *honestum* and unseemly.⁵² According to Andrew Dyck, 'Panaetius evidently regards *to prepon* as an infallible sign of the presence of the *kalon*. . . . Moreover, unseemly behaviour would, according to

94, appear to be a sure sign of the absence of the *kalon*.'[53] It follows that *honestum* is a necessary and sufficient condition for τὸ πρέπον and it is not reasonable to read these two notions as different. We can distinguish them conceptually (just as the *On Duties* indicates), but they necessarily coincide.

Although it has been argued that τὸ πρέπον was introduced by Panaetius specifically, there is no need to treat this notion as strictly existing outside the conceptual framework advocated by the early Stoics. The functional interpretation of beauty may very well have predated Panaetius within the Stoic tradition, and τὸ πρέπον can be said to be Panaetius' notion in the sense that he put a special emphasis on it. If *summetria* is a feature of *honestum*, and *honestum* necessarily coincides with τὸ πρέπον, a notion with a strong functional aspect, then *summetria* can be related to the functional theory of beauty. This is not, however, the only evidence for the theory of functional aesthetics in Stoicism.

It is noteworthy that beauty and utility are often cited in close proximity in Balbus' account of the Stoic theology in Cicero's *On the Nature of the Gods*, discussed in the previous Chapter 5. Providence, according to Balbus, has three objectives: 'to ensure first, that the universe is most suitably ordered for survival; secondly, that it is deficient in no respect; and above all, that its beauty is outstanding in its universal adornment'.[54] He also claims that the world could not have been better in regard to either utility or beauty as its parts exhibit exceptional coherence.[55] Although these statements do not reduce beauty to functionality (that is, Balbus does not say explicitly that the world is beautiful because of its utility), the proximity of the claims about the beauty of the world to the claims about the utility of the world is notable. Even if the relationship between the two properties is not spelled out in great technical detail, it is quite clear that the beauty and the utility of the world go hand in hand.

The functionality of the world can be described more precisely in metaphysical terms. Plutarch reports that, in his *On Motion*, Chrysippus argued that 'the world is a complete body, but the parts of the world are not complete because they are in certain ways relative to the whole and are not *per se*'.[56] The category of being relatively disposed, the fourth category in the Stoic theory of genera,[57] explains the relationship between the world as a whole and its constituent parts. Being relatively disposed refers to a kind of property that can appear and cease to exist without qualitative alteration, but in reference to something external.[58] Usually this category is explained by a simple example, such as 'a man on the left'. But Plutarch's passage shows that it can have a much more complex use. If the parts of the world are relatively disposed, they ought to be understood in reference to the cosmos as a whole. They have a nature, or function, in respect to the nature of the cosmos.

Similarly, in the Stoic definition of beauty as *summetria*, an object is said to be beautiful if its parts are *summetros* not only with each other but also with the whole. If being relatively disposed on a cosmic level has a certain functional meaning, then being disposed 'to the whole' on a smaller scale also quite plausibly has a functional meaning. There was, of course, a controversy within the Stoa regarding the category of 'relatively disposed' and its connection to virtue. On the one hand, Aristo argued that virtue is essentially only a single thing, and different kinds of virtues, such as courage and prudence, are relative dispositions. On the other hand, Chrysippus argued that every virtue constitutes its own quality as it is 'qualified' (τὸ ποιόν).[59] In the Chrysippean conceptual framework, beauty of the soul would arguably be a matter of a further differentiation of an already qualified thing in regard to an external factor, that is, the role assigned to human beings by the rational cosmic principle.

The proper functions

The category of relative disposition can be used to explain proper functions as well.[60] The proper functions (τὰ καθήκοντα) are actions in agreement with nature and can be interpreted as a functional notion. The most common definition of a proper function states that it is an act in accordance with nature.[61] The most broad and general understanding of this concept does not have aesthetic underpinnings. Animals and plants have proper functions[62] and certain simple actions performed by humans are proper functions as well,[63] yet none of these exhibit any kind of beauty. The proper functions do acquire certain aesthetic aspects, however, when the acting agent is the perfectly rational wise man.

In Cicero's *On Ends*, the Stoic spokesperson Cato explains that the first proper function is to preserve one's constitution, while the second is to pursue things that are in accordance with nature and to avoid those that are not. Once a person is able to perform this in a way which is fully consistent with his nature, he observes the regularity and harmony of such conduct (*viditque rerum agendarum ordinem et, ut ita dicam, concordiam*) and gains the understanding of the highest human good, which is praiseworthy and desirable for its own sake. This is the actual human good and *honestum* itself.[64] The harmony of behaviour described here seems to be similar to the beauty of the soul described in the Stoic definition of beauty as *summetria*. At the very least a person who is acting for the sake of *honestum* can be meaningfully described as having beauty of the soul. If this is the case, here the phenomenon of beauty has clear functional connotations.

This claim is also supported by a passage from Stobaeus that contains the Stoic definition of a right action as a proper function that possesses all the measures or numbers (τοὺς ἀριθμούς).[65] The importance of the phrase 'all the measures' is highlighted by Anthony Long in his article 'The Harmonics of Stoic Virtue'. The 'proper functions' are especially often described as having 'all the numbers' of virtue,[66] and Long argues that this phrase refers to a musical theory as follows:

> As he plays, the musician is moving with the notes of one tetrachord, or ascending or descending to a higher or lower tetrachord. So, by analogy, the Stoic sage at one time is exercising this or that subordinate virtue in the domain of justice, and at another time displaying a subordinate virtue in the domain of courage. . . . Just as the musician will fail if any of the notes in his mode is out of tune, so too virtue requires complete concordance between all its parts or 'numbers' . . . the conception of virtue as a harmony provides an illuminating analogy for the wise man's relationship with external nature as well as with himself. He may be pictured as someone whose character and actions are completely in tune with the causal system employed by cosmic nature.[67]

The wise man, thus, is directly comparable to the musician by virtue of the harmony of his actions, as his actions are organised in such a way as to be perfectly attuned with nature. The reading of this perfect attunement as resulting in beauty follows quite naturally, especially given the reference to music which Long rightly emphasises. The proper functions can, therefore, be a part of the phenomenon of beauty – and it seems fairly clear that the phenomenon described here is beauty – when the agent in question is wise. Even more importantly, the beauty described here consists of functionality, in the sense that it consists in living and acting in a way which is not only well structured, but also in accordance with nature, both individual and cosmic. It could be argued that the definition of beauty as *summetria* of parts with each other and with the whole already implies that aesthetic properties supervene on functionality. Although the definition clearly refers to the structure of a beautiful object, there is a condition of being *summetros* with the whole. As was argued above, the 'whole' referred to here might very well have the same meaning as in Chrysippus' claim that the parts of the world are relatively disposed to the whole, and thus it can be interpreted as a claim about functionality.[68] That is to say, this part of the definition implies that beauty is also functional, and that in order to be beautiful, an object has to perform adequately the role which this kind of object ought to fulfil. The proportionality of structure and functionality are not two distinct conditions for beauty, but two aspects of compositionality. The parts of a beautiful object are well composed not just in any respect, but by virtue of enabling the object to function as that kind of object. A composition, therefore, is only properly *summetros* if it has a functional structure.[69] While 'the *summetria* of parts with one another' refers to an internal relationship between parts within an object, 'the *summetria* of parts with the whole' concerns the role that an object has from the functional perspective as well as how the composition of its parts contributes to its playing of that role.

Beautiful vices?

If this reading is accepted, then it also helps to clarify the Stoic position regarding the problem of attributing aesthetic properties to virtues but not vices. As mentioned above, if it is assumed that beauty is produced when the parts simply 'fit together' and 'complement each other', then Plotinus is right in pointing out that the Stoics have trouble explaining why virtue, but not vice, is beautiful, as nothing seems to prevent vices from fitting together harmoniously. This problem could be tackled by denying that vices have the capacity to co-exist in a harmonious way. There is some evidence showing that this might have been the approach the Stoics took. In the *Tusculan Disputations*, for instance, viciousness (*vitiositas*) is described as a character that is 'inconsistent in the whole of life and out of harmony with itself' (*a se ipsa dissentiens*).[70] A similar claim is recorded by Stobaeus. Here, ignorance is said to be vice, which is contrary to moderation and which makes impulses unstable and fluttering (ἀκαταστάτους καὶ πτοιώδεις).[71] An unstable and fluttering impulse is defined as a passion (πάθος) by the Stoics.[72] Vices such as ignorance can be shown to be innately inharmonious by appealing to the description of passions. Galen, citing Chrysippus' *On Passions*, Book 1, records an elaborate explanation of the definition of passion as the excess of impulse that includes the following vivid illustration:

> οἷον ἐπὶ τοῦ πορεύεσθαι καθ' ὁρμὴν οὐ πλεονάζει ἡ τῶν σκελῶν κίνησις ἀλλὰ συναπαρτίζει τι τῇ ὁρμῇ ὥστε καὶ στῆναι, ὅταν ἐθέλῃ, καὶ μεταβάλλειν. ἐπὶ δὲ τῶν τρεχόντων καθ' ὁρμὴν οὐκέτι τοιοῦτον γίνεται, ἀλλὰ πλεονάζει παρὰ τὴν ὁρμὴν ἡ τῶν σκελῶν κίνησις ὥστε ἐκφέρεσθαι καὶ μὴ μεταβάλλειν εὐπειθῶς οὕτως εὐθὺς ἐναρξαμένων.

> When someone walks in accordance with his impulse, the movement of his legs is not excessive but commensurate with the impulse, so that he can stop or change whenever he wants to. But when people run in accordance with their impulse, this sort of thing no longer happens. The movement of their legs exceeds their impulse so that they are carried away and unable to change obediently, as soon as they have started to do so.[73]

The very nature of vice, then, is chaotic, and one could quite plausibly argue that, for the Stoics, the notion of harmonious vices is an oxymoron. Consequently, if vices cannot co-exist in a way that can be called harmonious, then they cannot be beautiful either.

There is another, somewhat related, way of denying that vices can harmoniously fit together and form beauty. In fact, if the Stoic conception of beauty is read as referring to the functional structure of a beautiful object, then their definition allows restricting the supervenience of aesthetic properties to those structures that properly fulfil the function of an object.[74] The Stoics maintain that the best in human beings is their rationality and it is in their nature to be rational.[75] Vice, meanwhile, is the cause of an unnatural and unhappy life.[76] Acting in a rational manner, therefore, constitutes acting in accordance with human nature and, therefore, fulfilling human functions. Subsequently, if it is accepted that beauty supervenes not just on any harmonious structure, but on a functional structure, it follows that vices cannot contribute to beauty, because they do not contribute to the human τέλος. The Stoics could deny that it is possible to act in a harmoniously vicious way, because vice is not functional by virtue of being not in accordance with human nature. Fitting vices together in a harmonious fashion for the Stoics is a bit like performing a dance at a singing competition. It might be a very good dance, but it cannot win, because that is not what the competition is for.

The two components of the Stoic definition of beauty render it a very flexible concept. This definition takes into account more than the internal coherence of parts within an object. Beauty has a functional aspect, since in order to be beautiful, an object must have appropriate properties for that kind of object. This stance has important philosophical implications. Chrysippus proposes what in contemporary terms is called broad aesthetic supervenience. This kind of supervenience differs from narrow aesthetic supervenience in respect to its scope of relevant factors. In contemporary aesthetics, broad supervenience is used to explain why an original masterpiece is more aesthetically valuable than its copy, even if the copy is very good. By virtue of having identical structural properties, both pieces ought to have identical supervening aesthetic properties. In order to support an intuition that the original piece of art has different aesthetic properties than its copy, broad supervenience is necessary, because this notion of supervenience takes into account the contextual and relational properties as well as the intrinsic properties of an object.[77]

Concluding remarks

All the explanations and arguments containing aesthetic terms discussed in the previous chapters are not only consistent but are also supported by the Stoic way of theorising *summetria*. The Stoic definition of beauty as *summetria* helpfully spells out the technical implications about the Stoic understanding of the aesthetic properties, although it is a notable piece of Stoic philosophy in its own right. Perhaps one of the most interesting aspects of their definition of beauty is providing a reference point from which a composition can be judged to be 'good'. Functionality is a reference point for composition, thus aesthetic properties in any given object depend on the composition of the parts attuned to the purpose of that object as a whole. Such a conceptualisation of aesthetic properties allows the Stoics to present a flexible and multi-layered theory that can account for the presence of beauty in simple physical objects, such as human bodies, complex physical objects, such as the world and even abstract objects, such as virtue. It becomes clear that the Stoic definition of beauty represents an interesting and significant development in ancient aesthetics once it is placed within the ancient aesthetic tradition. This will be shown in the following chapter.

Notes

1. Thompson (1992: 1007).
2. Hon and Goldstein (2008: 2): 'Symmetry in its current scientific usage refers either to a mathematico-logical relation or to an intrinsic property of a mathematical entity which under certain classes of transformations, such as rotation, reflection, inversion, or other abstract operations, leaves something unchanged – invariant. When an invariant property is maintained, it is the subject of group theory – a mathematical theory which explores, systematizes, and formalizes features that are preserved under the transformation.'

The Stoic Definition of Beauty as *Summetria*   165

3. Hon and Goldstein (2008: 1–2).
4. Galen *UP* 5.14 (3.395K).
5. The most substantial treatments of this Stoic concept are Horn (1989) and Bett (2010: 130–52), cf. McMahon (2009).
6. These passages are cited and discussed below.
7. Galen *Plac.* 5.3.15 (5.449K); tr. De Lacy, slightly amended. See also 5.2.46 (5.443K).
8. Although Galen attributes the definition of visual beauty as *summetria* to Chrysippus, he does not explicitly write that Chrysippus is the author. It is possible that Chrysippus was merely working with a definition proposed by Zeno or even some other Stoic. Yet even if Chrysippus is not the author of this definition, the only clear surviving attribution refers to him, therefore he must at least have advocated it.
9. See Cicero's *Off.* 1.98, although this account is typically attributed to Panaetius, not Chrysippus.
10. Arius Didymus 5b4–5b5 (Pomeroy)=Stobaeus 2.62, 15 W=*SVF* 3.278; the translation is mine.
11. The connection between beauty and health is a complicated issue. Whereas several sources make a very explicit connection between these two, and Bett (2010: 136) argues that 'this well-ordered state might just as well be called health as beauty', Galen records Chrysippus' distinction between health and physical beauty. In *Plac.* 5.3.13–15 (5.448–9K), Galen criticises Chrysippus for not distinguishing between health and beauty of the soul, as he distinguishes bodily beauty as the *summetria* of limbs from health as the *summetria* of elements. For this reason, I do not assume that Chrysippus proposed an equivalency between health and beauty.
12. This is argued in Graver (2002: 204–6). An elaborate study of this question can be found in Tieleman (2003: 290–320, especially 296–303).
13. *Tusc.* 4.31=*SVF* 3.279, tr. M. Graver. See also Philo *Mos.* 2.140=*SVF* 3.392.
14. See Graver (2002: 152–4) for an in-depth discussion of this text.
15. Plotinus *En.* 1.6.1, tr. A. Sheppard from Bychkov and Sheppard (2010), slightly changed to replace 'symmetry' with '*summetria*' and 'symmetrical' with '*summetros*'.

16. While Gerson (1994: 213) and Evangeliou (2000: 42–5) choose to read Plotinus' words as referring to a large unspecified group of thinkers or philosophers, it is also quite common to read Plotinus' attack as directed at the Stoics. See, for instance, Sheppard and Bychkov (2010: 186); Graeser (1972: 62); Beardsley (1966: 80). It is noteworthy that Galen also wrote that *all* physicians and philosophers claimed that beauty was *summetria* (*Plac.* 5.3.17 (5.449K)). It is hard to speculate what the relationship was between the Stoic and 'physicians and philosophers', but it is clear that this Stoic idea had some connection with a wider intellectual tradition, which will be discussed in the following chapter.
17. A thorough discussion of this topic can be found in Chapter 7.
18. This is made clear in the argument regarding a face which appears beautiful at one moment but not so at another; see Plotinus *En.* 1.6.1.
19. See Gatti (1996: 10–14).
20. Plotinus *En.* 1.6.1.
21. See especially Book 3, chapter 1.1–3. The physical beauty described here is probably that referred to in the fragments which define love as an attempt to form a friendship because of manifested beauty (Diogenes Laertius 7.130). It is noteworthy that beautiful youths who inspire love also show potential for virtue; see, for instance, Bett (2010: 141–4).
22. Bett (2010: 136): 'it is clear that according to the Stoics' conception of the soul, reason or the *hegemonikon* has a number of different aspects or functions, and that, in the wise person's soul, these aspects or functions will complement one another and fit together in a felicitous and harmonious way.'
23. Plotinus *En.*1.6.2.
24. Plotinus *En.* 1.6.1, tr. A. Sheppard, slightly changed by replacing 'symmetry' and 'symmetrical' with '*summetria*' and '*summetros*' respectively.
25. See Schmitt (2007: 60–3).
26. Plotinus *En.* 6.7.22, tr. Armstrong.
27. The argument itself can be found in Cicero *Fin.* 3.27, *Tusc.* 5.43; Plutarch *Mor.* 1039C–D.
28. Plutarch *Mor.* 1066C, tr. Cherniss.
29. Some commentators do, however, read the Stoic definition of beauty

The Stoic Definition of Beauty as *Summetria*   167

as suggesting that beauty originated from internal structure and parts' fitting together. Bett (2010: 136), for instance, argues as follows: 'For it is clear that according to the Stoics' conception of the soul, reason or the *hegemonikon* has a number of different aspects or functions, and that, in the wise person's soul, these aspects or functions will complement one another and fit together in a felicitous and harmonious way.'

30. Graver (2007: 29).
31. Diogenes Laertius 7.94=*SVF* 3.76, tr. Hicks: τὸ τέλειον κατὰ φύσιν λογικοῦ ὡς λογικοῦ. See also Sorabji (2000: 51).
32. Cicero *Fin.* 3.32=*SVF* 3.504.
33. Stobaeus 2.62, 15–63, 5 W=*SVF* 3.278, tr. from Tieleman (2003).
34. Tieleman (2003: 236–40).
35. Tieleman (2003: 237).
36. Parsons and Carlson (2008: 2) define functional beauty as follows: 'The basic idea of Functional Beauty is that of a thing's function being integral to its aesthetic character. Expressed slightly differently, the idea is that of a thing's aesthetic qualities emerging from its function or something closely related to its function, such as its purpose, use, or end.'
37. Plato *Hp. mai.* 290D–294E. See Barney (2010: 364–5) for a discussion of the Platonic notion of functionality and its relationship to beauty.
38. Xenophon *Mem.* 3.8.5–6.
39. Irwin (2010: 386–7) presents a survey and an analysis of Aristotle's use of τὸ καλόν in this way.
40. *Arete* ('virtue') can also be translated as 'excellence'. See, for instance, the translation of Aristotle *Eth. Nic.* 1167a in Crisp (2000: 171), cf. the brief discussion of this translation at (2000: 205).
41. Rogers (1993: 355). Xenophon's passage is *Mem.* 3.10.9–10.
42. Cicero *Off.* 1.98, tr. Atkins.
43. Dyck (1996: 240).
44. Cicero *Off.* 1.100.
45. Cicero *Off.* 1.97, tr. Atkins.
46. Cicero *Off.* 1.98, tr. Atkins.
47. There is a debate in Stoic scholarship on whether an agent's moral nature can be derived from her cosmic nature (and function) in Stoicism. Annas (1995: 162ff.) argues that such an explanation of

the Stoic ethical position is problematic, although see Betegh (2003: esp. 298–300) for an argument that the Stoic concept of τέλος, strongly influenced by the Stoic engagement with Plato's *Timaeus*, can be both cosmic and moral in its nature.

48. Lombardo (2002: 136).
49. See Chapter 3 for the argument that *honestum* is the Latin equivalent of τὸ καλόν. For the connection between *summetria* and *honestum*/τὸ καλόν, cf. Diogenes Laertius 7.100, tr. Hicks (slightly changed by replacing 'factors' with 'measures'): 'the reason why they characterize the perfect good as beautiful is that it has in full all the measures required by nature or has perfect proportion' (καλὸν δὲ λέγουσι τὸ τέλειον ἀγαθὸν παρὰ τὸ πάντας ἀπέχειν τοὺς ἐπιζητουμένους ἀριθμοὺς ὑπὸ τῆς φύσεως ἢ τὸ τελέως σύμμετρον). Here, the good is said to be beautiful because it has perfect proportion, that is, it is *summetros*. This is quite likely a reference to the definition of beauty as *summetria*. This phrase plays an important role in interpreting the Stoic notion of the proper function below.
50. Cicero *Off.* 1.93.
51. Cicero *Off.* 1.93.
52. Cicero *Off.* 1.94. It is also noteworthy that, in this passage, *honestum* is said to precede τὸ πρέπον.
53. Dyck (1996: 243). Note that although this citation uses the term τὸ καλόν, Cicero's text uses *honestum*. These terms are often treated as interchangeable in the scholarship.
54. *Nat. D.* 2.58, tr. Walsh.
55. *Nat. D.* 2.87.
56. Plutarch *Mor.* 1054 E–F=*SVF* 2.550=LS 29D, tr. Long and Sedley.
57. For this theory and its context see Menn (1999) and Sedley (1988: 259–63).
58. Simplicius *in Ar. Cat.* 166, 15–29=*SVF* 2.403=LS 29C.
59. Galen *Plac.* 7.1.12–15=*SVF* 3.259=LS 29E; Plutarch *Mor.* 440E–441D=LS 61B.
60. It is also related to the theory of *oikeiosis*; see Tieleman (2003: 185–6).
61. This claim can be found in a large number of texts. Plutarch, in *Mor.* 1069E=*SVF* 3.491, attributes it to Chrysippus.
62. Diogenes Laertius 7.107=*SVF* 3.493=LS 59C.

63. For instance, looking after one's body and health is a proper function (Diogenes Laertius 7.109=SVF 3.496).
64. Cicero *Fin*. 3.17=LS 59D.
65. Stobaeus 2.93, 14–18 W=SVF 3.500=LS 59K.
66. Long (1996: 210–12).
67. Long (1996: 218–19).
68. See Setaioli (2007: 50–1) for an argument that Seneca puts an emphasis on the beauty of the 'whole' in a way that seems to refer to the notion of τὸ πρέπον. Setaioli also traces this idea back to Chrysippus.
69. For the use of the terms 'structure' and 'composition', see Harte (2002: 14–16; 158–67). Since I am dealing with aesthetic rather than mereological problems, my use of these terms is not nearly as charged. I discuss structure as something an object *has* rather than *is*, to use Harte's distinction, because such a notion of structure is more relevant for aesthetic issues. I use 'composition' simply to denote the entirety of factors which render an object beautiful. Structure (especially proportionate structure) is one of them, but there can be other, more external factors, such as functionality. One might reason, for instance, that the good composition of a house requires both proportionality and functionality.
70. Cicero *Tusc*. 4.29, 34–5=LS 61O, tr. Long and Sedley.
71. Stobaeus 2.68, 18–23 W=SVF 3.663=LS 41I.
72. See Stobaeus 2.88, 8–90, 6 W=SVF 3.378=LS 65A. It is quite likely that this definition belonged to Chrysippus, because Galen's record shows that Posidonius addressed the criticism of this definition to Chrysippus in particular.
73. Galen *Plac*. 4.2.10–18 (5.368–370K)=SVF 3.462=LS 65J, translation by Long and Sedley. See also Stobaeus 2.88, 8–90, 6W=SVF 3.378, 389=LS 65A, which contrasts controllable erroneous opinions and uncontrollable passions, and Gill (2010: 152).
74. This explanation is not necessarily mutually exclusive with the first. The vices are, according to the Stoics, not only lacking in harmony, but also contrary to nature (see, for instance, Galen *Plac*. 4.2.10–18 (5.368–370K)=SVF 3.462=LS 65J).
75. See, for instance, Seneca *Ep*. 76.9–10=SVF 3.200a=LS 63D. Another relevant Stoic tenet is the claim that the τέλος of human life is living

in agreement with nature, which is held in common by all the early Stoics. See Stobaeus 2.75, 11–76, 8 W=LS 63B and Diogenes Laertius 7.87–9=LS63C, which show that Zeno, Cleanthes and Chrysippus advocated this idea, with slight emendations.
76. Plutarch *Mor.* 1044A=*SVF* 3.55=LS 63H.
77. Zangwill (2001: 43–4).

7

Aesthetics in Stoicism and Stoicism in Aesthetics

'The anatomist presents to the eye the most hideous and disagreeable objects; but his science is useful to the painter in delineating even a Venus or an Helen ... Accuracy is, in every case, advantageous to beauty, and just reasoning to delicate sentiment.'

David Hume, *An Enquiry Concerning Human Understanding*[1]

Having analysed the ways in which the Stoics used aesthetic terms and determined what theoretical implications this use underpins, one important question remains: that is, the question of the role that Stoic ideas played in the ancient debates on issues pertinent to aesthetics. Some of the debates that the Stoics engaged in have already been discussed. Plotinus' critique of the Stoic definition of beauty as *summetria*, for example, was discussed in the previous chapter in order to determine the implications of that definition. This chapter, meanwhile, is dedicated to painting the general picture of the place of Stoic views within the ancient tradition of aesthetics, with a special emphasis on the debates and the development of the ideas resulting from them. Given that the focus of this study is Stoicism, this account of ancient aesthetics will inevitably be limited to those debates that are pertinent to the topic, and thus it is not an exhaustive account. At the same time, it is worth stating from the outset that the Stoics engaged in the debates that were central and their influence was far more enduring than one might suspect.

The *summetriai*, the artistic theory

In the previous chapter, it was pointed out that the most important piece of evidence for the Stoic definition of beauty comes from Galen's treatise *On the Doctrines of Hippocrates and Plato*. In this passage, Galen claims that the Stoic theory is the same as the one proposed by Polycleitus. It is shown below that Galen is not quite right and the Stoic theory differed in several respects from Polycleitus' *Canon*, yet Galen's remark shows that Stoic thought is well integrated into the ancient Greek tradition. The Stoics were among the many philosophers influenced by the artistic theory typically attributed to Polycleitus. For this reason, the artistic theories are, arguably, the starting point of the enquiry into ancient Greek aesthetics.

Although far from being detailed, Galen's passage suggests that Polycleitus' theory referred mostly to ratios or the composition of an object.[2] Galen adds that Polycleitus was the first to give τὰς συμμετρίας of the body as well as making a statue in accordance with his theory.[3] Since Polycleitus is cited as talking about *summetria* in the plural, it does seem that in his work this term refers to specific ratios that govern the internal structural properties of a beautiful statue.[4] It is worth noting, however, that Polycleitus might not have been the inventor of the theory giving *summetriai*. Diogenes Laertius, while naming various people named Pythagoras active in the middle of the sixth century BC, also mentions Pythagoras the sculptor from Rhegium, who was the first to pay attention to rhythm and *summetria*.[5] It seems that Polycleitus' theory, however, was considered to be the theory of *summetria par excellence*. When listing the sculptors, Pliny the Elder describes Myron as being 'the first sculptor who appears to have enlarged the scope of realism, being more prolific in his art than Polycleitus and being more careful in his proportions (*symmetria*)'.[6] A little later he observes that Latin has no equivalent to the Greek term *summetria*, which Lysippus, another noted sculptor, followed attentively 'by the new and hitherto untried method of modifying the squareness of the figure of the old sculptors'.[7]

Although *summetria* is often associated with sculpture, it is also sometimes mentioned in relation to painting.[8] It also plays a significant role in the theories of architecture, as Vitruvius' *On Architecture* shows. According to Vitruvius, all buildings ought to possess strength, utility and beauty (*venustas*). He then explains what constitutes these properties. Strength comes from the solid foundation and the right choice of materials. Utility comes from the distribution of the parts which correspond to their purpose. Beauty, meanwhile, is produced by the pleasant appearance of the whole and the proportionality of its parts.[9] Later, in Book 3, Vitruvius explains that the design of temples comes from the *summetria* which depends on proportion (called ἀναλογία by Greeks). Then he defines proportion, in a way that is reminiscent of the Stoic definition of beauty, as follows: 'Proportion is the co-relation *(commodulatio)* of the fixed parts in the elements of the building and in the whole [building], [and] from this ratio *symmetria* is produced.'[10] As well as sharing some similarities, Vitruvius' description of *summetria* in *On Architecture* differs from the Stoic in one significant respect: it does not incorporate any references to functionality. Instead, proportionality consists of only a series of numbers representing ratios. This becomes clear when Vitruvius compares temples with a well-formed human body,[11] and then provides a rather in-depth description of the ideal proportions of a human body. From the chin to the top of the head is one tenth of the whole height, from chin to the crown of the head is one eighth, and so on.[12] This makes it clear that, in the context of the arts, *summetria* refers to a very specific and rather technical series of ratios that allows the depiction of, for example, human anatomy, although it could be used for other kinds of objects too. Numbers and mathematical calculations, therefore, constitute the theory of *summetriai* used by the artists.

The Pythagoreans

Numbers also play prominent explanatory roles in the accounts of beauty presented by the philosophers. Arguably, the Pythagoreans are the most famous advocates of the theory that explains everything in terms of numbers. It has been suggested that the Pythagoreans were the authors of the idea that beauty originates from the harmony of parts, which appears to be a conceptually similar (if not identical) stance to the one advocated by the Stoics.[13] Discussing the Pythagorean stance in general terms is, however, very difficult, as the history and even the identity of the Pythagorean school is non-monolithic. Pythagoreanism is divided into the mathematical and the acousmatic traditions.[14] The scope of this study does not allow discussing the Pythagorean stance in general, but it is possible to look at some representative evidence. Philolaus of Croton, for example, was one of the more noted Pythagoreans of the fifth century BC, and the extant fragments of his works are a valuable source for determining the views that can be reasonably associated with the Pythagorean school.

The similarity between the broadly Polycleitean *summetria* theory and the Pythagorean views is due to the role that mathematical explanation plays in both theories. Interestingly, the Pythagorean fragments rarely contain the term *summetria*. When they do, it is clear it is not a reductive explanation of aesthetic properties, as no surviving Pythagorean fragment identifies beauty with *summetria* in a reductive way. The Philolaus fragment that associates these two properties most explicitly can be found in Stobaeus, but it only states that *summetria* is beautiful as follows: 'Order and proportion are beautiful and useful, while disorder and lack of proportion are ugly and useless.'[15] Although this fragment attributes beauty to order and *summetria*, it does not explicitly state that there is a causal link between *summetria* and beauty, or that they share an identity in some sense.

Philolaus attributes a greater causal role to another often-employed term, *harmonia*, which at first sight appears to be very similar to *summetria*. *Harmonia*, however, is portrayed as a fundamental power which binds together the so-called limiters and unlimiteds into the world-order.[16] *Harmonia*, thus, tells us more about cosmology than aesthetics. Whereas the Pythagorean *harmonia* is a universal power which reconciles conflicting parts into unity, the theories of *summetria* merely explain that the *summetros* arrangement of parts produces a property of beauty in various objects. The Pythagorean view as represented by Philolaus, then, is rather different from both the artistic theory and the Stoic theory of *summetria*. Both the Pythagorean view and the artistic theory of *summetria*, nevertheless, share an insight which becomes extremely significant to the later philosophers, namely, that beauty can be explained in terms of numbers. If one says that Dion has a beautiful body, then it means that Dion's body is proportioned in a certain way and that proportion can be rendered in a series of very specific ratios. This idea is fairly fundamental to ancient Greek aesthetics, as it keeps on re-emerging in various forms and is used to posit various problems by later philosophers.

Plato

Of all ancient Greek philosophers who theorised beauty, Plato's views are probably the most studied. Ultimately, the Platonic account is distinctly original, but it is worth noting that Plato often uses the term *summetria* as a tool for theorising beauty. He often uses the term to denote good proportion,[17] measurements or ratio[18] and even appropriateness.[19] While these phenomena can be pertinent to the discussions of beauty, none of these passages explicitly describe beauty as nothing over and above *summetria*. The most pertinent passage for the discussion of how *summetria* is related to beauty is found in the *Philebus*. In the relevant section of this dialogue, Protarchus and Socrates discuss what the good is in a life that is devoted to pursuing a mixture of wisdom and pleasure.[20] After agreeing on the components of this mixture, Socrates states that the cause which renders any mixture valuable or valueless is obvious and known to everyone. Since Protarchus is perplexed by this claim, Socrates explains that this cause is τὸ μέτρον and ἡ συμμετρία.[21] After Protarchus agrees with this, Socrates states the following:

{ΣΩ.} Νῦν δὴ καταπέφευγεν ἡμῖν ἡ τοῦ ἀγαθοῦ δύναμις εἰς τὴν τοῦ καλοῦ φύσιν· μετριότης γὰρ καὶ συμμετρία κάλλος δήπου καὶ ἀρετὴ πανταχοῦ συμβαίνει γίγνεσθαι.
{ΠΡΩ.} Πάνυ μὲν οὖν.

{ΣΩ. Καὶ μὴν ἀλήθειάν γε ἔφαμεν αὐτοῖς ἐν τῇ κράσει μεμεῖχθαι.
{ΠΡΩ.} Πάνυ γε.
{ΣΩ.} Οὐκοῦν εἰ μὴ μιᾷ δυνάμεθα ἰδέᾳ τὸ ἀγαθὸν θηρεῦσαι, σὺν τρισὶ λαβόντες, κάλλει καὶ συμμετρίᾳ καὶ ἀληθείᾳ, λέγωμεν ὡς τοῦτο οἷον ἓν ὀρθότατ' ἂν αἰτιασαίμεθ' ἂν τῶν ἐν τῇ συμμείξει, καὶ διὰ τοῦτο ὡς ἀγαθὸν ὂν τοιαύτην αὐτὴν γεγονέναι.

Soc: But now we notice that the force of the good has taken refuge in an alliance with the nature of the beautiful. For measure and proportion manifest themselves in all areas as beauty and virtue.
Pro: Undeniably.
Soc: But we did say that truth is also included along with them in our mixture?
Pro: Indeed.
Soc: Well, then, if we cannot capture the good in one form, we will have to take hold of it in a conjunction of three: beauty, proportion, and truth. Let us affirm that these should by right be treated as a unity and be held responsible for what is in the mixture, for its goodness is what makes the mixture itself a good one.[22]

In this passage, Socrates states that there is a connection between beauty and *summetria*. Socrates claims that beauty, proportion and truth are unified in the good, and this claim shows that the members of this triad are separate entities that have a special relation amongst themselves.[23] There are two notable points about the Platonic treatment of *summetria* here. First, this notion is generalised here, it is clear that the issue at stake is more than just ratios.[24] The second and somewhat related point to note here is that, for Plato, beauty is not reducible to *summetria*; that is, this notion does not explain fully why some object is beautiful. In order to obtain a full explanation, it is necessary to refer to the Platonic Form.

In Plato's philosophy, Forms play a major causal role. Objects gain properties such as beauty by partaking in the Form of Beauty.[25] Interestingly, the motivation for positing the Form as the cause in general can be found in the texts discussing beauty.[26] The *Hippias Major* is an especially useful text for this purpose, although its authorship has been doubted.[27] Regardless of the question of whether Plato wrote this dialogue, it is an illuminating text. The dialogue contains the arguments that implicitly criticise the artistic theory of *summetria* and imply the need for the kind of explanation that can only be provided by positing Forms.

The dialogue starts with and then revolves around the question of what the beautiful is.[28] Hippias answers with confidence that a beautiful maiden is the beautiful.[29] The most important issue here is that Hippias provides an example instead of a definition.[30] The subsequent questioning by Socrates reveals this and some other interesting points. He suggests[31] that Hippias' answer does not explain what the beautiful is, by asking how a beautiful Elean mare, a beautiful lyre and a beautiful pot would compare to the maiden. Hippias is incensed by the example of the pot, but Socrates points out that a smooth, round and well-fired pot would have to be called beautiful.[32] The description of the pot is important not only because it mocks Hippias, but also because it shows that the target here is the theories that account for aesthetic properties in terms of formal properties, such as the shape, proportion or smoothness of a pot. Socrates here is pointing out that they describe certain features of beautiful objects but do not properly explain why they are beautiful. The pot is beautiful by virtue of one set of properties, while the maiden is beautiful by virtue of a different set of properties. Yet, crucially, these sets of properties are entirely different and the formal properties of the pot cannot explain the beauty of the maiden. Thus, we learn nothing about what beauty (or, to be more precise, the beautiful) actually is. The dialogue proceeds to discuss other definitions of beauty, some put forth by Hippias, some by Socrates, and it ends in *aporia*.

This claim is in line with what is said about *summetria* and beauty in the passage from the *Philebus* cited above. In Platonic metaphysics, saying that beautiful objects are *summetroi* would amount to naming one of the properties that beautiful objects have, rather than explaining why they are beautiful. *Summetria* might be a necessary condition for being beautiful (although it is impossible to assert this with certainty), but it is not a sufficient one. In Platonic thought, an account of beauty that includes no references to the Form of Beauty cannot adequately explain the origin of beauty.

Aristotle

Aristotle's contribution to aesthetics is very substantial. His brief discussion of catharsis alone has fuelled and informed debates until this day.[33] Although much of Aristotle's work on the philosophy of art survives, few texts in which he discusses the nature of aesthetic theories are extant. There is good reason to assume that these texts did exist, because Aristotle refers to them in the *Metaphysics*. This passage can be found in the context of refuting those who deny[34] that mathematics are of any use for moral philosophy and for understanding the beautiful. Aristotle makes his point as follows:

ἐπεὶ δὲ τὸ ἀγαθὸν καὶ τὸ καλὸν ἕτερον (τὸ μὲν γὰρ ἀεὶ ἐν πράξει, τὸ δὲ καλὸν καὶ ἐν τοῖς ἀκινήτοις), οἱ φάσκοντες οὐδὲν λέγειν τὰς μαθηματικὰς ἐπιστήμας περὶ καλοῦ ἢ ἀγαθοῦ ψεύδονται. λέγουσι γὰρ καὶ δεικνύουσι μάλιστα· οὐ γὰρ εἰ μὴ ὀνομάζουσι τὰ δ' ἔργα καὶ τοὺς λόγους δεικνύουσιν, οὐ λέγουσι περὶ αὐτῶν. τοῦ δὲ καλοῦ μέγιστα εἴδη τάξις καὶ συμμετρία καὶ τὸ ὡρισμένον, ἃ μάλιστα δεικνύουσιν αἱ μαθηματικαὶ ἐπιστῆμαι. καὶ ἐπεί γε πολλῶν αἴτια φαίνεται ταῦτα (λέγω δ' οἷον ἡ τάξις καὶ τὸ ὡρισμένον), δῆλον ὅτι λέγοιεν ἂν καὶ τὴν τοιαύτην αἰτίαν τὴν ὡς τὸ καλὸν αἴτιον τρόπον τινά. μᾶλλον δὲ γνωρίμως ἐν ἄλλοις περὶ αὐτῶν ἐροῦμεν.

Now since the good and the beautiful are different (for the former always implies conduct as its subject, while the beautiful is found also in motionless things), those who assert that the mathematical sciences say nothing of the beautiful or the good are in error. For these sciences say and prove a great deal about them; if they do not expressly mention them, but prove attributes which are their results or their definitions, it is not true to say that they tell us nothing about them. The chief forms of beauty are order and symmetry and definiteness, which the mathematical sciences demonstrate in a special degree. And since these (e.g. order and definiteness) are obviously causes of many things, evidently these sciences must treat this sort of causative principle also (i.e. the beautiful) as in some sense a cause. But we shall speak more plainly elsewhere about these matters.[35]

It is not clear what other works Aristotle has in mind here, but the passage offers a glimpse of Aristotle's more extensive views. Aristotle's argument is fairly straightforward. Those who deny the usefulness of mathematics for the understanding of the good and the beautiful are wrong, because *summetria* and order are forms of beauty and these are demonstrated mathematically. This shows that Aristotle's understanding of aesthetic phenomena is also greatly influenced by the artistic tradition which defines beauty in terms of formal properties. Aristotle is a notorious critic of Platonic metaphysics and one might wonder if, in this case, the problems he raises about the Forms might have motivated him to subscribe to a reductive theory of beauty as *summetria*. Aristotle also, however, does not equate beauty with *summetria* entirely, just like his teacher Plato. At the same time, *summetria* features in the passages where Aristotle does some work to define beauty. In the passage above, as well as in the *Topics*, Aristotle groups *summetria* together with order (ἡ τάξις) and definiteness (τὸ ὡρισμένον) as the main forms of beauty.[36] He does not, however, distinguish *summetria* as the necessary and sufficient condition of beauty.

More importantly, there are additional passages which indicate even more clearly that *summetria* is not a sufficient condition for beauty. According to Aristotle, the existence of beauty requires the presence of both good proportion (ἡ συμμετρία) and magnitude (τὸ μέγεθος). Without the latter, an object cannot be called beautiful. This is made very clear in the *Nicomachean Ethics* where Aristotle claims that in order to be beautiful, a body must possess magnitude. Short people, as a consequence, can be well proportioned, but not beautiful.[37] The definition of beauty as a combination of *summetria* and magnitude can be found in the *Poetics*[38] and in the *Politics*[39] as well, in the context of discussing the importance of size for the best government of the *polis*. According to these passages, *summetria* can exist independently of beauty. While it can account for some aspects of a beautiful phenomenon, beauty cannot be explained by the presence of *summetria* alone. Although Aristotle's views contain traces of the Polycleitean notion of *summetria*, it is, in fact, a distinct theory.

It seems that the problematic point about *summetria* according to Aristotle is entirely different from the one pointed out in the Platonic texts. The problem is not that *summetria* does not explain the beautiful itself, but that by defining beauty by means of *summetria*, one risks committing to absurd consequences. For example, if a *summetros* vase was so tiny that it is barely perceptible to human sight, a Polycleitean theorist would have to say it is beautiful, despite the fact that this beauty is not visible. Beauty, thus, is an object of sense perception, and an object cannot be called beautiful if it fails to produce a proper sensory impression. It would be possible to argue that beauty depends on a certain kind of functionality, although a different kind from the typically mechanical functionality discussed in, for example, Xenophon's *Memorabilia* or Plato's *Hippias Major*.

The Stoics

To sum up the points made above, the Stoic definition of beauty as *summetria* differs from the ways in which Plato and Aristotle used the term.[40] In certain respects, the Stoics agree with Aristotle, but their formulation is also notably different due to the explanatory primacy they assign to *summetria*. According to the Stoics, beauty is fully explained by the presence of *summetria*. This reductive understanding of beauty also constitutes the central difference between the Stoics and Plato.[41] The apt proportion of parts is the necessary and sufficient condition for beauty, and no additional explanation is required. This way, there is no need to posit complex theoretical devices, such as the theory of Forms. It is worth bearing in mind that the Stoic criticism of Plato's theory of Forms as unable to account for how immaterial Forms are able to have an impact on corporeal objects[42] is at the very least a relevant background and at most the central motivation here.

The Stoics defined beauty in a way that is closer to the Polycleitean account of *summetriai* than the philosophers preceding them, in the sense that, in their theory, beauty is explained, and explained fully, by *summetria*. At the same time, there is much more to the Stoic theorisation of *summetria* than the series of Polycleitean ratios. Arguably, the Stoic *summetria* is distinct because it is conceptualised as functional proportionality, that is, proportionality in reference to the function of an object. By theorising *summetria* in this way, the Stoics were able to avoid the drawbacks that Plato and Aristotle may have found in the simple artistic account of *summetriai*, while keeping the elegant reductivity of the theory. The notion of functional composition allowed them to explain how a single principle could unify diverse manifestations of beauty.

It is also quite noteworthy that the Stoic account allows the explanation of complex kinds of beauty, such as the beauty of abstract objects or unusually small objects. The odd consequence of Aristotle's view is that a well-proportioned, normally sized vase would be beautiful, while its exact but minute copy would not be. One might also wonder how the Aristotelian account would deal with objects whose aesthetic value is grounded in their minuteness, for example, an intricately engraved signet ring or a miniature painting. According to the Stoic view of *summetria*, one does not need to deny any explanatory power to the formal properties at all, but only to adjust the explanation to the nature of the aesthetic object. In a busy museum, for example, a person might get no chance to study an intricately carved signet ring in detail and miss seeing some of its properties, yet at the same time appreciate its aesthetic value arising precisely from its small size.

The influences of the Stoic theory

The return to a reductive way of accounting for aesthetic properties introduced by the Stoics was challenged by the resurgent Platonist tradition. An especially vivid example of the engagement between the broadly Platonist and the Stoic traditions is Plotinus' critique of the definition of beauty as *summetria*, discussed in the previous chapter. Plotinus' remarks can be read as representative not only of his own kind of Neoplatonism, but also of the position of any philosopher committed to advocating the existence of Forms. Plotinus, for instance, agrees that *summetria* plays a role in the account of aesthetic properties and the understanding of the arts, but this role is instrumental, overshadowed by the significance of the Forms.[43] Platonism and Neoplatonism dominated post-Hellenistic philosophy and thus, seemingly, the Stoic theory had hardly any successors. There is evidence to suggest, however, that the Stoic influence was, in fact, strongly present in certain scientific and rhetorical traditions.

Hermogenes of Tarsus, the second-century AD rhetorician, refers to something very much like the Stoic definition of beauty in his major treatise on style titled *On Types of Style*. To be precise, he compares the beauty originating from a composition in words to human beauty as follows:

> ἐπειδὴ γὰρ καθόλου τὸ κάλλος ἐστὶ συμμετρία μελῶν καὶ μερῶν μετ' εὐχροίας, δι' ὧν δὴ λόγος τις γίνεται, εἴτε ἰδεῶν ὅλων μιγνυμένων εἰς ταὐτὸν εἴτε καὶ τῶν ουμπληρούντων ἑκάστην ἰδέαν-ταῦτα γὰρ οἷον μέλη καὶ μέρη ἐστὶν αὐτοῦ . . .
>
> Beauty generally consists of symmetry and harmony and proportion in the various parts and limbs of the body, combined with a fresh and healthy complexion. That is also how the style is produced, whether you mix all the types together or concentrate on each one individually – for these are, as it were, the 'parts and limbs of the body'.[44]

The definition of beauty is not doing much work here; Hermogenes is simply using it to support his discussion of style. The elements of this definition are recognisably Stoic, and especially close to Cicero's record of the Stoic definition of beauty in the *Tusculan Disputations*,[45] in which colour is mentioned as one of the conditions. This shows that by the second century AD, the ideas that Cicero treated as distinctly Stoic had become part of the more general vocabulary. An even more striking case is found in another author working during the period of the Second Sophistic, Galen. After citing Chrysippus' definition of beauty as *summetria* in the *On the Doctrines of Hippocrates and Plato*, Galen adds that this notion of beauty is adopted by 'all physicians'.[46] This is a peculiar remark, but several passages from Galen's other treatise, *On the Utility of Parts*, not only illuminate the meaning of this claim but also show that Galen himself might have been one of these physicians.

The treatise *On the Utility of Parts* is a grand work dedicated to showing the brilliance of the teleological design of human anatomy. Although Galen claims the treatise is not polemical but rather focused on the exposition of this brilliance, some of his remarks show that the work is written as a counter-position to those who posit non-teleological explanations of various phenomena in human bodies.[47] The end of the treatise contains the 'Epode', a hymn to the designing powers of nature, which includes a rather personal description of awe and wonder arising from seeing an elephant for the first time. It is, therefore, perhaps unsurprising that beauty plays no small role in Galen's teleological account of human anatomy, as the impression of beauty invariably follows the discovery of functional design. Amongst the bodily parts that are described as beautiful or beautifully constructed are the coronas of the ulna,[48] the sponge-like bones lying in front of the meninges[49] and the placement of the kidneys.[50] These remarks are numerous, and it is clear that the terms used here are aesthetic, because Galen compares Nature to the craftsmen showing foresight for *analogias*.[51] Elsewhere in the treatise, when describing the proper sizing of the thorax, he states that all the body parts are in due proportion (*analogian*) to one another.[52] He also says that one cannot help but admire the tunic of the left side of the heart[53] due to the *summetria* found in its thickness and strength.

In this treatise, Galen shows himself not only to be interested in beauty but also to be versed in aesthetic theories. In book three of the same treatise, Galen argues that the beautiful arrangement of the heavenly bodies displays great wisdom and foresight. Then he addresses the problem of theodicy, and notes that due to the material from which humans are made, they cannot be as deathless and beautiful as heavenly bodies. Galen is presumably influenced by Plato's *Timaeus* here.[54] Subsequently, however, he adds that one might admire Pheidias' Zeus at Olympia for its ivory, gold and the size of the statue and turn away from the same statue made from clay. This is the sign of an uncultivated man, however. An artist, Galen argues, would recognise the art and appreciate the statue no matter what it is made of.[55] The idea that an architect appreciates the design itself rather than the appearance of an object can be found in Vitruvius' *On Architecture*. Vitruvius does not deny that the laymen can make proper aesthetic judgements in quite the same way as Galen does here, but he does note that the judgements of a layman and an architect are different because the latter can perceive beauty by thinking of the design, whereas the former has to see the object.[56]

Given his erudition and interest, it is unsurprising to find passages in *On the Utility of Parts* in which Galen's views about the nature of aesthetic properties are discussed in a fairly detailed way. It is surprising, however, to find recognisably Stoic themes in this discussion. Relatively early in the treatise, in book one, Galen cites Hippocrates on the shape of the hands and then comments as follows:

> καὶ γὰρ οὖν καὶ ὀφθαλμῶν καὶ ῥινῶν εὐφυῗαν ζητῶν ταῖς ἐνεργείαις συνάπτων αὐτῶν τὴν κατασκευὴν ἐξευρήσεις· αὕτη γάρ σοι κανὼν καὶ μέτρον καὶ κριτήριον εὐφυῗας τε καὶ κάλλους ἀληθινοῦ. οὐδὲ γὰρ ἄλλο τι τὸ ἀληθινὸν κάλλος ἐστὶ πλὴν τῆς ἀρίστης κατασκευῆς, ἣν ταῖς ἐνεργείαις κρινεῖς Ἱπποκράτει πειθόμενος, οὐ λευκότησιν ἢ μαλακότησιν ἤ τισιν ἑτέροις τοιούτοις, δι' ὧν τὸ κομμωτικόν τε καὶ νόθον, οὐ τὸ τῆς φύσεως οὐδὲ τὸ ἀληθινὸν ἐπιδείκνυται κάλλος.

> And so, if you are seeking to discover the proper form for the eye or nose, you will find it by correlating structure and action. In fact, this is your standard, measure, and criterion of proper form and true beauty, since true beauty is nothing but excellence of construction, and in obedience to Hippocrates you will judge that excellence from actions, not from whiteness, softness, or other such qualities, which are indications of a beauty meretricious and false, not natural and true.[57]

Galen uses language that can be traced to the Polycleitean tradition, that is, the canon and the criterion of beauty. Although Galen does not use the word *summetria* here, he does claim that the canon refers to the correlation between κατασκευή, structure, and action. Human bodily parts, thus, are beautiful if they are structured in a way which enables them to perform their acts, or in other words, to function appropriately. This is a strikingly Stoic way of conceptualising aesthetic properties.

Galen nowhere mentions Chrysippus. Instead, he ascribes this view to Hippocrates, despite the fact that the Hippocratic sayings he cites concerning anatomy do not imply anything as complex as the theorisation of aesthetic properties he provides. This is not, however, an empty attribution. Galen makes the connection between Hippocrates and the Stoics in a different treatise,[58] and it has been demonstrated that the key to understanding these claims is Galen's interaction with his contemporary Stoics and Stoicising doctors. To be precise, the significant influences here are figures such as Aeficianus, a Stoicising Hippocratic exegete. This Stoicising reading of Hippocrates led Galen to the appreciation and adoption of Stoic metaphysics, while maintaining his well-known rejection of the Chrysippean psychology and such views as the location of the *hegemonikon* in the heart.[59] It is quite likely that the Stoic conceptualisation of beauty was made convincing for Galen once it was incorporated into a medical context and reinterpreted within the Hippocratic exegetical tradition. In that case Galen would naturally attribute the idea to Hippocrates, whom he treats as the greatest authority in medicine.[60]

More generally speaking, Galen's passage shows a fascinating confluence of interests in aesthetics. After citing Chrysippus' definition of beauty and saying it is like that offered by Polycleitus, he says it is the definition adopted by all physicians in the *On the Doctrines of Hippocrates and Plato*. In the *On the Utility of Parts*, Galen himself uses a vocabulary that is strongly tied to the Polycleitean tradition (namely, the *Canon*). He references the argument about aesthetic agency that is also associated with the artistic tradition and can be cross-referenced to Vitruvius. In addition to this, close to this passage, Galen refers to the passage in Xenophon's *Symposium*, in which the functional theory of beauty is discussed. Socrates is said to be more handsome than any youth, because, for example, his bulging eyes make him see better, like a crab.[61] Galen's knowledge of these discourses on the arts and beauty could be due to the fact that Galen was extremely well educated.[62] Yet his claim that other physicians subscribe to a certain theory of beauty indicates that it was not unusual for those studying medicine to engage in discussions about the nature of beauty. This, moreover, shows that Stoic ideas travelled far and wide, and survived the rise of Platonism in fields that, although connected, are not entirely philosophical.

The case of Stoic ideas illuminates the ways in which the nature of aesthetic properties was discussed in antiquity and how the debates on this topic spread. These debates are not only scarcely confined within disciplinary bounds, but also the people participating in them adopt and adapt these views liberally. In this way, Stoic views on beauty suffered a rather peculiar fate. On the one hand, their account of beauty proved much more popular than rival accounts outside philosophy. By the third century AD, it was ubiquitous amongst doctors and rhetoricians. On the other hand, this meant that Stoic views were misattributed or treated as common, and the Stoics got less credit than they deserved for their elegant yet potent way of accounting for beauty.

Concluding remarks

One may wonder if the Stoics themselves might have been surprised by their legacy in aesthetics or, to put it differently, if the Stoics thought they had a theory of beauty. Despite the fact that the lack of evidence on early Stoicism inevitably leaves room for such scepticism, there are strong reasons to believe that the Stoic engagement with this topic was not an accident. It may very well be that all the extant remarks, arguments and conceptualisations of aesthetic properties in the Stoic corpus are not a clearly demarcated theory of the beautiful. These ideas permeate various metaphysical, epistemological and ethical arguments. There is no definite evidence that Chrysippus ever isolated his ideas on the beautiful and discussed them for their own sake, because his works survive only in fragments, yet there might have been a treatise or treatises on aesthetic questions that are not extant. It is impossible, therefore, to answer the question of whether the early Stoics considered themselves to have a theory of beauty with reference to the works they wrote or did not write.

It is possible, however, to argue on the grounds of the contents of the Stoic claims pertinent to beauty. They share a striking degree of consistency. The definition of beauty as *summetria*, for instance, states explicitly what other arguments imply in the use of the aesthetic terms τὸ καλόν and τὸ κάλλος. The evidence for every topic discussed in this book shares certain common theoretical grounds and assumptions with the evidence for all the other topics. There are, therefore, strong connections between the ways in which beauty is conceptualised not only within Chrysippus' fragments but also the Stoic corpus more generally. Even if Chrysippus and other Stoics never put all of their ideas on beauty into a single work but theorised the beautiful as a part of their other enquiries, their insights and arguments on the beautiful are substantial enough in their content to be treated as a theory of the beautiful.[63] The evidence of the extensive legacy of the Stoic ideas discussed in this chapter corroborates such a reading.

As a result, the significance of Stoic aesthetics is twofold. First, Stoic ideas played a fairly prominent role in the ancient debates on aesthetics and these ideas are much more influential than one might suspect, often reaching far beyond philosophical audiences and their polemics. Stoicism, thus, has a place within ancient aesthetics and the history of aesthetics more generally. Second, aesthetic issues permeate Stoicism thoroughly and, consequently, paying attention to Stoic views on matters relating to aesthetics means obtaining a fuller understanding of their system. Aesthetics, thus, has a place within the study of Stoicism, just as Stoicism has a place in aesthetics.

Notes

1. From Steinberg (1977: 4), original edn 1757.
2. See, for instance, Lombardo (2002: 30).
3. *Plac.* 5.3.16 (5.449K).
4. See Pollitt (1974: 14–15), who also argues that *summetria* in Polycleitus' thought denoted the proportionality of a structure.
5. Diogenes Laertius 8.47.
6. Plin. *Nat.* 34.19, tr. Rackham: ... *primus hic multiplicasse veritatem videtur, numerosior in arte quam Polyclitus et in symmetria diligentior.*

7. Ibid.: *non habet Latinum nomen symmetria, quam diligentissime custodiit nova intactaque ratione quadratas veterum staturas permutando.*
8. Philostratus the Younger *Imag.*, *Proem.* 4. See also Galen *Temp.* 1.9 (1.566K).
9. Vitruvius *De arch.* 1.3.2: *Haec autem ita fieri debent, ut habeatur ratio firmitatis, utilitatis, venustatis . . . venustatis vero, cum fuerit operis species grata et elegans membrorumque commensus iustas habeat symmetriarum ratiocinationes.*
10. Vitruvius *De arch.* 3.1.1, the translation is mine: '*Proportio est ratae partis membrorum in omni opere totiusque commodulatio, ex qua ratio efficitur symmetriarum.*'
11. Vitruvius *De arch.* 3.1.1–2.
12. Vitruvius *De arch.* 3.1.2.
13. McMahon (1999: 7–9); Tatarkiewicz (1970: 81).
14. See Horky (2013: esp. 3–5).
15. Stobaeus 4.1,49 W=DK 58 D4, tr. K. Freeman: ἡ μὲν τάξις καὶ συμμετρία καλὰ καὶ σύμφορα, ἡ δὲ ἀταξία καὶ ἀσυμμετρία αἰσχρά τε καὶ ἀσύμφορα.
16. Stobaeus 1.21,7d W=Frag. 6 (Huffman): περὶ δὲ φύσιος καὶ ἁρμονίας ὧδε ἔχει· ἁ μὲν ἐστὼ τῶν πραγμάτων, ἀΐδιος ἔσσα καὶ αὐτὰ μὰν ἁ φύσις θείαν τε καὶ οὐκ ἀνθρωπίνην ἐνδέχεται γνῶσιν πλάν γα ἢ ὅτι οὐχ οἷόν τ' ἦν οὐδενὶ τῶν ἐόντων καὶ γιγνωσκόμενον ὑφ' ἁμῶν γεγενῆσθαι μὴ ὑπαρχούσας τᾶς ἐστοῦς τῶν πραγμάτων, ἐξ ὧν συνέστα ὁ κόσμος, καὶ τῶν περαινόντων καὶ τῶν ἀπείρων. ἐπεὶ δὲ ταὶ ἀρχαὶ ὑπᾶρχον οὐχ ὁμοῖαι οὐδ' ὁμόφυλοι ἔσσαι, ἤδη ἀδύνατον ἦς κα αὐταῖς κοσμηθῆμεν, εἰ μὴ ἁρμονία ἐπεγένετο ᾡτινιῶν ἄν τρόπῳ ἐγένετο. τὰ μὲν ὦν ὁμοῖα καὶ ὁμόφυλα ἁρμονίας οὐδὲν ἐπεδέοντο, τὰ δὲ ἀνόμοια μηδὲ ὁμόφυλα μηδὲ ἰσοταχῆ, ἀνάγκα τὰ τοιαῦτα ἁρμονίᾳ συγκεκλεῖσθαι, εἰ μέλλοντι ἐν κόσμῳ κατέχεσθαι. See also Huffman (1993: 54).
17. *Ti.* 66A, D; 87D; 69B; *Sph.* 235D–236A; 228A.
18. *Resp.* 529D–530B.
19. *Lg.* 925A.
20. *Phlb.* 60D–61B.
21. *Phlb.* 64D–E.
22. *Phlb.* 64E–65A, tr. Frede in Cooper and Hutchinson (1997).

23. For a detailed discussion about the relationship between beauty, proportion and truth, see Frede (1997: 358–60).
24. Although in the *Timaeus* account of the creation of the world, the series of ratios are certainly present, see *Ti.* 80B for the explanation of music in terms of certain proportions of sounds. See also Chapter 4.
25. See *Parm.* 130E–131A. On the Form of Beauty in particular, see, for example, *Symp.* 211B. See also Hyland (2008: 17–18; 56–9); Dancy (2004: 289–90).
26. Although the unity of parts is also an important factor, see Asmis (1998: 389).
27. See Kahn (1985), although it is worth noting that nowadays *Hippias Major* is typically treated as an authentic Platonic text because the reasons for doubting its authorship are not considered to be quite sufficient.
28. The elenchus starts with Socrates asking 'εἰπὲ δή, ὦ ξένε,' φήσει, 'τί ἐστι τοῦτο τὸ καλόν;' (*Hp. mai.* 287D).
29. *Hp mai.* 288E: ἔστι γάρ, ὦ Σώκρατες, εὖ ἴσθι, εἰ δεῖ τὸ ἀληθὲς λέγειν, παρθένος καλὴ καλόν.
30. See Dancy (2004: 31–4) for the way the problem of definitions plays out in this dialogue in particular.
31. To be precise, Socrates is putting forth the questions and possible worries of the hypothetical questioners of Socrates. Hippias is supposed to be showing Socrates how to answer these queries. The dialogue is set up in a way which shows that Socrates is distancing himself from the critique of Hippias' views.
32. *Hp. mai.* 288D–E.
33. The scholarship on this topic is immense, as this notion has been interpreted in diverse ways, starting with the notorious interpretation of catharsis as the treatment of a pathological emotional state put forth by Jacob Bernays, Sigmund Freud's uncle by marriage, in 1857 (see Rapp (2015: 448–9). Recent interpretations are more nuanced; see, for example, the reading of catharsis as a psychological–moral response to aesthetic objects in Halliwell (2003). See Asmis (2015: 494–6) for an argument that Aristotelian catharsis was a response to the Platonic critique of poetry.
34. This presumably refers to sophists such as Aristippus. Earlier, at 13.996a, he writes that Aristippus spurned mathematics, because it

takes no account of good and evil. Even mechanical arts, such as cobbling, act for better or worse, but mathematics does not.
35. Aristotle *M* 13.1078a30–b6, tr. W. D. Ross.
36. *Top.* 116b21: τὸ δὲ κάλλος τῶν μελῶν τις συμμετρία δοκεῖ εἶναι. See also *Ph.* 246b3–246b19: ἔτι δὲ καί φαμεν ἁπάσας εἶναι τὰς ἀρετὰς ἐν τῷ πρός τι πὼς ἔχειν. τὰς μὲν γὰρ τοῦ σώματος, οἷον ὑγίειαν καὶ εὐεξίαν, ἐν κράσει καὶ συμμετρίᾳ θερμῶν καὶ ψυχρῶν τίθεμεν, ἢ αὐτῶν πρὸς αὐτὰ τῶν ἐντὸς ἢ πρὸς τὸ περιέχον· ὁμοίως δὲ καὶ τὸ κάλλος καὶ τὴν ἰσχὺν καὶ τὰς ἄλλας ἀρετὰς καὶ κακίας. Also see *Mu.* 397a6, a Pseudo-Aristotelian work, which also associates beauty with good arrangements, but in a different language, as follows: τῆς φύσεως ἐπὶ τῶν μειζόνων διδασκούσης ὅτι τὸ ἴσον σωστικόν πώς ἐστιν ὁμονοίας, ἡ δὲ ὁμόνοια τοῦ πάντων γενετῆρος καὶ περικαλλεστάτου κόσμου. τίς γὰρ ἂν εἴη φύσις τοῦδε κρείττων; ἣν γὰρ ἂν εἴπῃ τις, μέρος ἐστὶν αὐτοῦ. τό τε καλὸν πᾶν ἐπώνυμόν ἐστι τούτου καὶ τὸ τεταγμένον, ἀπὸ τοῦ κόσμου λεγόμενον κεκοσμῆσθαι.
37. *Eth. Nic.* 1123b6–8: ἐν μεγέθει γὰρ ἡ μεγαλοψυχία, ὥσπερ καὶ τὸ κάλλος ἐν μεγάλῳ σώματι, οἱ μικροὶ δ' ἀστεῖοι καὶ σύμμετροι, καλοὶ δ' οὔ.
38. *Poet.* 1450b34–1451a6.
39. *Pol.* 1326a33.
40. See Zagdoun (2000: 80). Zagdoun notes that the Stoics borrowed elements from other philosophers, but '*la définition stoïcienne du beau dans son ensemble est originale et serait incompréhensible sans une référence constante aux fondements du stoïcisme*'.
41. Recently, some scholars have argued that Plato's philosophy was influential to Stoicism not only polemically, but also in a positive way. The influence, however, might have been quite subtle. A. Long, for instance, argues as follows: 'When Zeno and Chrysippus read a Platonic dialogue and found ideas that to their mind were (or, properly developed, could be made to be) plausible, they were not constrained by the dialogue's own verdict on the ideas contained in it' (2013: 5). Recently, several edited volumes have been dedicated to exploring various aspects of the interaction between Plato and the Stoics, for instance, Bonazzi and Helmig (2007), Harte, McCabe, Sharples and Sheppard (2010) and Long (2013a).

42. Simplicius *In. Ar. Cat.* 217, 32–218, 1=*SVF* 2.389=LS 28L.
43. For the relationship between *summetria*, the intelligible word and the arts in Plotinus, see Heath (2012: 168–9).
44. Hermogenes of Tarsus *Id.* 1.12.20–28, tr. Wooten.
45. *Tusc.* 4.31=*SVF* 3.279; see the previous chapter for the discussion of this passage.
46. Galen *Plac.* 5.3.17 (5.449K): τὸ μὲν δὴ κάλλος τοῦ σώματος ἐν τῇ τῶν μορίων συμμετρίᾳ κατὰ πάντας ἰατροὺς καὶ φιλοσόφους ἐστίν.
47. See, for example, remarks against the Epicureans and Asclepiades of Bithynia in *UP* 1.20 (3.74K) and the attack on Anaxagoras on the issue of whether humans are intelligent because they have hands or have hands because they are intelligent (*UP* 1.3–4 (3.6–9K)).
48. *UP* 2. 15 (3.146K).
49. *UP* 8.7 (3.654K).
50. *UP* 5.6 (3.371K).
51. *UP* 2.16 (3.158K).
52. *UP* 13.6 (4.106K).
53. *UP* 6.16 (3.489K).
54. Plato *Ti.* 41D.
55. *UP* 3.10 (3.238–40K).
56. Vitruvius *De arch.* 6.8.10; See Augustine *Trin.* 9.6.11.
57. *UP* 1.9 (3.24–5K), tr. May.
58. *MM* 1.2 (10.15–16K); cf. *MM* 7.3 (10.462–3K).
59. See Tieleman (2009: 290–4) for the reconstruction of Galen's interaction with such figures as Aeficianus. See also Holmes (2015: 61–2).
60. See Craik (2017: 204–7) on Galen's attribution of Aristotelian teleology to Hippocrates.
61. Xenophon *Symp.* 5.4–5, cf. Sedley (2017: 40).
62. *Aff. Pecc. Dig.* 1.8 (5.41–2K).
63. This is contra Tsolis (2000: 211–13), who argues the opposite on the grounds of Kristeller's conception of aesthetics.

Bibliography

Algra, K. (2003), 'Stoic Theology', in B. Inwood (ed.), *The Cambridge Companion to the Stoics*, Cambridge: Cambridge University Press, pp. 153–78.

Algra, K., J. Barnes, J. Mansfeld and M. Schofield (1999), *Cambridge History of Hellenistic Philosophy*, Cambridge: Cambridge University Press.

Allen, J. (2001), *Inference from Signs: Ancient Debates about the Nature of Evidence*, Oxford: Clarendon Press.

Annas, J. (1995), *The Morality of Happiness*, New York: Oxford University Press.

Annas, J., and J. Barnes (1994), *Sextus Empiricus: Outlines of Scepticism*, Cambridge: Cambridge University Press.

Armstrong, A. (1966–88), *Plotinus: Enneads*, 7 vols, Cambridge, MA: Harvard University Press.

Arnim, H. F. A. von (1903–24), *Stoicorum Veterum Fragmenta*, 3 vols, Leipzig: Teubner.

Asmis, E. (1990), 'The Poetic Theory of the Stoic Aristo', *Apeiron* 23: 147–201.

Asmis, E. (1995), 'Philodemus on Censorship, Moral Utility, and Formalism on Poetry', in D. Obbink (ed.), *Philodemus and Poetry: Poetic Theory and Practice in Lucretius, Philodemus and Horace*, Oxford: Oxford University Press, pp. 148–77.

Asmis, E. (1998), 'Hellenistic Aesthetics: Philosophers and Literary Critics', in M. Kelly (ed.), *Encyclopedia of Aesthetics*, vol. 2, Oxford: Oxford University Press, pp. 389–91.

Bibliography 193

Asmis, E. (2004), 'Sound and Sense in Philodemus' *Poetics*', *Cronache Ercolanesi* 34: 5–27.

Asmis, E. (2007), 'Myth and Philosophy in Cleanthes' *Hymn to Zeus*', *Greek, Roman, and Byzantine Studies* 47: 413–29.

Asmis, E. (2015), 'Art and Morality', in P. Destrée and P. Murray (eds), *A Companion to Ancient Aesthetics*, Hoboken, NJ: Wiley-Blackwell, pp. 486–504.

Baltzly, D. (2003), 'Stoic Pantheism', *Sophia* 42 (2): 3–33.

Barnes, J. (1989), 'Antiochus of Ascalon', in M. Griffin and J. Barnes (eds), *Philosophia Togata: Essays on Philosophy and Roman Society*, Oxford: Oxford University Press, pp. 51–96.

Barnes, J. (ed.) (1992), *The Complete Works of Aristotle*, 2 vols, Clayton, GA: InteLex Corporation.

Barney, R. (2010), 'Notes on Plato on the *Kalon* and the Good', *Classical Philology* 105 (4): 363–77.

Beardsley, M. (1958), *Aesthetics: Problems in the Philosophy of Criticism*, New York: Harcourt, Brace.

Beardsley, M. (1966), *Aesthetics from Classical Greece to the Present*, New York: Macmillan.

Beech, D. (2009), 'Introduction: Art and the Politics of Beauty', in D. Beech (ed.), *Beauty: Documents of Contemporary Art*, London: Whitechapel Art Gallery, pp. 12–19.

Bell, C. [1914] (1987), *Art*, [London: Chatto & Windus] Oxford: Oxford University Press.

Bénatouïl, T. (2009), 'How Industrious Can Zeus Be?' in R. Salles (ed.), *God and Cosmos in Stoicism*, Oxford: Oxford University Press, pp. 23–45.

Bermúdez, J. L., and S. Gardner (ed.) (2003), *Art and Morality*, London and New York: Routledge.

Betegh, G. (2003), 'Cosmological Ethics in the *Timaeus* and Early Stoicism', *Oxford Studies in Ancient Philosophy* 24: 273–302.

Bett, R. (2010), 'Beauty and its Relation to Goodness in Stoicism', in A. Nightingale and D. Sedley (eds), *Ancient Models of Mind*, Cambridge: Cambridge University Press, pp. 130–52.

Blank, D. (2011), 'Reading Between the Lies: Plutarch and Chrysippus on the Uses of Poetry', *Oxford Studies in Ancient Philosophy* 40: 237–64.

Bobzien, S. (1996), 'Stoic Syllogistic', *Oxford Studies in Ancient Philosophy* 14: 133–92.

Bonazzi, M., and C. Helmig (eds) (2007), *Platonic Stoicism, Stoic Platonism: The Dialogue Between Platonism and Stoicism in Antiquity*, Leuven: Leuven University Press.

Botting, E. H. (ed.) (2014), *Mary Wollstonecraft: A Vindication of the Rights of Woman*, New Haven: Yale University Press.

Boudouris, K. (ed.) (2000), *Greek Philosophy and the Fine Arts*, vol. 2, Athens: International Centre for Greek Philosophy and Culture.

Boys-Stones, G. (1998), 'Eros in Government: Zeno and the Virtuous City', *The Classical Quarterly* 48 (1): 168–74.

Boys-Stones, G. (2007), 'Physiognomy and Ancient Psychological Theory', in S. Swain (ed.), *Seeing the Face, Seeing the Soul: Polemon's Physiognomy from Classical Antiquity to Medieval Islam*, Oxford: Oxford University Press, pp. 19–124.

Boys-Stones, G. (2019), 'The Myth of Inner Beauty in Plato', in P. Horky (ed.), *Cosmos in the Ancient World*, Cambridge: Cambridge University Press, pp. 108–21.

Breitenbach, A. (2012), 'Aesthetics in Science: A Kantian Proposal', *Aristotelian Society Lectures*, London: Senate House, University of London.

Brennan, T. (2005), *The Stoic Life: Emotions, Duties, and Fate*, Oxford: Clarendon Press.

Broad, C. (1925), *The Mind and Its Place in Nature*, London: Kegan Paul, Trench, Trubner & Co.

Broadie, S. (1999), 'Rational Theology', in A. Long (ed.), *The Cambridge Companion to Early Greek Philosophy*, Cambridge: Cambridge University Press, pp. 205–24.

Broadie, S. (2007), *Aristotle and Beyond: Essays on Metaphysics and Ethics*, Cambridge: Cambridge University Press.

Brunschwig, J., and M. Nussbaum (eds) (1993), *Passions and Perceptions: Studies in Hellenistic Philosophy of Mind*, Cambridge: Cambridge University Press.

Bury, R. G. (1933–49), *Sextus Empiricus: Works*, 4 vols, Cambridge, MA: Harvard University Press.

Bychkov, O. (2010), *Aesthetic Revelation: Reading Ancient and Medieval*

Texts after Hans Urs von Balthasar, Washington, DC: Catholic University of America Press.

Bychkov, O. (2011), Seneca, *On Benefits*, trans. Miriam Griffin and Brad Inwood, University of Chicago Press, *Notre Dame Philosophical Reviews*, <http://ndpr.nd.edu/news/25987-on-benefits/> (last accessed 28 May 2020).

Bychkov, O., and A. Sheppard (eds) (2010), *Greek and Roman Aesthetics*, Cambridge: Cambridge University Press.

Čelkytė, A. (2017), 'Epicurus and Aesthetic Disinterestedness', *Mare Nostrum* 7: 56–74.

Cherniss, H. (1976), *Plutarch: Moralia 13*, Cambridge, MA: Harvard University Press.

Classen, C. (1962), 'The Creator in Greek Thought from Homes to Plato', *Classica et Medievalia* 23: 1–22.

Clercq, R. (2013), 'Beauty', in B. Gaut and D. Lopes (eds), *The Routledge Companion to Aesthetics*, 3rd edn, London: Routledge, pp. 299–308.

Close, A. J. (1971), 'Philosophical Theories of Art and Nature in Classical Antiquity', *Journal of the History of Ideas* 32 (2): 163–84.

Collingwood, R. G. (1925), 'Plato's Philosophy of Art', *Mind* 134: 154–72.

Cooper, J., and D. Hutchinson (eds) (1997), *Plato: Complete Works*, Indianapolis and Cambridge: Hackett.

Craik, E. (2017), 'Teleology in Hippocratic Texts: Clues to the Future?' in J. Rocca (ed.), *Teleology in the Ancient World*, Cambridge: Cambridge University Press, pp. 203–16.

Crisp, R. (2000), *Aristotle: Nicomachean Ethics*, Cambridge: Cambridge University Press.

Dancy, R. (2004), *Plato's Introduction of Forms*, Cambridge: Cambridge University Press.

Danto, A. (2003), *The Abuse of Beauty*, Chicago: Open Court.

Davies, S., K. M. Higgins, R. Hopkins, R. Stecker and D. E. Cooper (eds) (2009), *A Companion to Aesthetics*, 2nd edn, Oxford: Wiley-Blackwell.

De Lacy, P. (1948), 'Stoic Views of Poetry', *American Journal of Philology* 69: 241–71.

De Lacy, P. (1978–84), *Galen: On the Doctrines of Hippocrates and Plato*, 3 vols, Berlin: Akademie Verlag.

Denham, A. (ed.) (2012), *Plato on Art and Beauty*, New York: Palgrave Macmillan.

Destrée, P. (2015), 'Pleasure', in P. Destrée and P. Murray (eds), *A Companion to Ancient Aesthetics*, Hoboken, NJ: Wiley-Blackwell, pp. 472–85.

Destrée, P., and P. Murray (eds) (2015), *A Companion to Ancient Aesthetics*, Hoboken, NJ: Wiley-Blackwell.

Diels, H., and W. Kranz (eds) (1951–2), *Die Fragmente der Vorsokratiker, griechisch und deutsch*, 3 vols, Berlin: Weidmannsche buchhandlung.

Dirac, P. (1963), 'The Evolution of the Physicist's Picture of Nature', *Scientific American* 208 (5): 45–53.

Donoghue, D. (2003), *Speaking of Beauty*, New Haven: Yale University Press.

Douglas, A. (1990), *Cicero: Tusculan Disputations II and V*, Warminster: Aris and Phillips.

Dover, K. J. (1978), *Greek Homosexuality*, London: Duckworth.

Dover, K. J. (1994), *Greek Popular Morality in the Time of Plato and Aristotle*, Indianapolis: Hackett.

Dutton, D. (2009), *The Art Instinct: Beauty, Pleasure, and Human Evolution*, Oxford: Oxford University Press.

Dyck, A. R. (1996), *A Commentary on Cicero De Officiis*, Ann Arbor: University of Michigan Press.

Engler, G. (1990), 'Aesthetics in Science and in Art', *The British Journal of Aesthetics* 30 (1): 24–34.

Evangeliou, C. (2000), 'Portraits of Plotinus and the Symmetry Theory of Beauty', in K. Boudouris (ed.), *Greek Philosophy and the Fine Arts*, vol. 2, Athens: International Center for Greek Philosophy and Culture, pp. 38–48.

Everett, C. C. (1882), *The Science of Thought: A System of Logic*, Boston: Hall and Whiting.

Farquharson, A. (1944), *The Meditations of the Emperor Marcus Aurelius*, Oxford: Clarendon Press.

Fitzgerald, W. (2016), *Variety: The Life of a Roman Concept*, Chicago: University of Chicago Press.

Flew, A. (1975), *Thinking About Thinking (Or, Do I Sincerely Want to be Right?)*, Glasgow: Fontana.

Fortenbaugh, W. W. (2006), *Aristo of Ceos: Text, Translation, and Discussion*, New Brunswick, NJ: Transaction.

Fowler, B. H. (1989), *The Hellenistic Aesthetic*, Bristol: Bristol Classical Press.

Frede, D. (1997), *Platon: Philebos. Übersetzung und Kommentar von Dorothea Frede*, Göttingen: Vandenhoeck & Ruprecht.

Frede, D. (2002), 'Theodicy and Providential Care in Stoicism', in D. Frede and A. Laks (eds), *Traditions of Theology: Studies in Hellenistic Theology*, Leiden: Brill, pp. 85–119.

Frede, D., and A. Laks (eds) (2002), *Traditions of Theology: Studies in Hellenistic Theology*, Leiden: Brill.

Frede, M. (1987), *Essays in Ancient Philosophy*, Minneapolis: University of Minnesota Press.

Frede, M. (1999), 'The Stoic Conception of the Good', in K. Ierodiakonou (ed.), *Topics in Stoic Philosophy*, Oxford: Clarendon Press, pp. 71–94.

Freeman, K. (1948), *Ancilla to the Pre-Socratic Philosophers: A Complete Translation of the Fragments in Diels' Fragmente der Vorsokratiker*, Oxford: Blackwell.

Gál, O. (2011), '*Unitas Multiplex* as the Basis of Plotinus' Conception of Beauty: An Interpretation of *Ennead* V.8', *Estetika: The Central European Journal of Aesthetics* 48 (2): 172–98.

Gatti, M. L. (1996), 'Plotinus: The Platonic tradition and the foundation of Neoplatonism', in L. P. Gerson (ed.), *The Cambridge Companion to Plotinus*, Cambridge: Cambridge University Press, pp. 10–37.

Gaut, B. (2009), 'Morality and Art', in S. Davies, K. Higgins, R. Hopkins, R. Stecker and D. Cooper (eds), *A Companion to Aesthetics*, Oxford: Wiley-Blackwell, pp. 428–31.

Gerson, L. (1990), *God and Greek Philosophy*, London: Routledge.

Gerson, L. (1994), *Plotinus*, London: Routledge.

Gill, C. (1983), 'Did Chrysippus Understand *Medea*?' *Phronesis* 28 (2): 136–49.

Gill, C. (1996), *Personality in Greek Epic, Tragedy, and Philosophy: The Self in Dialogue*, Oxford: Clarendon Press.

Gill, C. (2006), *The Structured Self in Hellenistic and Roman Thought*, Oxford: Oxford University Press.

Gill, C. (2010), 'Stoicism and Epicureanism', in P. Goldie (ed.), *The Oxford Handbook of Philosophy of Emotion*, Oxford: Oxford University Press, pp. 143–66.

Gill, C., and R. Hard (1995), *The Discourses of Epictetus*, London: Everyman.

Gould, J. (1970), *The Philosophy of Chrysippus*, Leiden: Brill.

Graeser, A. (1972), *Plotinus and the Stoics*, Leiden: Brill.
Grahn-Wilder, M. (2018), *Gender and Sexuality in Stoic Philosophy*, Cham: Palgrave Macmillan.
Grand-Clement, A. (2015), 'Poikilia', in P. Destrée and P. Murray (eds), *A Companion to Ancient Aesthetics*, Hoboken, NJ: Wiley-Blackwell, pp. 406–21.
Graver, M. (2002), *Cicero on The Emotions: Tusculan Disputations 3 and 4*, Chicago: University of Chicago Press.
Graver, M. (2007), *Stoicism and Emotion*, Chicago: University of Chicago Press.
Gutzwiller, K. (2007), *A Guide to Hellenistic Literature*, Oxford: Blackwell.
Haake, M. (2004), 'Documentary evidence, literary forgery, or manipulation of historical documents? Diogenes Laertius and an Athenian honorary decree for Zeno of Citium', *The Classical Quarterly* 54 (2), 470–83.
Halliwell, S. (1991), 'The Importance of Plato and Aristotle for Aesthetics', in J. Cleary (ed.), *Proceedings of the Boston Area Colloquium in Ancient Philosophy*, vol. 7, New York: Routledge, pp. 321–48.
Halliwell, S. (2002), *The Aesthetics of Mimesis: Ancient Texts and Modern Problems*, Princeton: Princeton University Press.
Halliwell, S. (2003), 'The moral psychology of catharsis', *Les Études Philosophiques* 67 (4): 499.
Halliwell, S. (2009), 'Plato', in S. Davies, K. M. Higgins, R. Hopkins, R. Stecker, and D. E. Cooper (eds), *A Companion to Aesthetics*, 2nd edn, Oxford: Wiley-Blackwell, pp. 472–4.
Halliwell, S. (2012), '*Amousia*: Living Without the Muses', in I. Sluiter and R. M. Rosen (eds), *Aesthetic Value in Classical Antiquity*, Leiden: Brill, pp. 15–45.
Hankinson, R. (2001), *Cause and Explanation in Ancient Greek Thought*, Oxford: Oxford University Press.
Hard, R., and C. Gill (2014), *Epictetus: Discourses, Fragments, Handbook*, Oxford: Oxford University Press.
Harte, V. (2002), *Plato on Parts and Wholes: The Metaphysics of Structure*, Oxford: Oxford University Press.
Harte, V., M. M. McCabe, R. Sharples and A. Sheppard (eds) (2010), *Aristotle and The Stoics Reading Plato*, London: Institute of Classical Studies.

Heath, M. (2012), *Ancient Philosophical Poetics*, Cambridge: Cambridge University Press.
Heck, E., and A. Wlosok (2005–11), *Lactantius Divinarum Institutionum*, vols 3–4, Monachii et Lipsiae: Saur.
Hicks, R. (1924), *Diogenes Laertius: Lives of Eminent Philosophers*, Cambridge, MA: Harvard University Press.
Holmes, B. (2015), 'Reflection. Galen's Sympathy', in E. Schliesser (ed.), *Sympathy: A History*, Oxford: Oxford University Press, pp. 61–9.
Hon, G., and B. Goldstein (2008), *From Summetria to Symmetry: The Making of a Revolutionary Scientific Concept*, Dordrecht: Springer.
Horky, P. S. (2013), *Plato and Pythagoreanism*, New York: Oxford University Press.
Horn, H.-J. (1989), 'Stoische Symmetrie und Theorie des Schönen in der Kaiserzeit', *Aufstieg und Niedergang der römischen Welt* 36 (3): 1454–1472.
Huffman, C. (1993), *Philolaus of Croton: Pythagorean and Presocratic: A Commentary on The Fragments and Testimonia with Interpretive Essays*, Cambridge: Cambridge University Press.
Hume, D. [1757] (1985), *Essays: Moral, Political Literary*, ed. Eugene F. Miller, Indianapolis: Liberty Classics.
Hunter, R., and D. Russell (2011), *How to Study Poetry/De Audiendis Poetis by Plutarch*, Cambridge: Cambridge University Press.
Hyland, D. (2008), *Plato and the Question of Beauty*, Bloomington and Indianapolis: Indiana University Press.
Ierodiakonou, K. (1993), 'The Stoic Division of Philosophy', *Phronesis* 38 (1): 57–74.
Ierodiakonou, K. (2005), 'Empedocles and Colour and Colour Vision', *Oxford Studies in Ancient Philosophy* 29: 1–37.
Ierodiakonou, K. (2005a), 'Ancient Thought Experiments: A First Approach', *Ancient Philosophy* 25 (1): 125–40.
Inwood, B. (1985), *Ethics and Human Action in Early Stoicism*, Oxford: Clarendon Press.
Inwood, B. (2007), *Seneca: Selected Philosophical Letters*, Oxford: Oxford University Press.
Inwood, B. (2012), 'How Unified is Stoicism Anyway?' *Oxford Studies in Ancient Philosophy*, suppl., 223–44.

Ioppolo, A. M. (2012), 'Il concetto di nella filosofia di Aristone di Chio', *Elenchos* 33 (1): 43–68.

Irwin, T. (2010), 'The Sense and Reference of *Kalon* in Aristotle', *Classical Philology* 105 (4): 381–96.

Jackson, F. (1982), 'Epiphenomenal Qualia', *Philosophical Quarterly* 32: 127–36.

Janko, R. (2000), *Philodemus 'On Poems' Book 1*, Oxford: Oxford University Press.

Janko, R. (2011), *Philodemus 'On Poems' Books 3–4 with the Fragments of Aristotle On Poets. With an Unpublished Edition by Cecilia Mangoni*, Oxford: Oxford University Press.

Jones, A. (2017), *A Portable Cosmos: Revealing the Antikythera Mechanism, Scientific Wonder of the Ancient World*, New York: Oxford University Press.

Kahn, C. H. (1985), 'The Beautiful and the Genuine', *Oxford Studies in Ancient Philosophy* 3: 261–87.

Kant, I. [1790] (2007), *Critique of Judgement*, ed. N. Walker, trans. J. C. Meredith, Oxford: Oxford University Press.

King, J. (1945), *Cicero: Tusculan Disputations*, Cambridge, MA: Harvard University Press.

Kintsch, W. (2012), 'Musings about Beauty', *Cognitive Science* 36: 635–54.

Kirwan, J. (1999), *Beauty*, Manchester and New York: Manchester University Press.

Konstan, D. (1997), *Friendship in the Classical World*, Cambridge: Cambridge University Press.

Konstan, D. (2012), 'Epicurean Happiness: A Pig's Life?', *Journal of Ancient Philosophy* 6 (1): 1–22.

Konstan, D. (2014), *Beauty: The Fortunes of an Ancient Greek Idea*, Oxford: Oxford University Press.

Kosman, A. (2010), 'Beauty and the Good: Situating the *Kalon*', *Classical Philology* 105 (4): 341–62.

Kraut, R. (2013), 'An Aesthetic Reading of Aristotle's Ethics', in V. Harte and M. Lane (eds), *Politeia in Greek and Roman Philosophy*, Cambridge: Cambridge University Press, pp. 231–50.

Kristeller, P. (1951), 'The Modern System of the Fine Arts', *Journal of the History of Ideas* 12 (4): 496–527.

Kuisma, O. (2003), 'Plotinus: Beauty, Virtue, and Aesthetic Experience', *Acta Philosophica Fennica* 72: 65–82.
Laurand, V. (2007), 'L'eros pédagogique chez Platon et les Stoïciens', in M. Bonazzi and C. Helmig (eds), *Platonic Stoicism, Stoic Platonism: The Dialogue between Platonism and Stoicism in Antiquity*, Leuven: Leuven University Press, pp. 63–86.
Lesses, G. (1993), 'Austere Friends: The Stoics and Friendship', *Apeiron* 26 (1): 57–75.
Levinson, J. (2011), 'Beauty is Not One: The Irreducible Variety of Visual Beauty', in E. Schellekens and P. Goldie (eds), *The Aesthetic Mind: Philosophy and Psychology*, Oxford: Oxford University Press, pp. 190–207.
Lewis, C. I. (1946), *An Analysis of Knowledge and Valuation*, La Salle, IL: The Open Court Publishing Company.
Lewis, E. (2010), 'Diogenes Laertius and the Stoic Theory of Mixture', *Bulletin of the Institute of Classical Studies* 35 (1): 84–90.
Lombardo, G. (2002), *L'Estetica Antica*, Bologna: Il Mulino.
Long, A. A. (1996), 'The Harmonics of Stoic Virtue', in A. A. Long, *Stoic Studies*, Cambridge: Cambridge University Press, pp. 210–12.
Long, A. A., and D. Sedley (eds) (1987), *The Hellenistic Philosophers*, 2 vols, Cambridge: Cambridge University Press.
Long, A. G. (2013), 'Introduction', in *Plato and the Stoics*, ed. A. G. Long, Cambridge: Cambridge University Press, pp. 1–10.
Long, A. G. (ed.) (2013a), *Plato and the Stoics*, Cambridge: Cambridge University Press.
Mansfeld, J. (1999), 'Sources', in K. Algra, J.Barnes, J. Mansfeld and M. Schofield (eds), *The Cambridge History of Hellenistic Philosophy*, Cambridge: Cambridge University Press, pp. 3–30.
Mansfeld, J. (1999a), 'Theology', in K. Algra, J.Barnes, J. Mansfeld and M. Schofield (eds), *The Cambridge History of Hellenistic Philosophy*, Cambridge: Cambridge University Press, pp. 452–78.
Marchant, E. (2013), *Xenophon: Memorabilia; Oeconomicus*, Cambridge, MA: Harvard University Press.
McAllister, J. (1996), *Beauty and Revolution in Science*, Ithaca and London: Cornell University Press.
McMahon, J. (1999), 'Towards a Unified Theory of Beauty', *Literature and Aesthetics* 9: 7–27.

McMahon, J. (2005), 'Beauty', in B. Gaut and D. Lopes (eds), *The Routledge Companion to Aesthetics*, 2nd edn, London: Routledge, pp. 307–19.

McMahon, J. (2009), 'Beauty as Harmony of the Soul: the Aesthetic of the Stoics', in M. Rossetto, M. Tsianikas, G. Couvalis and M. Palaktsoglou (eds), *Greek Research in Australia: Proceedings of the Eighth Biennial International Conference of Greek Studies*, Adelaide: Flinders University Department of Languages, pp. 54–63.

Menn, S. (1999), 'The Stoic Theory of Categories', *Oxford Studies in Ancient Philosophy* 17: 215–47.

Meredith, J. C. (1978), *'The Critique of Judgement' by Immanuel Kant*, trans. with analytical indexes by J. C. Meredith, Oxford: Clarendon Press.

Mill, J. S. [1843] (1919), *A System of Logic*, London: Longmans, Green and Co.

Mothersill, M. (2009), 'Beauty', in S. Davies, K. Higgins, R. Hopkins, R. Stecker and D. Cooper (eds), *A Companion to Aesthetics*, Oxford: Wiley-Blackwell, pp. 166–71.

Mynott, J. (2009), *Birdscapes: Birds in Our Imagination and Experience*, Princeton: Princeton University Press.

Nehamas, A. (2001), 'A Promise of Happiness: The Place of Beauty in a World of Art', The Tanner Lectures on Human Values, delivered at Yale University, 9–10 April.

Nehamas, A. (2007), *Only a Promise of Happiness: The Place of Beauty in a World of Art*, Princeton: Princeton University Press.

Nussbaum, M. (1990), *Love's Knowledge: Essays on Philosophy and Literature*, Oxford: Oxford University Press.

Nussbaum, M. (1993), 'Poetry and the Passions: Two Stoic Views', in J. Brunschwig and M. Nussbaum (eds), *Passions and Perceptions: Studies in Hellenistic Philosophy of Mind*, Cambridge: Cambridge University Press, pp. 97–149.

Nussbaum, M. (1995), 'Eros and the Wise: The Stoic Response to a Cultural Dilemma', *Oxford Studies in Ancient Philosophy* 13: 231–67.

Obbink, D. (ed.) (1995), *Philodemus and Poetry: Poetic Theory and Practice in Lucretius, Philodemus and Horace*, Oxford: Oxford University Press.

Obbink, D., and P. Waerdt (1991), 'Diogenes of Babylon: The Stoic

Sage in the City of Fools', *Greek, Roman and Byzantine Studies* 32 (4): 355–96.

O'Meara, D. (2014), 'The Beauty of the World in Plato's *Timaeus*', *Schole* 8 (1): 24–33.

Onians, J. (1979), *Art and Thought in the Hellenistic Age: The Greek World View 350–50 BC*, London: Thames & Hudson.

Opsomer, J. (2017), 'Why Doesn't the Moon Crash into the Earth? Platonist and Stoic Teleologies in Plutarch's *Concerning the Face Which Appears in the Orb of the Moon*', in J. Rocca (ed.), *Teleology in the ancient World*, Cambridge: Cambridge University Press, pp. 76–91.

Paley, W. (1802), *Natural Theology*, London: R. Edwards.

Parsons, G., and A. Carlson (2008), *Functional Beauty*, Oxford and New York: Oxford University Press.

Peponi, A.-E. (2012), *Frontiers of Pleasure: Models of Aesthetic Response in Archaic and Classical Greek Thought*, Oxford: Oxford University Press.

Perl, E. D. (2007), 'Why Is Beauty Form? Plotinus' Theory of Beauty in Phenomenological Perspective', *Dionysius* 25: 115–28.

Pinker, S. (1997), *How the Mind Works*, London: The Penguin Press.

Pollitt, J. J. (1974), *The Ancient View of Greek Art: Criticism, History, and Terminology*, New Haven and London: Yale University Press.

Pomeroy, A. (ed.) (1999), *Arius Didymus: Epitome of Stoic Ethics*, Atlanta: Society of Biblical Literature.

Porter, J. I. (1996), 'The Philosophy of Aristo of Chios', in R. B. Branham and M.-O. Goulet-Cazet (eds), *The Cynics: The Cynic Movement in Antiquity and its Legacy*, Berkeley: University of California Press, pp. 156–89.

Porter, J. I. (2009), 'Is Art Modern? Kristeller's "Modern System of the Arts" Reconsidered', *British Journal of Aesthetics* 49: 1–24.

Porter, J. I. (2010), *The Origins of Aesthetic Thought in Ancient Greece: Matter, Sensation and Experience*, Cambridge: Cambridge University Press.

Powers, N. (2012), 'The Stoic Argument for the Rationality of the Cosmos', *Oxford Studies in Ancient Philosophy* 43: 245–69.

Price, A. (2002), 'Plato, Zeno, and The Object of Love', in M. Nussbaum and J. Sihvola (eds), *Sleep of Reason: Erotic Experience and Sexual Ethics in Ancient Greece and Rome*, Chicago: University of Chicago Press, pp. 170–99.

Rackham, H. (1931), *Cicero: On Ends*, Cambridge, MA: Harvard University Press.

Rackham, H. (1938), *Pliny the Elder: Natural History*, Cambridge, MA: Harvard University Press.

Rackham, H. (1942), *Cicero: The Paradoxes of the Stoics*, Cambridge, MA: Harvard University Press.

Rapp, C. (2015), 'Tragic Emotions', in P. Destrée and P. Murray (eds), *A Companion To Ancient Aesthetics*, Hoboken, NJ: Wiley-Blackwell, pp. 438–54.

Reesor, M. (1954), 'The Stoic Concept of Quality', *The American Journal of Philology* 75 (1): 40–58.

Reydams-Schils, G. (2013), 'The Academy, the Stoics and Cicero on Plato's *Timaeus*', in A. G. Long (ed.), *Plato and the Stoics*, Cambridge: Cambridge University Press, pp. 29–58.

Rogers, K. (1993), 'Aristotle's Conception of τὸ καλόν', *Ancient Philosophy* 13: 355–71.

Roman, L. (2014), *Poetic Autonomy in Ancient Rome*, Oxford: Oxford University Press.

Ross, D. (1907), *A Theory of Pure Design: Harmony, Balance, Rhythm*, Boston: Houghton, Mifflin.

Rusch, H., and E. Voland (2013), 'Evolutionary Aesthetics: an Introduction to Key Concepts and Current Issues', *Aisthesis. Pratiche, Linguaggi E Saperi Dell'Estetico* 6 (2): 113–33.

Salles, R. (2018), 'Why is the Cosmos Intelligent?' *Rhizomata* 6 (1): 40–64.

Sartwell, C. (2004), *Six Names of Beauty*, London: Routledge.

Scade, P. (2010), 'Stoic Cosmological Limits and Their Platonic Background', in V. Harte, M. M. McCabe, R. Sharples and A. Sheppard (eds), *Aristotle and the Stoics Reading Plato*, London: Institute of Classical Studies, pp. 143–83.

Schmitt, A. (2007), 'Symmetrie und Schönheit. Plotins Kritik an hellenistischen Proportionslehren. Ihre unterschiedliche Wirkungsgeschichte in Mittelalter und Früher Neuzeit', in O. Lobsien and C. Olk (eds), *Neuplatonismus und Ästhetik. Zur Transformationsgeschichte des Schönen*, Berlin and New York: De Gruyter, pp. 59–84.

Schofield, M. (1999), *The Stoic Idea of the City*, Chicago: University of Chicago Press.

Schofield, M., and M. Nussbaum (eds) (1982), *Language and Logos: Studies* in *Ancient Greek Philosophy Presented to G. E. L. Owen*, Cambridge: Cambridge University Press.

Scruton, R. (2009), *Beauty*, Oxford: Oxford University Press.

Sedley, D. (1988), 'The Stoic Criterion of Identity', *Phronesis* 27 (3): 255–75.

Sedley, D. (2002), 'The Origins of Stoic God', in D. Frede and A. Laks (eds), *Traditions of Theology: Studies in Hellenistic Theology, Its Background and Aftermath*, Leiden: Brill, pp. 41–84.

Sedley, D. (2007), *Creationism and Its Critics in Antiquity*, Berkeley: University of California Press.

Sedley, D. (2017), 'Socrates, Darwin, and Teleology', in J. Rocca (ed.), *Teleology in the Ancient World: Philosophical and Medical Approaches*, Cambridge: Cambridge University Press, pp. 25–42.

Setaioli, A. (2007), 'Some Ideas of Seneca's *On Beauty*', *Prometheus* 33: 49–65.

Sheppard, A. (1987), *Aesthetics: An Introduction to the Philosophy of Art*, Oxford: Oxford University Press.

Sluiter, I., and R. M. Rosen (eds) (2012), *Aesthetic Value in Classical Antiquity*, Leiden: Brill.

Sommerstein, A. (2008), *Aeschylus: Fragments*, Cambridge, MA: Harvard University Press.

Sorabji, R. (1982), 'Myths about Non-Propositional Thought', in M. Schofield and M. Nussbaum (eds), *Language and Logos: Studies in Ancient Greek Philosophy Presented to G. E. L. Owen*, Cambridge: Cambridge University Press, pp. 295–314.

Sorabji, R. (2000), *Emotion and Peace of Mind: From Stoic Agitation to Christian Temptation*, Oxford: Oxford University Press.

Staley, G. (2009), *Seneca and the Idea of Tragedy*, Oxford: Oxford University Press.

Steinberg, E. (ed.) (1977), *An Enquiry Concerning Human Understanding: A Letter from a Gentleman to his friend in Edinburgh by David Hume*, Indianapolis: Hackett Publishing.

Stephens, W. (1996), 'Epictetus on Stoic Love', *Oxford Studies in Ancient Philosophy* 14: 193–210.

Tatarkiewicz, W. (1970), *The History of Aesthetics*, The Hague: Mouton.

Tatarkiewicz, W. (1972), 'The Great Theory of Beauty and its Decline', *Journal of Aesthetics and Art Criticism* 31: 165–80.

Thompson, D. W. (1992), *On Growth and Form*, New York: Dover.

Tieleman, T. (1996), *Galen and Chrysippus on the Soul: Argument and Refutation in the 'De Placitis', Books II–III*, Leiden: Brill.

Tieleman, T. (2003), *Chrysippus' On Affections: Reconstruction and Interpretations*, Leiden: Brill.

Tieleman, T. (2009), 'Galen and the Stoics, or: The Art of Not Naming', in C. Gill, T. Whitmarsh and J. Wilkins (eds), *Galen and the World of Knowledge*, Cambridge: Cambridge University Press, pp. 282–99.

Tieleman, T. (2016), 'The Early Stoics and Aristotelian Ethics', *Frontiers of Philosophy in China* 11 (1): 104–21.

Todd, R. (1976), *Alexander of Aphrodisias on Stoic Physics: A Study of the 'De Mixtione' with Preliminary Essays, Text, Translation and Commentary*, Leiden: Brill.

Tolstoy, Leo (1995), *What Is Art?*, trans. R. Pevear and L. Volokhonsky, London: Penguin Books.

Tsolis, T. (2000), 'The Meaning and Content of So-Called Aesthetic Terms in Stoic Thinking', in K. Boudouris (eds), *Greek Philosophy and the Fine Arts*, vol. 2, Athens: International Center for Greek Philosophy and Culture, pp. 206–14.

Usher, S. (1974), *Dionysius of Halicarnassus: The Critical Essays*, vol. 2, Cambridge, MA: Harvard University Press.

Vogt, K. (2008), *Law, Reason, and the Cosmic City: Political Philosophy in the Early Stoa*, New York: Oxford University Press.

Walsh, P. G. (1997), *Cicero: On the Nature of the Gods*, New York: Clarendon Press.

Walton, K. (2007), 'Aesthetics: What? Why? And Wherefore?' *Journal of Aesthetics and Art Criticism* 65 (2): 147–61.

White, S. (2012), 'Stoic Selection: Objects, Actions, and Agents', in A. Nightingale and D. Sedley (eds), *Ancient Models of Mind*, Cambridge: Cambridge University Press, pp. 110–29.

Wiater, N. (2011), *The Ideology of Classicism: Language, History, and Identity in Dionysius of Halicarnassus*, New York: De Gruyter.

Williamson, T. (1994), *Vagueness*, London: Routledge.

Wolfsdorf, D. (2013), *Pleasure in Ancient Greek Philosophy*, Cambridge: Cambridge University Press.

Woolf, R. (2001), *Cicero: On Moral Ends*, Cambridge: Cambridge University Press.

Wooten, C. H. (1987), *Hermogenes' On Types of Style*, Chapel Hill: University of North Carolina Press.

Wynne, J. (2012), 'God's Indifferents: Why Cicero's Stoic Jupiter Made the World', *Apeiron* 45: 354–83.

Zagdoun, M.-A. (2000), *La Philosophie Stoïcienne de l'art*, Paris: CNRS Editions.

Zangwill, N. (2001), *The Metaphysics of Beauty*, Ithaca and London: Cornell University Press.

Zangwill, N. (2003), 'Beauty', in J. Levinson (ed.), *The Oxford Handbook of Aesthetics*, Oxford: Oxford University Press, pp. 325–43.

Zilioli, U. (2014), *The Cyrenaics*, Hoboken, NJ: Taylor & Francis.

Index Locorum

Aeschylus
Fr.361: 79

Aetius
1.7.33: 134n.21, 137n.53
1.10.5: 134n.31
4.11.1–4: 43n.16

Alexander of Aphrodisias
In Aristotelis topicorum libros octo commentaria
181.2–6: 45n.40

De mixtione
216.7–11: 135n.35
216.14–217.1: 110, 136n.43
217.7–9: 109
217.13–19: 112
217.30–1: 137n.50
2.17.32–218.6: 110–11
226.24–9: 109, 117

Aristotle
Metaphysica
13.996a: 178
13.1078a30–b6: 72n.22, 178

De mundo
397a6: 190n.36

Ethica Nicomachea
1098b30–1: 30
1099a31–b6: 30
1123b6–8: 179
1153b17–19: 30
1167a: 167n.40

Physica
246b3–246b19: 190n.36

Poetica
1450b34–1451a6: 179

Politica
1326a33: 179

Topica
116b21: 179

Arius Didymus
2.7.7–7a: 28–9
5b4–5b5: 71n.15, 98n.37, 146
5b9: 91
7b: 88
11s: 91

Athenaeus
546F: 45n.45

Athenagoras
Legatio sive supplication pro Christianis
4.1: 134n.13

Augustine
De trinitate
9.6.11: 191n.56

Aulus Gelius
Noctes Atticae
7.1.1–13: 139n.65
9.5.2: 46n.48

Calcidius
Commentaria in Platonis Timaeum
294: 137n.51

Chrysippus
Quaestiones logicae
3, 9.7–12: 82

Cicero
Academica
2.36: 142n.103
2.93: 76n.59

De finibus bonorum et malorum
2.9–10: 45n.44, 123
3.17: 160
3.20–1: 71n.18
3.22–3: 46n.52
3.26: 47, 61, 96n.13
3.27: 61, 166n.27
3.28: 61
3.29: 56, 61
3.32: 152
3.33: 75n.48
3.43: 31
3.44: 31–2
3.49: 75n.48
3.50: 35
3.51: 45n.39
3.57: 75n.48
3.58: 35
3.62: 99n.51
3.74: 96n.14
3.75: 97n.23, 87
4.50: 76n.59

De natura deorum
1.39: 137n.51
2.12–15: 101
2.12: 43n.16
2.16: 133n.8
2.43: 121
2.58: 122, 158
2.75–6: 128
2.87: 158
2.88: 102
2.93: 105
2.145: 122
3.26: 101, 102, 104

De officiis
1.93: 157
1.94: 157
1.95: 65
1.97: 157
1.98: 165n.9, 156, 157
1.100: 156

Paradoxa Stoicorum
2.17–18: 96n.17
5.33–4: 96n.12
5.34–5: 83–4
6.52: 96n.16

Tusculanae disputationes
4.29: 162
4.31: 90, 146–7, 182
4.34–5: 162
5.43: 62, 166n.27
5.44: 56

Clement of Alexandria
Paedagogus
3.11.74: 92

Diogenes Laertius
2.87–8: 45n.41
2.108: 96n.6
7.39: 24n.61
7.46–8: 85
7.52: 127
7.53: 43n.15
7.60: 14
7.83: 85

7.85–6: 46n.50, 70n.10
7.87–9: 97n.32, 169–70n.75
7.89: 71n.17
7.94: 152
7.98: 70n.6
7.99: 57
7.100: 51, 57, 96n.14, 87, 88, 157
7.101: 57
7.102: 20n.8, n.10, 27
7.104–5: 28
7.107: 168n.62
7.109: 168n.63
7.119: 97n.22
7.121–2: 96n.12
7.122: 97n.23
7.124: 99–100n.53
7.129: 93
7.130: 91, 93, 166n.21
7.134: 135n.36
7.135–6: 134n.20, 134n.21
7.138–9: 137n.52
7.147: 137n.51, 138n.58
7.151: 137n.50
7.156: 134n.21, 113
7.160: 35–6
7.180: 15, 23n.44, 96n.7
7.199: 15
7.201: 15
7.202: 15
8.47: 172
10.136–7: 45n.43

Dionysius of Hallicarnasus
De compositione verborum
4.20–1: 16

Epictetus
Dissertationes
1.20.1–5: 137n.54
1.28.6–10: p.15
2.23.30–5: 36–7, 97n.35
4.11.25–6: 99n.45

Epicurus
Epistula ad Herodotum

43–4: 134n.17
45: 104n.16

Epistula ad Menoeceum
127–8: 45n.45, 46n.46
129–31: 46n.47

Sententiae Vaticanae
33,59: 46n.47

Galen
De propriorum animi cuiuslibet affectuum dignotione et curatione
1.8 (5.41–2K): 191n.62

Methodo Medendi
1.2 (10.15–16K): 191n.58
7.3 (10.462–3K): 191n.58

De placitis Hippocratis et Platonis
4.2.10–18 (5.368–70K): 162, 169n.74
5.2.46 (5.443K): 165n.7
5.3.13–15 (5.448–9K): 165n.11
5.3.15 (5.449K): 145
5.3.16 (4.449K): 172
5.3.17 (5449K): 166n.16, 182
7.1.12–15: 168n.59

De plenitudine
7.525, 9–14: 111

De temperamentis
1.9 (1.566K): 188n.8

De usu partium
1.3–4 (3.6–9K): 191n.47
1.9 (3.24–5K): 184
1.20 (3.74K): 191n.47
2.15 (3.146K): 183
2.16 (3.158K): 183
3.10 (3.238–40K): 183
5.6 (3.371K): 183
5.14 (3.395K): 144–5
6.16 (3.489K): 183
8.7 (3.654K): 183
11.14 (3.905K): 134n.13
13.6 (4.106K): 183

Hermogenes of Tarsus
Περὶ ἰδεῶν λόγου
1.12.20–8: 182

Homer
Ilias
2.212–23: 44n.36

Lactantius
Divinae institutiones
3.25: 43n.19

De ira dei
13.9–10: 139n.65

Lucretius
De rerum natura
2.216–50: 134n.18

Marcus Aurelius
3.2: 139n.67
4.40: 135n.34
6.16: 137n.55
8.50: 139n.65

Musonius Rufus
4.1: 43n.19

Olympiodorus
In Platonis Gorgiam commentaria
21.1: 114

Origen
Commentarii in evangelium Joannis
2.10: 96n.5, 97n.22

Philodemus
De signis
1.2–4.13, 6.1–14: 142n.103

Philo of Alexandria
De posteritate Caini
133: 56

Quaestiones in Genesin
4.99: 96n14

De vita Mosis
2.140: 165n.13

Philostratus the Younger
Imagines
Proem. 4: 188n.8

Plato
Euthydemus
281D–E: 33

Gorgias
467C–468E: 33

Hippias maior
287D: 177
288D–E: 177
288E: 177
290D–294E: 155

Leges
925A: 188n.19

Meno
87E–88A: 33
88D–E: 44n.27

Respublica
368E–371E: 72n.22
399E: 124
472A: 96n.6
529C: 140n.77
526D–530B: 188n.18

Parmenides
130E–131A: 189n.25

Philebus
60D–61B: 175
64D–E: 175
64E–65A: 175–6

Sophista
228A: 188n.17
235D–236A: 188n.17

Symposium
184D–185B: 99n.50
204C–205A: 95n.2
211B: 189n.25

Timaeus
28C–29A: 106
29E: 106
30A: 106
35A–B: 106
37B–C: 106
37D–38B: 106
39D: 123
40A: 123
41D: 191n.54
66A: 188n.17
66D: 188n.17
69B: 188n.17
80B: 189n.24
87D: 188n.17

Pliny the Elder
Naturalis Historia
34.19: 172

Plotinus
Enneades
1.6.1: 147–8, 148, 149–50
1.6.2: 141n.85, 149
5.8.1: 125
5.8.4: 125
5.8.6: 125
5.8.10: 125
6.7.22: 151

Plutarch
Moralia
440E–441D: 168n.59
1038F: 72n.25, 60
1039C–D: 60, 166n.27
1041E: 43n.15
1044A: 170n.76
1044C–E: 101, 138n.63, 118–19, 139n.65, 120, 127
1048A: 44n.29
1054E–F: 158–9
1057A–B: 96n.10
1057E–1058A: 79–80, 97n.27
1058A: 82
1066C: 151
1069E: 168n.61
1077C–E: 137n.52
1078E: 137n.50
1089D: 46n.47, n.48

De facie quae in orbe lunae apparet
138n.59

Pompeius
14.6: 96n.6

Seneca
Ad Lucilium epistulae morales
76.9–10: 97n.34, 169n.75
88.25–8: 87n.21
113.15–16, p.120
118.8: 77n.63
118.9: 33
118.10–11: 65–6
118.11: 33
119.15: 139n.65
120.1–3: 58–9
120.3: 65
121.6–15: 40

Sextus Empiricus
Adversus mathematicos
7.151–7: 97n.33
7.416: 76n.59
8.275–6: 142n.102
9.75–6: 107
11.22: 70n.8
11.64–7: 23n.43, 35
11.99–100: 49

Pyrrhoneae hypotyposes
2.104–7: 129–30
2.141–2: 130
2.142–3: 130–1

Simplicius
In Aristotelis categorias commentarium
166,15–29: 168n.58
217,32–218,1: 191n.42

Stobaeus
1.21,7d: 174
1.155,5–11: 110
1.136,21–137,6: 134n.30
2.62: 71n.15, 146
2.62–3: 98n.37, 153.
2.66: 91
2.67, 5–12: 85
2.68, 18–23: 162
2.75,11–76,8: 169n.75
2.77, 16–27: 70n.7
2.79–80: 28–9
2.81–2: 88
2.88,8–90,6: 169n.72, 169n.73
2.93, 14–18: 52, 160
2.109,10–110,4: 46n.53
2.115: 91
4.1,49: 174

Syrianus
In Aristotelis metaphysica commentaria
105,21–5: 134n.31

Vitruvius
De architectura
1.3.2: 173
3.1.1: 173
3.1.1–3: 149, 173
6.8.10: 184

Xenophon
Memorabilia
3.8.5–6: 155
3.10.9–10: 155

Symposium
5.4–5: 185

General Index

ἀριθμοί, 51–3, 57, 160
ἴσος, 145
καλοσκἀγαθος, 7–8
παράδοξα, 81–2
τέλος, 39, 49, 61, 68, 115, 155, 157, 163
τὸ κάλλος, 16, 27, 47, 145, 187
τὸ καλόν, 7–8, 16, 50–5, 67, 69, 187
  in Aristotle, 22n.30, 155
  and *honestum*, 55, 59
τὸ πρέπον/*decorum*, 155–8
  and *honestum*, 157–8

Alexander of Aphrodisias, 108–12, 117
analogia, 173, 183
animals
  beauty of, 101, 118–20, 126
  have proper functions, 159
  recognise τὸ καλόν, 49–50, 128
  teleological function of, 155
Apollodorus (the Stoic), 27
Aratus, 14
Aristo of Chios, 35–6, 38, 41, 159
Aristotle, 5–11, 30–2, 108, 178–81
  on *kalon*, 22n.30, 155
  Metaphysics, 178
  Nicomachean Ethics, 30, 179
  Poetics, 179
  Politics, 179
  Topics, 179

Brennan, T., 34

Chrysippus, 12–16, 27, 31, 42n.3,
  44n.29, 56–8, 60–1, 63, 65, 68,
  76n.59, 82, 85, 101–4, 108–12,
  114–20, 122, 124, 126–7, 136n.47,
  137n.57, 138n.63, 139n.65, 145–8,
  151, 153, 157–9, 161–3, 165n.8,
  165n.11, 169n.68, 169n.72
Cicero
  On Duties, 155–8
  On Ends, 30–2, 35, 45n.39, 47, 56,
    61–3, 87, 123, 152, 160
  On the Nature of the Gods, 43n.16,
    101–5, 120–3, 128, 158
  Tusculan Disputations, 56, 62, 90,
    146, 162, 182
Cleanthes, 14, 101, 114–16, 137n.57
cognitive impression, 82–3, 140–1n.83
colour, 90, 122–4, 126, 147–9, 151, 182
common conceptions, 31, 43n.16
Cyrenaics, 39

Darwin, C., 6, 10
design
  of architecture, 173, 184–5
  argument from, 102–5, 133n.8, 183
  human anatomy, 122, 183
  rational, 107–8, 113, 117, 121
Destrée Pierre and Murray Penelope, 5
Diogenes Laertius, 14, 15, 27–8, 33, 35,
  38, 51–60, 63–5, 67, 85, 87, 91, 93,
  113, 116, 127, 130, 152, 172

General Index   215

Diogenes of Babylon, 14, 73n.29, 75n.48, 75n.49, 97n.25
Dionysus of Halicarnasus, 15–16
Dover, K., 7–8
Dutton, D., 6–7
Dyck, A., 156–8

emotions, 62, 74n.41, 146, 147, 189n.33
Epictetus, 15, 36–8, 97n.35, 98n.45
Epicureanism, 14, 38–9, 49–50, 104–5, 128, 129, 132
Eubulides, 96n.6

Forms (Platonic), 11, 19, 125, 176–7, 180, 181
formal properties, 22n.30, 52–3, 58, 66, 67–8, 72nn20,22,24, 78, 89–90, 95, 106, 121, 126, 131–2, 140n.82, 144, 177, 179, 181
Frede, M., 52

Galen, 144–8, 162, 165n.11, 172, 182–6
Gill, C., 67–8

Halliwell, S., 5, 20n.5, 20n.16, 21n.22, 189n.33
happiness, 29–36, 38–9, 41, 48, 55, 65, 68, 85, 88
harmonia, 174
health and disease, 10, 27, 33, 35, 39, 90, 113, 117, 145–7, 153, 165n.11
Hecato (the Stoic), 27, 58, 60, 61, 73n.29, 75n.49
Hermogenes of Tarsus, 182
Homer, 25n.63, 36, 82
  Iliad, 36
  Odyssey, 82
Hon, G. and Goldstein, B., 144
honestum, 65–6, 160; *see also* τὸ καλόν; τὸ πρέπον/*decorum*
Hume, D., 8

Inwood, B., 44n.27, 65

Kant, I., 8–10
Kirwan, J., 125–6
Kristeller, P. O., 4–7, 191n.63

Levinson, J., 10
Lombardo, G., 157
Long, A. A., 160–1
Lysippus (the sculptor), 172

McMahon, J., 11
music, 9, 14, 24n.60, 85, 160–1
Musonius Rufus, 43n.19
Myron (the sculptor), 172

Neoplatonism, 124–5, 181

objectivity/subjectivity, 8–9, 69–70

painting, 122, 173
Panaetius, 155, 157–8
Peponi, A.-E., 5
Pheidias, 183
Philodemus, 14
Philolaus of Croton, 174–5
philosophical education, 92–4
Plato, 5–11, 13, 19, 33, 124, 175–7, 179–81, 183
  Euthydemus, 33
  Hippias Major, 155, 176–7, 180
  Philebus, 175–7
  Republic, 6, 72n.22
  Timaeus, 105–7, 123, 183
pleasure, 27, 38–40, 49–50, 91, 123, 175
Pliny the Elder, 172
Plotinus, 8, 124–6, 147–52, 154, 162, 165–6n.16, 171, 181
Plutarch, 25n.63, 56, 60–1, 63, 74n.46, 78–82, 87, 89, 93, 101, 118–20, 138n.63, 151, 158–9
poetry, 14–15, 21n.25, 25n.63, 156–7
Poikilia, 120–4, 148
Polycleitus, 149, 172, 179–80, 185
Porter, J., 5, 140n.82
Posidonius, 13, 14, 169n.72
Posidonius' sphere, 102–3, 127
proper functions/ τὰ καθήκοντα, 52, 57, 159–61
Pythagoras of Rhegium (the sculptor), 172

rationality
    of the creation of the world), 103–17, 121, 126, 130–2
    of god, 103, (119), 112–13, 116, 119
    of humankind, 32, 93, 157, 163
    of virtue, 48, 68, 85, 152
    wise man, 82–6, 89, 94, 160
ratio-based proportionality, 106, 149, 154, 172–3, 175–6, 180
rhetoric, 15–16, 114, 182, 186
Rogers, K., 155

sculpture, 14, 172
Sedley, D., 100n.54, 102–3, 135n.36
Seneca, 14–15, 33–4, 40, 55–60, 63, 65–7, 69, 74n.43, 96n.21, 120, 123
Socrates, 33–4, 155, 175–7, 185, 189n.31
sorites, 82, 76n.59

Tatarkiewicz, W., 1–4
techne, 108, 113–17, 137n.54, 153
theodicy, 117–20, 124, 151, 183
Tieleman, T., 153
Tolstoy, L., 74n.41
tragedy, 14–15

varietas, 123–4; *see poikile*
Vitruvius, 149, 173, 183, 185

Xenophon, 155, 180, 185

Zangwill, N., 10
Zeno of Citium, 45n.39, 73n.37, 92–3, 99n.53, 114–16, 137n.57, 165n.8, 170n.75, 190n.41
Zeno of Elea, 81

EU representative:
Easy Access System Europe
Mustamäe tee 50, 10621 Tallinn, Estonia
Gpsr.requests@easproject.com

www.ingramcontent.com/pod-product-compliance
Lightning Source LLC
Chambersburg PA
CBHW070352240426
43671CB00013BA/2477